Keine Gewalt! No Violence!

Keine Gewalt! No Violence!

How the Church Gave Birth to Germany's
Only Peaceful Revolution

ROGER J. NEWELL

WIPF & STOCK · Eugene, Oregon

KEINE GEWALT! NO VIOLENCE!
How the Church Gave Birth to Germany's Only Peaceful Revolution

Wipf & Stock
An Imprint of Wipf and Stock Publishers
199 W. 8th Ave., Suite 3
Eugene, OR 97401

www.wipfandstock.com

PAPERBACK ISBN: 978-1-5326-1282-4
HARDCOVER ISBN: 978-1-5326-1284-8
EBOOK ISBN: 978-1-5326-1283-1

Manufactured in the U.S.A.   OCTOBER 9, 2017

Cover photo: The Ring Road, Leipzig, Germany, October 9, 1989.
From left to right: Karl Barth, Dietrich Bonhoeffer, Christian Führer, Albrecht Schönherr, Martin Niemöller, Heino Falcke

To my brother, Clifford Sturges Newell,
whose love of history has always been an inspiration.

The church is only a church if it is there for everyone.

—DIETRICH BONHOEFFER

Contents

Introduction | 1

1   Dietrich Bonhoeffer: To Seize the Wheel Itself | 15

2   Martin Niemöller: From U-Boat to Pulpit to Concentration Camp | 26

3   Against the Stream: How Karl Barth Reframed Church-State Relations | 44

4   Barth beyond Barmen | 67

5   Guilt, Forgiveness and Foreign Policy: The Stuttgart Declaration of 1945 | 78

6   The Church and the Cold War: In Search of a Third Way | 107

7   The Wilderness Era: A Forty-Year Journey to a Peaceful Revolution | 127

8   From the Sanctuary to the Street | 154

Epilogue: Unlearned Lessons, Hopeful Anticipations | 174

Appendix I   *Theological Declaration of Barmen May 1934: An Appeal to the Evangelical Congregations and Christians in Germany* | 193

Appendix II   *The Stuttgart Declaration: Declaration of the Council of the Evangelical Church in Germany October 19, 1945* | 198

Acknowledgments | 201

Bibliography | 205

Introduction

CANDLES AND PRAYERS: THEOLOGICAL WEAPONS AT THE END OF THE COLD WAR

IN MAY OF 2007 my wife and I organized a study tour for students from our university to visit sites of special significance in European church history. We would start in Rome and conclude our tour in Berlin. In planning for Germany, I naturally wanted to include a stay in Martin Luther's Wittenberg as a Reformation sight not to be missed. As I studied maps and booked accommodation, I seemed to recall stories about a church in nearby Leipzig that had played a special role in the "year of miracles" when the East German State (the German Democratic Republic or GDR) collapsed and all of Germany reunited after forty years of postwar division.

Questions began to race through my mind. How was it possible that a marginalized church in the middle of East Germany could play any role, let alone a decisive one, in the transformation of modern Europe? For that matter, there was the larger question of how it was possible that Germany, divided for forty years by the bitterest of ideological divides, had come to be reunited before the astonished eyes of Western society. As far as I knew, no scholar or journalist saw it coming. Why had such a major revolution come so unexpectedly? Perhaps a visit to this church might offer some "local knowledge" to help us gain perspective. Perhaps we could talk with someone who actually knew something about these strange happenings now nearly two decades past.

With a mustard seed of hope, I "googled" Leipzig, and the name of the church: *Nikolaikirche*. I was pleased to find that the church had a website; however, it was mostly in German. With the help of my German-speaking daughter, I dashed off an email *auf Deutsch* to inquire about a possible visit

1

while we were in the area. Within a week, I received a reply from the wife of one of the pastoral staff. In English she wrote that her husband would be happy to meet with us on the proposed day. But my elation turned to anxiety when she requested that we bring along a translator because "*Mein Mann hat kein Englisch*" (my husband does not speak English). Since my German was basically at an advanced kindergarten level, I was puzzled. How, from the Pacific Northwest of America, could I arrange for a German translator to meet us in the middle of the former East Germany? As I pondered this "so close but so far" situation, I seemed to recall an alumnus who had moved back to Germany (his father was German, his mother American). This was a good five years ago at least and even then I had not known him well. In checking with our alumni relations staff, a name was recovered: Tim Buechsel. Yes, now I remembered. Apparently, Tim was living somewhere in this country of eighty million people, but alas the alumni office had no forwarding address. I "googled" again. I found a Tim Buechsel who played on a semi-pro basketball team and worked as a youth pastor in the city of Weimar. There was even a team picture and he looked vaguely familiar. Yes, that might be the Tim Buechsel I knew, since Tim had played on our college team. It was worth sending an email inquiry, reintroduce myself and ask: would he be able to join us for a day and translate for us? In just a few days I received an email from Tim, saying yes, he remembered me; that he lived about an hour's drive from Leipzig and would be delighted to meet us at the church and act as our translator! It had all fallen together in less than a week.

Now all our group had to do was show up on time and meet these two Germans at the city center church in Leipzig. Four months, an all-night train ride from Zurich, and a confusing episode regarding our booking at a youth hostel later, twenty of us were walking from the train station along the *Nikolaistrasse* toward the *Nikolaikirche*. At the front of the church I spied what must be our tall translator introducing himself to someone dressed in modest, but distinctly un-clerical garb who had grey, short, spiky hair and wore the multi-pocketed blue denim vest so popular among German men. It was indeed one of the pastors, with the unlikeliest of names, Christian Führer, the same person in fact who had written the church's website material about the events of 1989. He would shortly be telling us a story we would not forget.

After brief introductions, the pastor, followed by Tim, led us straight into the church, past a few curious visitors, right to the main altar. There, with Tim as a most competent translator, he briefly introduced us to the history of the church, its tradition of music (including the link with J. S. Bach's *Thomaskirche* a ten-minute walk away) and one or two highlights of its various architectural renovations. Before leading us into a little room just off to the side of the altar, Tim later reminded me that Führer made an odd remark about how where we were now standing, for centuries past, only priests were allowed access. Out of all the things he had said thus far, this one made Führer's eyes light up.

We settled into the former priests' room and after everyone had found somewhere to sit, the pastor asked us each to introduce ourselves by name and field of study. Then he began to tell us his story. Pastor Führer now spoke in the first person about his time as pastor here, beginning in the early 1980s. He reminded us that it was a time of increasing tension between East and West. NATO and Soviet missile warheads had been stationed to face each other right where the Cold War's trench cut Germany in half. On both sides of the Berlin Wall, Germans grew increasingly anxious that Germany could become the battleground for Europe's third war in the same century, except this one would be of unthinkable nuclear proportions. People grew very afraid as they listened to politicians on both sides of the divide prefer the rhetoric of strident accusation to calm negotiation. (As I listened, I could recall President Reagan's famous rebuke of the Soviet Union as "the evil empire." I learned later that Erich Honecker, the East German head of state, spoke regularly about NATO's "imperialist aspirations"). But in a one-party state like the German Democratic Republic, where could people discuss their worries? To even voice such concerns over foreign or domestic policies in public was tantamount to disloyalty and charges of sedition.

This was the brooding climate in which Pastor Führer opened the doors of the church to young people who were anxious to discuss such things. Gradually as we listened, it dawned on me that Führer was not narrating to us the events he had been told about by others. He was describing things with the unique details of an eyewitness and primary organizer, taking us through to the events which would culminate in the nonviolent revolution of November 1989.

From the notes I intensively scribbled that day, certain key points stood out. First there was an initial gathering way back in 1981, in which he invited people with concerns about peace and the arms race to meet at the church. My notes said Führer arranged it for around 10 o'clock at night. (Why so late I wondered? To avoid unwanted Stasi attention?) He expected maybe ten or so people to come and let off some steam. But to his astonishment, by word of mouth, ten times that number showed up. They were mostly young, many of them dissidents who were not getting along with the governing SED (Socialist Unity party of Germany) in East Germany, which of course was a one-party state.

Führer next described how he brought everyone right to the central altar where he brought us, sat them on the center floor of the church surrounded by the choir stalls. In other words, he hadn't stuck them in some sterile classroom building somewhere marginal. After introductory words and a greeting, he laid a large rough wooden cross on the floor in the middle of where everyone was seated. To facilitate some order in the discussion, he invited anyone who wished to express a frustration or concern to take a candle, light it, and speak the concern aloud as they placed their candle on or around the cross. As I listened, it struck me that Pastor Führer had with great simplicity transfigured a potentially angry political discussion into a prayer meeting with the cross of the crucified Jesus at the center of the conversation. If the dissidents were surprised to find themselves at a prayer meeting, it was now Pastor Führer's turn for surprise as every single person lit a candle, and shared a concern in what turned out to be the most significant prayer meeting in the forty-year history of the GDR. As the sharing continued past midnight, the bare wooden cross gradually transformed into a glowing cross beaming with light. It was a harbinger of a future transformation which no one sitting there would have dared imagine.

Later I mused further how Führer had seamlessly joined political discussion to Christ-centered prayer. We in the West are more comfortable with a clean separation of church and state. Of course, even in the home of this separation, the United States, the Baptist pastor Martin Luther King Jr. had joined together the Christian gospel in a civil rights movement that had permanently changed the segregated ways of American society. But Dr. King was assassinated twenty-five years before and the GDR was an officially communist-atheist state. This was the context in which these young people, who were alienated from a state which had taught and trained them in an atheistic worldview, now sat with Pastor Führer around a cross filled with light from a hundred candles. The collective mood was so full of openness, freedom and acceptance no one wanted to leave.

There was one more unlikely connection Führer mentioned. At the beginning of his introduction to the *Nikolaikirche*, Führer noted that before the Reformation came to Leipzig, only priests could enter the altar area where we were seated. As I have mentioned already, Tim our translator later reminded me that Führer's eyes had twinkled when he made the comment about the exclusivity of this room for the clergy, because he opined that for long centuries the church had put itself in charge of controlling access to God. Instead of opening paths for the masses to meet God, the leaders created barriers, giving themselves special privileges reinforced by liturgical solemnity, intimidating building structures, surrounded by inward-focused gatherings divorced from the city streets and civic affairs. All this would change. As I read later in the Nikolai brochure:

When we open up the church to everyone who has been forced to keep silent, has been slandered or maybe even imprisoned, then no one can ever think of a church again as being simply a kind of religious museum or a temple for art aesthetics. On the contrary, Jesus is then really present in the church because we are trying to do what he did and what he wants us to do today. This is the hour of the birth of "Nikolai church—Open for everyone," also for protest groups and those living on the margin of society.

Throw open the church doors! The open wings of a church door are like the wide open arms of Jesus: "Come to me, everyone who is troubled and burdened, I will relieve you!" And they came and they come! The threshold is low, for atheists and those in wheelchairs."[1]

From this first gathering Führer would eventually arrange what he called "peace prayers" (*Friedensgebet*) to meet every Monday evening at 5 p.m. to pray for peace in both local and international situations of conflict. Years later, the prayers were sometimes followed by the people walking into the streets, carrying candles to witness for peace and for freedom, including permission for visas for foreign travel, permission to express ecological concerns and putting pressure on the government for increasing openness and democratic reforms. In contrast to the other demonstrations in the GDR, the gatherings in Leipzig were by far the largest and also the most peaceful.

Führer telescoped the years down to a moment of tension which followed a fraudulent local election in May 1989, in which the party reported that it had received 98 percent of the votes cast. The public was outraged by such a flagrant deception. Calls for reform grew louder. People were tired of always waiting for travel visas; some were fleeing to the West by way of Hungary. Pastor Führer summed up the next few decisive events as follows.

In early May, the police blocked all driveways to the church, seeking to shut down the Monday prayer meetings, which they had determined had become a cover for political insurrection. Nevertheless the crowds only increased.

On October 7, Soviet Union president Mikhail Gorbachev, the author of the movement for openness, *Perestroika*, arrived in Berlin to celebrate the fortieth anniversary of the GDR. The government did not want this occasion to be used for any kind of public expression of discontent. In Leipzig, for ten long hours police battered and bullied defenseless demonstrators who made no attempt to fight back as they were carted away in trucks.

In this heightened atmosphere, just two days later, Monday, October 9, the peace prayers were scheduled. The government warned protestors that

1. Führer, *Spiritual Church Guide*, 20.

any further demonstrations would not be tolerated. All day long the police and military tried to intimidate the populace with a brutal show of force. During the day, the military and Stasi shut down schools and shops early in the city and built roadblocks. The police carried guns loaded with live ammunition. Soldiers with tanks were mobilized and surrounded the central area. Rumors circulated that the government intended to use the "Chinese Solution" as it was called, to solve the problem of ongoing public dissent. It was reported to Führer that extra hospital beds and blood plasma had been assembled in the Leipzig hospitals. As I listened to the mention of "Chinese Solution" I only later realized that Führer was alluding to the massacre that had taken place but a few months earlier, in June 1989, on the Square of Heavenly peace (Tianenmen) in Beijing, China, where an estimated one thousand unarmed protesters had been massacred by government forces.

To neutralize and perhaps disrupt the prayer meeting, one thousand SED party members and Stasi went early to the church; six hundred had filled up the nave by two o'clock. As Führer describes it in the brochure:

> They had a job to perform, like the Stasi personnel who were on hand regularly at the peace prayers. What has not been considered was the fact, that these people were exposed to the word, the gospel and its impact! I always appreciated that the Stasi members heard the Beatitudes from the Sermon on the Mount every Monday. Where else would they hear these?[2]

So the stage was set, the actors assembled for the climactic Monday evening prayer service. Despite all the threats, all the attempts to minimize any public display of dissent, the early closing of the schools and businesses, huge numbers had come to the peace prayers, not only at *Nikolaikirche* but at churches throughout the city which had agreed to be open as well. That evening the atmosphere and the prayers for peace were serenely calm. As he concluded the service and prepared to send the people out with a blessing, Pastor Führer made a final plea for the people to refrain from any form of violence or provocation, to break the chain of violence just like Jesus had taught in the Sermon on the Mount. Once again the Sermon on the Mount was read aloud to the people (including the ever present Stasi). A specially moving paraphrase is set in italics in the church pamphlet:

> Then with Jesus there was One,
> Who said: Bless the poor!
> And not: Money makes you happy.
> Finally there was One Who said: Love your enemies!

2. Führer, "Events in Fall 1989," 1.

And not: Down with the opposition!

Finally there was One Who said:

The first will be the last!

And not: The status quo will remain untouched.

Finally there was One Who said:

He who risks his life and loses it, he will triumph!

And not: Be cautious!

Finally there was One Who said: You are the salt!

And not: You are the cream.

Finally there was One Who died as He lived![3]

As the doors opened for people to depart, something unforgettable happened: the two thousand people leaving the sanctuary were welcomed by tens of thousands waiting outside with candles in their hands. That night an estimated seventy thousand people marched around the city loop. Though the police and the military were everywhere, Pastor Führer said: "Our fear was not as big as our faith. . . . Two hands are necessary to carry a candle and to protect it from extinguishing so that you can not carry stones or clubs at the same time."[4] Instead of shouting hostilities or throwing stones, people cradled their candle flames. As Führer wrote: "There were thousands in the churches. Hundreds of thousands in the streets around the city center. But: Not a single shattered shop window. This was the incredible experience of the power of non-violence."[5]

It was, he said, as though Jesus' spirit of nonviolence seized the masses and became a physical, peaceful force. Soldiers and police engaged in conversations with demonstrators. Then after a few hours, everyone withdrew.

It was an evening in the spirit of our Lord Jesus for there were no winners and no defeated, nobody triumphed over the other, nobody lost his face. There was just a tremendous feeling of relief.[6]

As Tim our translator relayed these words, a moment came when he was overcome with emotion, and began to quietly weep. Back in 1989 he had been only a boy. Now for the first time as an adult he was hearing an intimate eyewitness tell the story which had led to the nonviolent reunification of his country. How to describe it? Amid thousands of dissenters, military and armed police, and potential provocations from the Stasi or an

3. Führer, *Protestant Lutheran Church of St. Nikolai*, 14.

4. Führer, "Events in Fall 1989," 1.

5. Ibid., 2.

6. Ibid., 1.

angry youth, not one act of violence had broken out. Not a shop window, not a single pane of glass was broken.

> Born of the people and not just preached but practiced in a consistent manner: an earth-shaking course of events, a miracle of Biblical proportions! When had we ever had a successful revolution before? And then, best of all, the very first time without any bloodshed. The unification of Germany this time without war and victory and the humiliation of other people and nations. That GOD held HIS protecting hand over all of us—Christians as well as non-Christians, people in grassroots groups and the police, regime critics and comrades, those who wanted to escape the Iron Curtain and those working for the Stasi (state security) those in the tanks and those protesting on the streets—and let us succeed in our peaceful revolution after so much brutal violence to which Germany in the 20th century subjected other nations, in particular the nation in which JESUS was born into, can only be described with the word blessing: A blessing on this Church, on this city, on the whole of Germany.[7]

It was reported that Horst Sindermann, a key member of the Central Committee of the GDR, summed up both the extensive preparations of the authorities as well as their inability to know how to respond to the events of the evening. "We had planned everything. We were prepared for everything. But not for candles and prayers."[8]

When Pastor Führer had finished his retelling of those special events, a time for question and answer followed. Then he thanked us for our visit and asked that God would bless our continued study. We gathered our coats and daypacks, everyone shook his hand, said our goodbyes and in silence walked out into the bustling streets of Leipzig.

I had not anticipated that a visit to Leipzig eighteen years after these unprecedented events would have stirred up such emotion. Perhaps the gravity of what we were hearing touched us through the witness of our translator Tim, when he paused to gather himself amid the emotion stirred by Führer's firsthand report. A few weeks later back in Oregon, I began to read the student journals. Each had recorded their impressions of the visit to the *Nikolaikirche*. Each described something of the impact made as they heard firsthand about the events of 1989. The following quotations from journals give a taste of what we experienced that day.

---

7. Führer, *Protestant Lutheran Church of St. Nikolai*, 23.
8. Ibid., 22.

This was an amazing experience; we have been touring these places in which history-making things happened four to six hundred years ago. At the *Nikolaikirche*, though, we were talking to the pastor who had been at the church when history had been made, where Christians and non-Christians alike had met for prayer meetings which eventually exploded out of the church into the streets: a completely peaceful protest which brought down the division created by the governments of East and West Germany.

I was expecting to hear a lecture about how the fall of communism affected Leipzig and how these peace prayers were a part of the fall. Instead we actually got to talk with one of the pastors that put all of this on. It was a very moving experience because I did not realize that those people that were involved in the prayers were risking their lives and that this pastor knew these people might die because they were resisting the government. This man told us that this did not happen because of him; it happened because of the Holy Spirit. Wow!

It was the most incredible hour and twenty minutes of my college career! Listening to his version of the peace movements, the prayer meetings, the people and God's power, gave me chills. I felt as if I had stepped back into a time capsule stopped on October 9, 1989 when communism fell. All I can say is that seeing Pastor Führer, talking to him and seeing first hand where everything took place, was one of the overwhelmingly powerful events that has and will make a lasting impression on me.

I had been thinking on this subject lately anyway: what is greatness? We so often see it in such human terms—Who impacted the most people? Who made the greatest mark in history? Whose statue, erected after their death, is the largest? It is so engrained within me to think of these things being great, it's kind of scary to consider thinking otherwise. But I read once that God's history book looks very different than our human one; I do believe that this is true. He does not desire that we impact others or history; we must do justly, love mercy and walk humbly with our God. And that is enough.

As I read their reflections, the church historian part of me began to think about the many tumultuous years of church struggles in Germany from Luther onward. I imagined Luther, on that October day in 1989, peering down from some celestial viewing station to watch the city where he once debated the redoubtable Dr. Eck. What would the father of the German Reformation have made of seventy thousand marchers armed only with prayers and candles streaming out of the church into the city to challenge a dictatorial government? Would he have felt vindicated or confounded that the Protestant church had become the cradle for nonviolent social and political change on such a massive scale? We know he eventually came to strongly oppose Thomas Müntzer's peasant rebellion. But what would he have thought of peasant pitchforks turned into candles and prayers? And what about Müntzer himself, perhaps sitting in a neighboring cloud observing these event? Might these two have finally been united in joy at such a sight? Had the descendants of Germany's Reformation at last found a way to join the gospel of God's righteousness with the raw world of political and social transformation in the spirit of the Sermon on the Mount?

Transformation: From Propaganda to Carnival

Pictures and images often connect us to the real potency within cultural change more effectively than concepts. An image that discloses the energy unleashed by Kaiser Wilhelm's declaration of World War I is the billboard *Germania*, displayed in the German History Museum in Berlin. At the top it reads: *Deutschland, August, 1914*. Looking like an archetypal figure from a Wagnerian opera, *Germania* represents the female soul of the German people. She stands majestic, steel-eyed, and beautiful, grasping the sword of justice to exact a fitting revenge upon her enemies. Dramatically she represents the collective longing for a great destiny rekindled and enemies defeated.

Or consider the moving images designed twenty years later by Leni Riefenstal in her classic piece of propaganda, *The Triumph of the Will*. Riefenstal wanted to focus an entire nation's imagination on the Nazi's torchlight processions staged on Nuremberg's parade grounds. Her goal was to communicate the emotion of the Nazi movement through images of row upon row of marching soldiers armed with weapons and torches. These images would reach into local theatres in every city and village in Germany. The sight and sounds would awaken a sense of the German people restored after the humiliating failure of World War I and the weakness of the Weimar Republic.

I doubt one can imagine a greater contrast to Riefenstal's images of martial power than the scenes from the Leipzig marches captured by amateur photographers and cameramen.[9] Neither stylized nor romantic, they disclose a carnival-like array of ordinary citizens, youthful dissidents, mothers, husbands, old age pensioners—armed only with hope. But there they go, strolling cautiously along the ring road of Leipzig in their hundreds and thousands, wielding not rocks but candles, saying prayers, chanting slogans like "*Wir sind das Volk*" (We are the People!) as they peacefully encircle the city, not knowing whether around the next corner they might walk into a frontal assault from the omnipresent police or the soldiers. Over the following weeks, children joined as well, but not on October 9. "They did not bring their children, because you had to fear for your life."[10] Amid the danger of that night, a unique energy of cultural disenchantment spilled onto the streets. Instead of giving vent to the seductions of getting even with one's enemies, it was as if a peaceful spell of reconciliation had been cast over everyone. Controversially, mercy was extended even to the Stasi and apparatchiks of the discredited regime. This way of being a People (*Volk*) together was unknown to the designer of *Germania* or Leni Riefenstahl. Whereas 1933 birthed a society of destiny based on the exclusion of communists, social democrats, Jews and Gypsies, 1989 brought together Christians, atheists, dissidents, soldiers, Stasi, and pensioners onto the streets in a stunning event of reconciliation that had not been predicted by any political pundits, East or West. How was it possible?

The Plan of This Study

The task of interpreting the meaning of both propaganda and current events is part of the ongoing challenge that scholars and journalists set themselves. My goal in the chapters which follow is to offer an interpretation of October 9, 1989, that sets it in the context of the turbulent history of the German Protestant Church and its relation to the German state. Long before visiting Leipzig's *Nikolaikirche*, I have been intrigued by the story of the church's resistance to National Socialism. I knew it was a "mingled yarn" of courageous resistance and embarrassing acquiescence. But my visit to Leipzig provoked me to revisit the story of the church's long struggle with the German state.

9. Perhaps the most thorough depiction is the Beller documentary *The Burning Wall: Dissent and Opposition Behind the Berlin Wall* (2002). In addition to scenes from the October 9 march, this film includes several interview clips with Pastor Führer as he animatedly describes the October 9 events.

10. Führer, extended interview (Nov 6, 2009).

Were there connecting threads of both people and beliefs that joined the church's failed resistance to Hitler with the peaceful revolution of 1989? Why was the church unable to stop the Nazis and yet fifty years later provide both the space and strategy by which a totalitarian government was brought to its knees and nonviolently removed from power?

The chapters that follow tell the backstory of the relevant theological debates and figures in church politics leading to the moment when the church became the cradle for Germany's only nonviolent revolution. As I considered the best way to frame this half-century-long story of the church's struggle, I wrote a follow-up email to Pastor Führer, asking him who were the influences behind his own pastoral engagement with a nation's political life? Had he specific inspirations or influences from the church struggles of the Nazi era? I listed several names from the past. On behalf of her husband, his wife Monika replied, naming three persons, Barth, *Bonhoeffer* and Niemöller as "good friends," with Bonhoeffer's name in bold. But speaking of her husband, she added, "But he isn't a man of books, but a man of action."[11] I adopted this testimony as my starting point to trace how these witnesses guided the next generation of pastors, and in particular, Christian Führer, as they sought to bear witness to the gospel in a highly charged political context. I will describe something of how these three in particular wrestled with the competing loyalties of church and state, and how each gave witness to a distinctive way of being the church in the world. As their stories unfold, we will also see how their engagement was taken up by their students and younger colleagues, including Pastor Führer.

Let me repeat: that the church was able to make such a contribution to Germany's reunification is well worth pondering. Think of it: an institution marginalized in every way possible by the state education system, stripped of its traditional privileges, ridiculed by the government and the media as a dinosaur. Nevertheless it became the catalyst for a transformation that enabled a great but troubled nation to be peacefully reunited—something unprecedented in German history. And if the enormity of Germany's nonviolent reunification is not enough to render one speechless, there is a further enormous surprise closely connected here. That is, the Cold War itself, with its horrific nuclear arsenals, its rhetoric of fear, its cultural barricades both literal and spiritual, came to an end without a shot being fired. The recent alarm about the emergence of a new Cold War between Russia and the United States should not diminish but highlight the unique accomplishment of the Gorbachev and Reagan/Bush era.

11. Personal correspondence with Christian and Monika Führer. The central influence of Bonhoeffer for the 1989 revolution has been noted by others. Cf. Moses, "Bonhoeffer's Reception," 296.

I have a final motive in revisiting this story: perhaps a clearer under-standing of this modern miracle may help us (both Christians and non-Christians) explore hopeful analogies in our own violent times. As Pastor Führer was fond of putting it, "Anyone who does not believe in miracles is not a realist."[12] From the perspective of the previous half-century of church-state relations in Germany, I now see that Pastor Führer's invitation to pray around the cross in 1981 joined together what Dietrich Bonhoeffer called "prayer and righteous action." Though it was impossible to anticipate or predict, that 1981 prayer meeting was not a random event. Nor was it by chance that *Nikolaikirche* members formed a nonviolent ring around the Stasi headquarters on the night of October 9, and chanted *"Keine Gewalt!"* (No Violence! No Provocation!). These were enacted prayers centered in the gospel, with a lineage going back to resistance begun in 1933. The following chapters tell the story of how in the short term, the church's resistance failed. Nobody, no person, no institution, no nation was able to stop Germany from launching a global war. In fact the church's own resistance too often dissolved into acquiescence. But from this struggle a new kind of church emerged with a theology that was to impact Germany far out of proportion to its numbers.

To trace the development of Leipzig's peculiar theological weapons—prayers and candles—we must go back to the 1930s, as the newly elected National Socialist government began its seductive courtship of the Protes-tant Church in Germany. There is a sentence Führer quoted in the church brochure which offers a summary of the trajectory we shall study: *The church is only a church if it is there for everyone. Dietrich Bonhoeffer.*[13] Again, this citation was not a casual choice. As I have noted already, Monika Führer listed Bonhoeffer's name in bold as one of her husband's "good friends." To help us truly understand the *Annus Mirabilis* which was 1989 we will turn first to Bonhoeffer's experiments in fashioning a church that existed not simply for its own members. Of course, as the Third Reich swept to power, to live from this counter-vision meant that a clash between church and state was inevitable.

12. Quoting the founding prime minister of Israel, David Ben-Gurion. Führer, fore-ward to *Und Wir Sind Dabei Gewesen.*

13. Führer, *Protestant Lutheran Church of St. Nikolai,* 23.

1

Dietrich Bonhoeffer
To Seize the Wheel Itself

Cheap grace is the mortal enemy of our church.
Our struggle today is for costly grace.

—DIETRICH BONHOEFFER[1]

WITHIN MONTHS OF SWEEPING to power, the new Reich government of
Adolf Hitler signed a historic treaty or *Concordat* with the Vatican (July 8,
1933), gaining itself a new level of international respect. Not only did Rome
reverse its previous condemnations of National Socialism, it agreed to dis-
band its political organizations, including the Center Party, since the days of
Bismarck the major Catholic voice in German political life. With the stroke
of a pen all Roman Catholic political resistance to Hitler's National Socialist
State ceased to exist. In exchange, the new government promised Rome full
autonomy for her educational institutions and associations. Perhaps most
importantly, the *Concordat* opened the way for millions of German Roman
Catholics to serve and fully embrace the new National Socialist State.[2] Far
from satisfied at this immense consolidation of power, Hitler now sought to
shape and reform Germany's other great Christian tradition, the Protestant
Church, into his idyllic vision of coordination (*Gleichschaltung*), whereby
all cultural organizations were harmonized into the purposes of the Third
Reich. With remarkable political savvy, Hitler turned his full attention

1. Bonhoeffer, *Discipleship*, 43.
2. Scholder, *Churches and the Third Reich*, 1:381–413.

toward the Protestants, enticing and intimidating the children of Luther to join his revival of national honor and military-industrial strength.[3]

It was a heady moment for the church to be courted by this strong new leader risen from the ranks of the common folk of the nation. Indeed over the next months, it nearly collapsed into a department of state. As we will see in the next chapter, Hitler's plans were thwarted through a remarkable chain of events. But unlike 1989, the church failed to create a successful counter-revolution. How did it happen that on the one hand, Hitler's plan to completely assimilate the church floundered while on the other the church was unable to derail Hitler's fraudulent dream? The primary clue for both the church's tragic failure and its later success lies embedded in the life and ministry of Pastor Dietrich Bonhoeffer.

As part of his reflection on the four years since the Nazi rise to power, Bonhoeffer wrote *Discipleship*, which his friend and biographer Eberhard Bethge described as an impassioned analysis of how Luther's theology of grace became hijacked by German nationalism.[4] A Lutheran pastor of impeccable academic and social pedigree, Bonhoeffer declared Luther's homeland to be in a state of cultural emergency regarding the meaning of *grace*. It was as though a bishop of Rome attacked the legitimacy of apostolic succession. With Luther's famous attack on the indulgence seller Tetzel in the background, Bonhoeffer accused his own church of selling off the legacy of the Lutheran Reformation into bargain-basement goods. Luther's cornerstone doctrine of the justification of the sinner had been deformed into the justification of sin.[5] Of course that great word, *justification*, was retained as a centerpiece of church syntax but it had been emptied of semantic integrity, collapsed into a system, and projected as an interpretation of history in which the German *Volk* had been conned into playing the starring role.

With a diatribe in keeping with Luther's attack on Tetzel, Bonhoeffer summed up the church's betrayal in two discordant words: "cheap grace."

> Cheap grace is preaching forgiveness without repentance; it is baptism without the discipline of community; it is the Lord's

---

3. Unless otherwise indicated I will normally use the word "church" to refer to the Protestant Church in Germany (*Evangelische* in German). This is because, apart from notable exceptions, by signing the *Concordat* the Catholic Church separated itself from any resistance to the new state, at least until 1937 and Pius XI's encyclical. See ch. 4. Moreover, the flow of our story heads eastward to the GDR side of a postwar divided Germany, which historically was the land of Luther, with Catholics comprising only 14% of the GDR population in 1949 and by 1989, only 4%. Moses, "Church Policy," 8. Also, Spotts, *Churches and Politics in Germany*, 22–43.

4. Bethge, *Dietrich Bonhoeffer*, 375.

5. Ibid., 43.

Supper without confession of sin; it is absolution without personal confession. Cheap grace is grace without discipleship, grace without the cross, grace without the living, incarnate Jesus Christ.[6]

Outwardly of course, Germans still drank from the traditional Lutheran vessels, but in fact like ravens they had "gathered around the carcass of cheap grace" and "imbibed the poison which has killed the following of Jesus among us," leaving behind a place of spiritual carnage where millions of souls were being killed.[7]

The Tipping Point

What had provoked this withering attack? The lead-up to Hitler had been a lengthy gestated synthesis of Christianity, patriotism and idealist philosophy. But the entire idolatrous edifice reached its tipping point with the coming to power of National Socialism. The actual signal which alerted Bonhoeffer came in April 1933 when the *Aryan clause* became the law of the land. This law disqualified those of Jewish origin, regardless of religion, from holding any form of employment by the state. As if this wasn't disturbing enough, the authorities of Bonhoeffer's regional church in and around Berlin, the Prussian *Landeskirchen*, took the fatal step in *coordination*, by adopting it, thereby forbidding those of Jewish descent from the office of pastor.[8] Estimates of the number of pastors affected vary between thirty and ninety.[9] But for Bonhoeffer it wasn't the numbers. The point is that within months of the launch of Hitler's Third Reich, Bonhoeffer sensed an emergency had arisen and the church utterly unprepared for the challenge.

In fact, only weeks prior to the synod's corrupting decision, Bonhoeffer had met with several younger theologians at the request of the revered director of the Bethel Institute, Friedrich von Bodelschwingh Jr., to help draft a confession to address the emerging crisis. As it happened, it wasn't published at the time and was later revised and toned down by Martin Niemöller, who was yet to grasp the nettle of the crisis. But Bonhoeffer's text forcefully rejected the teachings of the coordinators, the so-called German Christians and unlike the later Barmen document boldly linked the crisis

6. Ibid., 44.

7. Ibid., 53.

8. Bethge, *Dietrich Bonhoeffer*, 237. To be precise, the decision was made to adopt the paragraph for future clergy, while permitting current clergy of Jewish ancestry to continue.

9. Hockenos, *Church Divided*, 20. According to Barnett the higher number includes Aryan pastors with non-Aryan wives (*For the Soul of the People*, 324).

with the Jewish question. "Christians descended from the Gentile world must expose themselves to persecution rather than give up, voluntarily or by force, even in one respect, their brotherhood with the Jewish Christians in the Church which has been established through Word and sacrament."[10]

Why was Bonhoeffer nearly alone in making such a vigorous and principled rejection of the Aryan clause at this time? No doubt his close friendship with Franz Hildebrandt, a Jewish convert and fellow pastor, sensitized and clarified for him the issue. Moreover, his recent year of study at Union Theological Seminary in New York was next door to Harlem, the famous African American cultural center, where his friend and fellow student Frank Fisher, himself an African American, introduced him to regular worship and teaching Sunday school. Clearly the Union Seminary experience granted him an unusual empathy for ethnic minorities caught up in a racist society. For Bonhoeffer, it meant that upon returning home his eyes were painfully open to the ugliness of German racism to which his fellow Germans were blind. Without a doubt, Bonhoeffer was in full agreement with the blunt assessment that Karl Barth had already published in 1933:

> The fellowship of those belonging to the church is not determined by blood, therefore, not by race, but by the Holy Spirit and Baptism. If the German Evangelical Church excludes Jewish-Christians, or treats them as of a lower grade, she ceases to be a Christian Church.[11]

Hence for Bonhoeffer, to exclude baptized Jews from full partnership in church constituted a *statu confessionis*, that is, a crisis in which the church's fundamental identity was at risk. Shall the church declare that in Christ there are neither Jews nor Greeks? Shall it speak aloud to the *Volk* that the blood of Christ into which we are baptized is thicker than any racial blood? For a national church (and Europe had few of any other kind) to return to ethnic exclusivity would be to relapse into a paganism of a scale unknown since the days of Constantine's nephew, Julian the Apostate. Ironically, Bonhoeffer warned that an Aryan Church would be a "Jewish Church," that is, like the "foolish Galatians" who based Christianity on a legal/racial prerequisite. This time, however, instead of circumcision, the prerequisite was race.[12] That his church passed by on the other side while the Aryan laws were enacted provoked Bonhoeffer to remark that a greater danger than the election of the

10. Quoted in Scholder, *Churches and the Third Reich*, 1:458. The original document with Bonhoeffer's strong influence, particularly in regards to the Jews, only became known from the publication of the biography by Bethge in 1959.

11. Barth, *Theological Existence Today!*, 52.

12. Bonhoeffer, *Berlin*, 372.

German Christian Ludwig Müller as *Reichsbishop* was an orthodox church that ignored the Sermon on the Mount. In other words, Müller, even though handpicked by Hitler, might have been able to subscribe to orthodox doctrine.[13] The Prussian Synod's adoption of the Aryan clause meant for Bonhoeffer that church and state relations had collapsed into chaos. "It is precisely here *in our attitude toward the state*, that we must speak out with absolute sincerity for the sake of Jesus Christ and of the ecumenical cause. It must be made quite clear—terrifying though it is—that we are immediately faced with the decision: National Socialist *or* Christian."[14]

Immediately following the synod vote, Bonhoeffer, Hildebrandt and other members of the opposition retreated to Martin Niemöller's manse in the Berlin suburb of Dahlem. Bonhoeffer and Hildebrandt argued that the time had come to resign in protest from the church. But the others resisted such a decisive step as too extreme a response for what in the end affected a mere handful of pastors. Bonhoeffer followed up with a quick letter to Barth, asking his counsel. When in reply Barth too advised a period of waiting, Bonhoeffer felt completely isolated. This was the relational context in which he decided to accept a pastorate of two German-speaking congregations in London and withdraw from the turbulence of Berlin.[15]

Reading Bethge's biography of his friend offers a firsthand account of Bonhoeffer's sense of the unfolding tragedy which overtook the church; how in fact Bonhoeffer's voice did not carry the day even among those, like Niemöller and Barth, who would become pillars of the resistance launched by the Confessing Church (*Bekennende Kirche*).[16] Yes, Barth boldly sent a copy of *Theological Existence Today!* to Adolf Hitler, but he refrained from making the Jewish question central to his own resistance. Even though he would be the principal author of the celebrated Barmen Declaration the following year, he would make no mention of vulnerable populations in Germany nor abuses of human rights.[17] In a 1967 letter thanking Bethge for sending a copy of the Bonhoeffer biography, Barth not only praised Bonhoeffer for being so clear sighted on the centrality of the Jewish question but lamented his own silence. He writes:

13. Bethge, *Dietrich Bonhoeffer*, 183.

14. Ibid., 192.

15. Ibid., 237.

16. Ibid., 238.

17. For Barnett this absence is because Barmen was a "negotiated and strategic compromise" in order to win unity against the German Christians from across the Protestant spectrum. Barnett, "Barmen," 17–23. As we will see, Barth himself acknowledged that he tailored his words to gain a consensus.

> Especially new to me was the fact that in 1933 and the years fol-
> lowing, Bonhoeffer was the first and almost the only one to face
> and tackle the Jewish question so centrally and energetically. I
> have long since regarded it as a fault on my part that I did not
> make this question a decisive issue, at least publicly in the church
> conflict (e.g., in the two Barmen Declarations I drafted in 1934).[18]

However, Barth's silence would not be permanent. A major change in
Barth's thinking on church and state relations would lead him to include a
series of outspoken public statements regarding the Jewish Question. But
this development would have to await his own deepening reflections which
grew out of his experience of deportation from Germany and marginalization within Basel.[19]

Bonhoeffer's Silence

However, Bonhoeffer's clear grasp of this core issue creates its own puzzle.
Despite Barth's praise for Bonhoeffer's early support of Jewish rights, how
should we interpret the lack of a single comment concerning Jewish mistreatment or the Aryan paragraph in *Discipleship*? What we do find there
is a profound universal defense of human dignity based on the incarnation.
Through the incarnation, Bonhoeffer says, the entire human race recovers
the dignity of the image of God. "Whoever from now on attacks the least of
the people attacks Christ."[20] But this eloquent defense of the "least" stands
without concrete application to specific persons or groups in the Third
Reich. How should we interpret this lack of concrete application to the political situation of the moment?

Perhaps by the time *Discipleship* was published (1937) silence regarding the Jews was a survival tactic in a totalitarian society. Perhaps it was
partly rhetorical, letting the reader supply the concrete implications. Bethge
describes a moment in 1940 when he and Bonhoeffer heard the announce-
ment that France had surrendered. Sitting at an open-air café when the news
was announced, the crowd around them erupted in celebration. Bethge
watched dazed as Bonhoeffer joined the cheering crowd in standing to give
the Hitler salute. Bonhoeffer whispered, "Raise your arm. Are you crazy?"
Later he explained: "We shall have to run risks for very different things now,

---

18. Barth, *Letters, 1961–1968*, 250.
19. See ch. 4 for the details of Barth's later outspokenness.
20. Bonhoeffer, *Discipleship*, 285.

but not for that salute."[21] In his 1937 devotional best seller, Bonhoeffer did not run that risk.

Perhaps the struggle within Bonhoeffer ran more deeply than tactics. In 1933 he experienced another conflict between state policy and the cost of discipleship when his brother-in-law Gerhard Leibholz's father died. Though Leibholz's father was Jewish and had never been baptized, the family asked Dietrich to take the funeral service. Bonhoeffer wavered, consulting his general superintendent for advice, and was strongly recommended against taking a service for a Jew at that moment.[22] A few months later, Bonhoeffer wrote anguished words to his brother-in-law:

> I am tormented by the thought . . . that I didn't do as you asked me as a matter of course. To be frank, I can't think what made me behave as I did. How could I have been so much afraid at the time? It must have seemed equally incomprehensible to all of you, and yet you said nothing. But it preys on my mind . . . because it's the kind of thing one can never make up for. So all I can do is to ask you to forgive my weakness then. I know now for certain that I ought to have behaved differently.[23]

The personal failure to risk his standing within church structures was part of Bonhoeffer's struggle. Another evidence of struggle was the previously mentioned decision just as events were heating up in Berlin in 1933 to withdraw to the relative tranquility of a pastorate in London. When later Bonhoeffer wrote to Karl Barth explaining his actions, he admitted that he did not tell him beforehand for fear that Barth might talk him out of going. Barth minced no words in response, bluntly admonishing him that he was needed in Berlin.

> Think only of one thing: that you are a German, that your church's house is on fire, that you know enough, and know well enough how to say what you know, to be able to help, and in fact you ought to return to your post by the next ship! Well, let's say, with the one after that. But I cannot tell you explicitly and urgently enough that you belong in Berlin and not in London.[24]

Finally, there was also the "almost" escape to the safety of an American lectureship only months before war began with Poland. Was this a last attempt to avoid the task he must bear? He wrote to the American theologian

21. Bethge, *Dietrich Bonhoeffer*, 585.
22. Ibid., 209.
23. Quoted in Bethge, *Dietrich Bonhoeffer*, 209.
24. Quoted in Bonhoeffer, *London*, 41.

Reinhold Niebuhr that it was a mistake to have come, that his task was to be with his people.[25] All these instances can be debated back and forth, but together, they offer a glimpse of Bonhoeffer's struggle with the risks involved and help us see why he himself refused to view his own path as a sort of heroic performance. He understood too well what kept the church from standing up for others. It was only day by day that his own journey of resistance led him to the simple path, "daring to do what is right" as part of an ordinary disciple's road to freedom.

Taking Stock

Bonhoeffer's inner struggle is reflected in the German title of his prison writings, *Widerstand und Ergebung* (Resistance and Submission) which the English translation blandly retitled *Letters and Papers from Prison.*[26] Writing many risks later from a prison cell, Bonhoeffer both pays tribute to Barth and also criticizes his unofficial teacher. As the crisis wore on, he regretted that "in the nonreligious interpretation of theological concepts he [Barth] gave no concrete guidance, either in dogmatics or ethics."[27] In an outline for the book he hoped to write, there is a section entitled "taking stock of Christianity." Here Bonhoeffer shines a laser light that illumines the church's failure in two simple but profound sentences: "Church defending itself. No risk taking for others." The essence of his lament is that whenever the Confessing Church dared to speak up, it was never on behalf of others, but only for itself. This failure he now viewed as evidence of the absence of a personal faith in Christ.[28] The prison cell granted Bonhoeffer a new clarity from below: the church's problem had to do not with tactics, rather something was missing at the core of its doctrine of the church. "No risk taking for others" was the converse of no faith in Jesus. Discipleship and theological confession belonged indissolubly together.

Resisting the State

Already in his 1933 essay, Bonhoeffer identified three implications for church/state relations were the church to confess the gospel faithfully.

25. Niebuhr, "To America and Back," 165.

26. Cf. Bonhoeffer, *Letters and Papers.*

27. Ibid., 429.

28. Ibid., 500.

The State that threatens the proclamation of the Christian message negates itself. There are thus three possibilities for action that the Church can take vis-a-vis the State: *first* (as we have said) questioning the State as to the legitimate State character of its actions, that is, making the State responsible for what it does. *Second* is service to the victims of the State's actions. The Church has an unconditional obligation toward the victims of any societal order, even if they do not belong to the Christian community. "Let us work for the good of all." These are both ways in which the Church, in its freedom, conducts itself in the interest of a free State. In times when the laws are changing, the Church may under no circumstances neglect either of these duties. The *third* possibility is not just to bind up the wounds of the victims beneath the wheel but to seize the wheel itself. Such action would be direct political action on the part of the Church. This is only possible and called for if the Church sees the State to be failing in its function of creating law and order, that is, if the Church perceives that the State, without any scruples, has created either too much or too little law and order . . . such as the obligatory exclusion of baptized Jews from our Christian congregations or a ban on missions to the Jews. In such a case, the Church would find itself in *statu confessionis*, and the State would find itself in the act of self-negation.[29]

In laying out these possible lines of action, Bonhoeffer says that timing and tactics have a place. After all, according to Jesus' parable, there is a time to be wise as a serpent, like the children of this world (Luke 16:8). But there can be no illusions about the cost. Of course it was neither inevitable nor foreseeable that ten years later Bonhoeffer would be arrested for his role in the plot to assassinate the head of the German state. The twists and turns of his next ten years—pastoral duties in Spain, studies in New York, Berlin, pastorate in London, cancelling plans to travel to India and meet Gandhi, returning to supervise an illegal seminary, engagement to marry, conspiracy work—these were the improvisational acts of a free man, yet one who, like Luther, was also a servant, bound by his commitment to follow Jesus.[30]

29. Bonhoeffer, *Berlin*, 365–66.

30. "A Christian is a perfectly free lord of all, subject to none. A Christian is a perfectly dutiful servant of all, subject to all." Luther, "Freedom of a Christian," 277.

Bonhoeffer and the 1989 Revolution

What was it, even from the earliest days of Bonhoeffer's resistance, that so impacted the church's witness in East Germany? First and foremost, there was Bonhoeffer's prescient awareness that the Jewish question was the defining question for the church; that to deny the Jew before the state was to deny Jesus as Lord of the church. As early as his doctoral thesis, *Sanctorum Communio*, Bonhoeffer described the church as the place where through faith in Christ, one is granted the gift of freedom to love the other.[31] But it was only the final months of his life when he spoke of Jesus as "the man for others," employing a title Bethge describes as "at once confession, hymn, prayer and interpretation."[32] In this designation Bonhoeffer gathered up the longings that had haunted even his earliest writings. It was the phrase upon which he "hung his heart" for it expressed in an utterly concrete and social way that to know the incarnate God always joins us in solidarity with our neighbor.[33]

To leap forward to 1989, this title explains why Bonhoeffer was the essential theologian for the church in East Germany, a society where "the others" might be dissidents, atheists, apparatchiks, state security police (the dreaded *Stasi*) or any combination thereof. If Jesus is "the human being for others" there can be only one clear and distinct path for his church. This is why Bonhoeffer's way, despite his absence at his brother-in-law's funeral, his sojourn in a safe London parish, his "mistaken" flight to America, could not in the end be the path of a private pilgrim seeking inner peace or outer safety. It was not a casual choice for Pastor Führer to include in the *Nikolaikirche* brochure Bonhoeffer's words: "The church is only a church if it is there for everyone."[34] Nor was it just a coincidence that the *Nikolaikirche* motto was *Ofen für Alles* (open for everyone.)

Neither at the adoption of the Aryan laws, nor in response to the savage persecution of *Krystalnacht* (The Night of Broken Glass) did the church speak any word of public protest and solidarity on behalf of the others. True, the church's resistance prevented a total apostasy, a collapse into a religious bureau of the National Socialist State. But only by "hanging its heart" upon

31. Bonhoeffer, *Sanctorum Communio*, 166–70.

32. Bethge, *Dietrich Bonhoeffer*, 790. Cf. *Letters and Papers*, 501. It is interesting that Barth's *Doctrine of Creation*, published in 1948, uses the subtitles "Jesus, Man for God" and "Jesus, Man for Other Men" as the titles respectively of chs. 44 and 45 on what it means to describe human beings as created for covenant partnership. Barth, *CD*, III/2, 55, 203.

33. Bethge, *Dietrich Bonhoeffer*, 99.

34. Führer, *Protestant Lutheran Church of St. Nikolai*, 23. The quotation from the prison writings is slightly different: "The church is church only when it is there for others." Bonhoeffer, *Letters and Papers*, 503.

the christological title bequeathed by Bonhoeffer would it become the mustard seed of revolution which toppled a totalitarian government in 1989.

Meanwhile, another pastor's journey sheds further light both on the courage of the church's resistance as well as why it failed to incorporate the solidarity of standing alongside the other. To Martin Niemöller's story we turn next.

2

Martin Niemöller
From U-Boat to Pulpit to Concentration Camp

I am aware that this League cannot save the Church and move the world; but I am equally aware that we owe it to the Lord of the Church and to the brethren to do today what lies within our power, and that caution and restraint today already signify failure, because those in great distress lack proof of our fraternal solidarity. So let us act.

—MARTIN NIEMÖLLER[1]

THE CHURCH/STATE VISION WHICH NURTURED NIEMÖLLER

IN HIS LETTER WRITTEN to his fellow pastors in September 1933, Martin Niemöller wrote with clarity and boldness that, whatever the outcome, they must resist the changes happening in Germany. Yet in many ways Niemöller was the unlikeliest critic of the head of the German State in its hour of national renewal. Hitler's popularity during his first year as chancellor was unparalleled. Niemöller had himself voted for him—twice. One would be hard-pressed to find anyone more patriotic in all of Germany than Martin Niemöller.

---

1. From the letter that launched the Pastors' Emergency League. Quoted in Scholder, *Churches and the Third Reich*, 1:484.

As a youth, Niemöller combined love of country with a love of sailing by joining the navy, later serving with energy and skill as a U-boat commander during the Great War (or World War I as it later came to be known). In many ways Niemöller was the product of the German triumvirate which united Lutheran theology, patriotic nationalism and military prowess. It was a synthesis which identified grace as God's promise of national renewal; faith as trust in God's providential guidance of the German people through history; the communion of saints as the community of the *Volk*; God's covenant as the special bond with the German people; law as obedience to national values; sin as the neglect of national duties. Somehow mysteriously, the Holy Spirit joined all these blessings together and poured them upon the German Volk.[2] This was the relationship between church and state that Martin Niemöller had inherited and internalized.

Today it is easier to see how all the "Christian" nations of Europe who designed and implemented the Great War were guilty of making an unequal yoke between the Christian religion and patriotic militarism. Church historians have amply documented the impact of nationalism in the preaching and popular piety in *both* Britain and Germany in the era leading up to August 1914. But a careful study will reveal that the strongest bond between church and state was forged by Germany.[3] It was the norm for German worship services to include flags in the sanctuary along with patriotic hymns. More typically, British clergy would strike a self-critical tone, at times warning of the dangers inherent in excessive patriotism.[4] At a distance of a century, the marriage of religion to militarism at the heart of Europe may be hard to imagine, but under stress the distance can still collapse. For instance, when I served as a pastor in a United Reformed Church in England shortly after the Falklands War, a respected elder requested that we sing "I Vow to Thee My Country" on Remembrance Sunday. Being a recent arrival from the United States, I looked up the words in the hymnal. To my surprise I discovered an unapologetic nationalism throughout this popular hymn. There was no hint of any ameliorating confession of sin nor any balanced prayer for judgment and mercy, such as one finds, for instance, in G. K. Chesterton's "O God of Earth and Altar." It is doubtful one could have found in a Prussian hymnal a more idolatrous mingling of flag and altar than the following stanza.

---

2. According to Wilhelm Prussel. Cf. Hoover, *God, Germany and Britain*, 133.

3. Jenkins, *Great and Holy War*, 74–76.

4. Ibid., 89. Even so, Hoover cites many examples of a British-style marriage of altar and nationalism, including Archbishop of Canterbury Randall Davidson and the highly regarded Studdert-Kennedy. Hoover, *God, Germany and Britain*, 24, 123, 131.

> I vow to thee, my country, all earthly things above,
> Entire and whole and perfect, the service of my love:
> The love that asks no question, the love that stands the test,
> That lays upon the altar the dearest and the best;
> The love that never falters, the love that pays the price,
> The love that makes undaunted the final sacrifice.[5]

Being a US citizen, the elder kindly excused me for not being swept along with nostalgia for the days of the British Empire. Moreover, to her credit, she also acknowledged how these lyrics could have been sung by "a good Nazi." The request was set aside. But it gives one pause: if after two devastating world wars and the loss of empire, a pious Scottish elder in the 1980s was still nostalgic to sing this hymn, one can only imagine the general mood of church-going folk when Britain's Empire was popularly viewed as the White Man's Burden to civilize and proclaim salvation to the nations of the world.

Growing up a pastor's son in Kaiser Wilhelm's Germany, Niemöller recalls being nurtured by two dogmas: "a good Christian is a good citizen, and a good Christian is a good soldier."[6] When after early hopes of decisive victory were dashed, those raised on this diad were thrown into confusion. Moreover, defeat was compounded by an acute sense of injustice. The Treaty of Versailles was widely believed to be so vindictive that instead of experiencing defeat as a call for self-examination and reorientation for the sins which led to such a failure, the wounded German soul reached for the "stab in the back" legend from the German epic of the Nibelung in which Siegfried the hero was stabbed by treachery. Like Siegfried, the German armies were unbeatable in battle except for the betrayal of the politicians back home who settled for an armistice before the country had felt the full pain of an Allied invasion. Many ached to replace the disgrace of Versailles. How would Germany recover its pride against those who had trampled on her honor?[7]

In history, the cry for justice is repeatedly the cloak worn by the desire for revenge. This sense of having been unfairly scapegoated by the Allies, helps us understand why Germany's defeat did so little to deconstruct Germany's *Gott mit uns* (God with us) synthesis. Certainly for Niemöller, the aftermath of war was a most un-contemplative time as a newly married man entered into training for Christian ministry. To keep a roof over his head and food on the

5. Spring-Rice, "I Vow to Thee My Country," in Parry, *Congregational Praise*, hymn 810.

6. Quoted in Bentley, *Martin Niemöller*, 8.

7. To anticipate 1989, it is striking how a justice came to German soil in which, for once, no one was "getting back" at anyone else.

table, he worked around the clock while attending seminary classes. With two children soon coming one after the other, the family might have gone hungry had his wife, Else, not unraveled the gold lace from his old uniforms which were promptly sold to the jeweler for melting down.[8]

During the postwar years inflation in Germany was beyond belief. On Monday, a loaf of bread might cost a million marks; on Tuesday two million. To even try to keep up with this financial meltdown, employers paid their workers daily rather than weekly. Against this backdrop of imminent social collapse, Niemöller worked day and night, convinced that the best help he could offer his stricken country was to teach people the knowledge of Christ as Lord and how to diligently attend to God's Word.[9]

Given his church and military background, Niemöller was no friend of the parliamentary democracy imposed upon Germany by the Allies. For Niemöller, the Weimar Republic was a sorry, truncated fabrication, lacking a Kaiser father figure and divorced from the church in a manner foreign to Lutheran German history. Nor had Niemöller sympathy for communism's plea for a class-based worker uprising. He joined the Academic Defense Corps, a reserve fighting unit of right-wing students, commanding a battalion which saw action in halting an attempted *Spartacist* (communist) insurrection.[10] It was not a radical step when in 1924 Niemöller first voted for the National Socialist party. In 1931 he avidly read Hitler's autobiography, *Mein Kampf*. In the spring of 1933 he voted Nazi again, this time in their breakthrough election, which as it turned out, was the last multiparty election in Germany for many years.[11]

In retrospect, Niemöller's voting path mirrored that of many faithful churchgoing folk deeply attachment to the triad of faith, patriotism and military strength. Like many Germans, Niemöller projected upon Hitler the embodiment of a strong moral message, the recovery of traditional values and the restoration of the nation's honor after the Versailles humiliation. The Nazi platform had no irritating secular tone. Article 24 of the party stated clearly its intention to promote "positive Christianity in the spirit of Martin Luther."[12] In his victory speech on becoming chancellor in the fateful January of 1933, Hitler declared "Christianity the unshakable foundation of the moral and ethical life of our people."[13] He also claimed the two main

---

8. Schmidt, *Pastor Niemöller*, 69.

9. Ibid., 63.

10. Ibid., 62–69.

11. Bentley, *Martin Niemöller*, 48.

12. Schmidt, *Pastor Niemöller*, 85.

13. Quoted in Cochrane, *Church's Confession*, 85.

Christian traditions in Germany (Roman Catholic and Protestant) were "the bedrock of state and family life" that would remain unchanged. Clearly such words were intended to reassure traditional value voters like Niemöller. Had Hitler an ounce of antagonism toward Christianity, he kept it well hid.[14]

Riding this patriotic wave came the *Deutsche Christen Bewegung* (German Christian movement), with its platform of uniting Nazism and Christianity in keeping with the Nazi policy of *Gleichschaltung* (coordination). The age-old regional governance within the Protestant church would soon be unified under the providential guidance of the *Führer*. However, this was the beginning of a dramatic change for Protestants, who since the Reformation had divided themselves into local government regions (*Landes*), which both reflected and contributed to the historic German reticence about political unity for the nation. Most *Landeskirchen* were Lutheran; some were Reformed; others (through the actions of Prussian King Frederick William III in 1817), a union of Reformed and Lutheran. It's easy to forget that Germany only became a united nation under one sovereign in 1871, later even than Italy (1861). For the German Christian movement, the Nazi *Gleichschaltung* was a tangible sign of God's providential hand in history, merging together the gifts of "race," "nation," and "honor." Through these intra-historical revelations God was active, disclosing to Germany her future.[15] During the early months of his chancellorship, Hitler repeatedly spoke of providential convergence. The German Christian movement convinced itself that Hitler's rise signaled nothing less than God's blessing and guidance for a Germany now risen from the ashes of humiliation.[16]

At this sensitive moment the highly regarded Göttingen theologian Emanuel Hirsch articulated the feelings of many when he openly declared Hitler to be Germany's opportunity for rebirth.[17] Hirsch became the leading *Volk* theologian. According to his diagnosis, parliamentary democracy was nothing but the political engine of selfish individualism that had proved itself incapable of binding society together on a path of common duty and service to a greater good. Germany must repent of the false path of Weimar democracy. The starting point for Hirsch was the *Volk* hearing God's voice in history through their God-given capacity for making conscientious decisions. That is the stuff of history: living out great moments in which a people claim their meaning and destiny through strong decisions. In the emergence of a gifted,

14. After the first eight weeks of his premiership, Hitler would never again so frequently and ardently implore God and make use of Christian symbols. Scholder, *Churches and the Third Reich*, 1:222.

15. Cochrane, *Church's Confession*, 71.

16. Bentley, *Martin Niemöller*, 49.

17. Ericksen, *Theologians under Hitler*, 124.

natural leader rising from the workers themselves, the time had come for Germany to affirm her strength by confirming Adolf Hitler as their strong leader (*Der Führer*). Hitler would be the one to unite, discipline and call forth the sacrificial spirit necessary for Germany to reach her true destiny under God's providence. Church support for this German Christian Movement would confirm these events as God's moment of restoration.[18]

Such a merger of state and church, *Volk* and gospel, met receptive soil in Niemöller. In fact, the whole tenor of both Hirsch and the *German Christians* seemed perfectly designed to stir the heart of this pious war veteran. In nearly every way it is an irony, analogous to Saul the Jewish Pharisee becoming Paul the Apostle to the Gentiles, that Niemöller became an international symbol of Christian resistance to Hitler. What provoked this pious war veteran to become Hitler's most public adversary?

Ever awkwardly honest, Niemöller confessed the alarm bell that roused him was not the treatment of Jews. Regarding non-Aryans, he was closer to those, like Paul Althaus, the respected "moderate" professor from Erlangen, who argued that based on 1 Corinthians 8 (unnecessary stumbling blocks), German evangelism and mission were best served when the church drew its clergy from its own people. Therefore Jewish Christians can quite legitimately be asked to step aside from public ministry, especially since the Jewish people were a major cause of Germany's collapse into Weimar secularism.[19] At this point in time, Niemöller was blind to the treatment of *the other* as the essential sign of Christ's presence in the church.

It was Hitler himself who lifted the veil from Niemöller's eyes. It happened after the Nazi's breakthrough election in March 1933, when he chose to bring the full weight of his office upon the church by using the power of the state and the party to ensure that his personal choice for Reich Church bishop, Ludwig Müller, would lead the newly organized Protestant Church in Germany. The plan was to reorganize the twenty-eight traditional regional Protestant churches (*Landeskirchen*) under one Reich bishop and thus conform the church to the Führer principle (*Führerprinzip*) in keeping with the new Germany. The German Christian movement seemed ideally suited to become Hitler's tool to implement this coordination. Richard Evans suggests that Hitler's real ambition was to create a new kind of National Church, one that would eventually integrate Nazi teachings about race and nationalism into the church's core, and eventually win over the mass of Catholics as well.[20] Already in July Hitler had signed an agreement (*Concordat*) with the

18. Ibid., 135.
19. Ibid., 108–9.
20. Evans, *Third Reich in Power*, 223.

Catholic Church, guaranteeing independence for its schools in exchange for abandoning its traditional political role in Germany through the Center Party. Now Hitler would proceed to eliminate all Protestant opposition by its *coordination* under his chosen representative. The church elections which followed were accompanied by the worst forms of manipulation.[21] The last straw came on the night before the elections when Hitler himself made an unprecedented intervention by giving a national radio address to endorse his friend Müller for the *Reichsbishop* post.[22] As a result, the July 23 church elections swept the German Christians to victory. To Niemöller, this was no conscientious decision that would help Germany claim its destiny (Hirsch). It was a naked grab for power which disrespected the historic freedom of Protestantism in Germany. "I was absolutely disgusted that a head of state should act in this way. From that moment onwards, I didn't believe that there would be any support for the autonomous existence of Protestant churches so long as Hitler had the say."[23]

As for the Jewish question, Niemöller's view was complex. When the 1933 civil service law (Aryan paragraph) forbade non-Aryans from holding public office in the state, 28 percent of higher civil service officers in Prussia lost their jobs.[24] But for Niemöller, laws governing the employment or civil rights of Jews or any minority had nothing to do with the church's mandate. Moreover, there was a long-standing anti-Semitic tendency within German culture, with awkward quotations antedating Luther himself. All this was part of Niemöller's baggage. During Hitler's rise to power, the church was silent about the mistreatment of many subgroups, including communists, democratic socialists, and trade unionists, many of whom were systematically rounded up and murdered. Of course, the communists were self-proclaimed atheists, not friends but sworn enemies of the church. Why should the church intervene? Niemöller's oft-quoted refrain of the postwar years makes this point with a precise historical chronology that is rarely noticed.

> They came for the communists and I did not speak up because I was not a communist.
> Then they came for the socialists and I did not speak up because I was not a socialist.
> They came for the union leaders but I did not speak up because I was not a union leader.

21. The grim details of these manipulations and the complicity of many church leaders are in Scholder *Churches and the Third Reich*, vol. 1.

22. Bentley, *Martin Niemöller*, 59–60.

23. Quoted in Bentley, *Martin Niemöller*, 60.

24. Barnett, *For the Soul of the People*, 129.

They came for the Jews and I did not speak up because I was not a Jew.

Then they came for me and there was no one left to speak up for me.[25]

With unforgettable rhetoric, Niemöller touched the essence of the Confessing Church's failure and in so doing confirmed Bonhoeffer's dictum: *the church for others.* "We acted as if we had only to sustain the church. Afterwards from the experience of those bygone years, we learned we had a responsibility for the whole nation."[26] But that the church had responsibility for its neighbors in 1933, especially the awkward kind who were indifferent or hostile to the church, was not on Niemöller's radar. Niemöller did not fully rethink his religious nationalism until the aftermath of war and his preaching tour following the Stuttgart declaration.[27]

However, despite all resistances, the Jewish question pressed itself upon the church at the infamous Brown Synod, September 5–6, 1933. This was the moment when the Prussian General Synod voted to apply the state's Aryan laws of April to the church.[28] From now on, in parallel with state regulations, only Aryans could be employed by the church. Non-Aryan pastors or those married to non-Aryans were to be dismissed. Now Niemöller resisted. The state had interfered with the freedom of the church to govern itself by its own beliefs, particularly the belief that the unity of the church was not a matter of race but of grace. Moreover, Niemöller was alarmed about the personal livelihood of the ethnically Jewish pastors threatened with expulsion from their charges. What could be done? After several preliminary conversations and false starts, Niemöller agreed to organize a group to tackle the crisis created by the synod decision.[29] They named themselves the Pastors' Emergency League (*Pfarrernotbund*). Immediately a circular letter (which I quoted at the start of this chapter) was sent to every pastor in every *Landeskirchen* inviting them to pledge sole allegiance to Scripture, protest

25. Quoted in Littell, "Niemöller, Niebuhr and Wannsee," in Locke and Littell, *Remembrance and Recollection*, 9. Littell comments that Niemöller's list has often been either contracted or expanded, its order revised, by those wishing to trade on the "name brand" of the church struggle for other agendas. Conway notes that after diligent effort, the original context and use by Niemöller has yet to be unearthed. What is clear is that Niemöller used it on numerous occasions and in various wordings. Cf. Conway, "Political Theology of Martin Niemöller," 540.

26. Quoted in Bentley, *Martin Niemöller*, 66.

27. Bentley, *Martin Niemöller*, 163.

28. Scholder, *Churches and the Third Reich*, 1:480.

29. For all the details of negotiation see Scholder, *Churches and the Third Reich*, 1:475ff.

any violation of the fundamentals of the church confession, support those who would be persecuted by these violations, and in conclusion, to testify that with the entrance of the Aryan paragraph into the church, the church's confession had already been so violated. Niemöller arranged for a Council of Brethren (not a council of bishops with its suggestion of hierarchy and its proximity to the Führer principle) to steer the league's course. By the end of January 1934, out of a nation with eighteen thousand Protestant (*Evangelische*) pastors (Lutheran, Reformed and United), over seven thousand had taken this pledge.[30] It was organized resistance the Nazis could not ignore. Moreover, as Scholder has argued, though the resistance was taken up at the point of the church's freedom to govern itself and not be simply a bureau of state, "the hidden theme" of the church struggle was the Jewish question.[31] What might have happened if the Confessing Church had made this hidden theme its public manifesto we shall never know. What we do know is what happened when in 1989 pastors like Christian Führer opened the arms of the church wide to those who were being persecuted.

But even prior to January, the fact that a virulent form of heresy and racism infected the German Christian movement had ostentatiously displayed itself. At the infamous Sports Palace rally of November 13, some twenty thousand fervent German Christians cheered as the organizer, Dr. Reinhold Krause, gave a stunning speech in which he went public with the previously hidden disrespect for the Old Testament (with its "Jewish money morality, stories of cattle-dealers and pimps") and even the "unheroic theology of rabbi Paul with his inferiority complex."[32] Krause called for the church to be liberated from everything un-German in its worship and confession, to recover the pure teachings of Jesus "which coincide completely with the teachings of national socialism—and of that we may be proud." From now on an "exaggerated presentation of the crucified Jesus was to be avoided because the Third Reich needed proud men and not slaves."[33] Such borderline blasphemy at a major public event of the Protestant Church was widely reported in both the foreign as well as the German press. The very next day Niemöller went with his brother, Wilhelm, also a pastor, and Pastor Gerhard Jacobi, to Bishop Müller, demanding Krause's suspension and that of all clergy who attended the rally.[34]

30. Bentley, *Martin Niemöller*, 70.
31. Scholder, *Churches and the Third Reich*, 1:322.
32. Quoted in Bentley, *Martin Niemöller*, 75.
33. Scholder, *Churches and the Third Reich*, 1:553.
34. Ibid., 554.

It was during this period of crisis that Niemöller began to search his heart regarding the content of his own faith. Despite his native sympathies that seemed aligned with Hitler's leadership, was his own soul really centered on a trinity of God, country and militarism? While these awkward questions began to rise within him, Niemöller came into growing contact with Karl Barth. As professor of Reformed theology at Bonn, Barth was heavily involved in similar struggles with the German Christians in the Rhineland area of Germany. Especially important to Niemöller were thirty-six hours Barth spent in Berlin to lecture and hold discussions only two weeks prior to Krause's outburst.[35] Despite many disagreements about strategy, over the next weeks and months, Barth's analysis would gradually break apart Niemöller's unequal yoking of German nationalism and Christian discipleship. Niemöller now realized he had been in grave danger of substituting the gospel of Luther's courageous German spirit for the gospel of the faithfulness of Jesus Christ.[36]

Meanwhile, Nazi excesses only kept coming. The Aryan paragraph, withdrawn by Müller after the Sports Palace furor, was soon reinstituted by the Prussian *Landeskirchen*. Quite deviously, Müller handed over all church youth work to the control of the Hitler Youth Movement. When protests by Niemöller (and others) followed, the now *Reichsbishop* Müller issued a "Muzzling Decree" forbidding pastors to discuss church controversies during worship services. The Pastors' Emergency League responded by reading from their pulpits a declaration accusing Müller of bringing strife into the church. Another PEL declaration confronted German Christian doctrines. In such an environment, President Hindenburg announced to chancellor Hitler that he had lost confidence in Bishop Müller. Perceiving a crisis, Hitler agreed to discuss the deteriorating situation with both the German Christian leadership and their opponents on January 24, 1934.[37] As PEL leader, Niemöller was invited.

Confrontation with Hitler

On his way out the door of the manse for this famous meeting, Niemöller was stopped by a phone call from a fellow pastor. In the conversation, Niemöller mentioned plans to send a memorandum on the situation to President Hindenburg. At one point Niemöller expressed the hope that Hindenburg would offer Chancellor Hitler . . . here Niemöller paused, and

35. Ibid., 538–39.
36. Bentley, *Martin Niemöller*, 104.
37. Ibid., 84.

either his wife or his housekeeper suggested the words, "extreme unction." Niemöller repeated the little joke down the telephone.[38]

It was later that day, with the Hitler-clergy meeting barely underway, that Hitler surprisingly asked Gestapo leader Hermann Göring to speak first. Göring then read a telegram from the secret police which explained that the morning phone conversation of Niemöller had been tapped. The report claimed that Niemöller was strategizing to use Hindenburg to pressure Hitler to make accommodations with the church. Hitler flew into a rage at what he called "outrageous backstairs politics" that tried to drive a wedge between him and Hindenburg. Niemöller attempted to explain to Hitler and the others that the concerns of the PEL were not directed *against* the Reich but *for the sake* of the Reich. Hitler sharply retort to Niemöller: "You leave concern for the Third Reich to me and look after the church!"[39] As the meeting came to a close, which in typical German fashion meant a fair amount of shaking hands with the host, Niemöller, as he shook Hitler's hand, took the opportunity to respond to Hitler's angry accusations. Bentley records Niemöller's recollections of what he said next:

> A moment, ago, Herr Reich Chancellor, you told us that you would take care of the German people. But as Christians and men of the church, we too have a responsibility for the German people, laid upon us by God. Neither you nor anyone else can take that away from us.[40]

Hitler did not reply and turned aside. Such drama was too much for nearly all the pastors in the room. For those who had hoped a personal meeting with Hitler would lead to Müller's resignation, the day was an utter failure.[41] Most in attendance blamed Niemöller for causing unnecessary upset.[42] Within a few days, the PEL suffered over two thousand resignations—as the negative verdict spread about the events and Niemöller's role

---

38. Ibid. In German this is a pun, "buttering up" and/or last rites. Barnett, *For the Soul of the People*, 51.

39. Quoted in Scholder, *Churches and the Third Reich*, 2:41.

40. Quoted in Bentley, *Martin Niemöller*, 87.

41. Bethge records that Bonhoeffer (who was not at the meeting) was also disappointed by the failure to change Hitler's mind in regards to Müller. Bethge, *Dietrich Bonhoeffer*, 372.

42. Schmidt, *Pastor Niemöller*, 94.

in the upset.[43] Hitler had succeeded in isolating Niemöller and the PEL geographically from the rest of the church.[44]

Despite what was clearly a setback, in retrospect we can glimpse something other than defeat, for with a few words spoken face to face with Hitler, Niemöller had shaken the Lutheran tradition of strict separation of powers between church and state. By a profound intuition, Niemöller had asserted the church's God-given responsibility to intervene.[45] Later that same day, despite his outward calm, Niemöller predicted to his wife that Hitler would have his revenge. That same evening the Gestapo came to the house and confiscated the PEL files. A few days later a bomb exploded inside the house, setting the roof on fire. In March, Müller dismissed Niemöller from his pastoral office. Of course, Niemöller resisted and with the help of the Dahlem parish council the revocation was rescinded. But he had become a marked figure. Every public worship service now had secret police observing and taking notes.

Most painful for Niemöller was the response from his fellow clergy. Among the forty who met that day with Hitler, only one (Karl Koch) did not blame him for the negative tone and outcome.[46] On January 27, just three days later, the Lutheran bishops present issued a statement unanimously affirming their "unconditional loyalty" to the Reich and the Führer, and condemned all criticisms of the state and the Nazi movement.[47] Immediately Niemöller wrote them on behalf of the PEL Council of Brethren, to declare that their "slick surrender of the gospel and thus also of the church" had left him deeply hurt and shaken.[48]

Shortly thereafter, Niemöller gathered himself by taking a holiday. It was during this time of calm before the storm that he wrote his WWI memoir, *From U Boat to Pulpit* which soon became a best seller.[49] On his return he continued to speak boldly and publicly about the dangers facing Germany from "false gospels" and "wolves in sheep's clothing." If someone was detained or arrested, he read their name aloud from the pulpit and asked for prayers. Scholder records one such example when the following verses appeared in a weekly regional newspaper around this time:

43. The resignations were largely in the regions where the bishops attending the meeting wished to dissociate themselves from Niemöller. Bentley, *Martin Niemöller*, 88.

44. Scholder, *Churches and the Third Reich*, 2:52.

45. Gerlach, "From Pirate on the High Seas to Angel of Peace," in Locke and Littell, *Remembrance and Recollection*, 46.

46. Bentley, *Martin Niemöller*, 87.

47. Cochrane, *Church's Confession*, 32. Scholder, *Churches and the Third Reich*, 2:44.

48. Quoted in Scholder, *Churches and the Third Reich*, 2:44.

49. Bentley, *Martin Niemöller*, 94.

"A Vision"

Church service. The opening hymn has ended. The pastor stands at the altar and begins:

"non-Aryans are requested to leave the church."

No one moves.

"Non-Aryans are requested to leave the church immediately."

Again all remain quiet.

"Non-Aryans are requested to leave the church immediately."

Thereupon Christ comes down from the altar cross and leaves the church.[50]

When the editor of the paper was sent to a concentration camp for this, Niemöller protested to the Reich minister of Interior in the name of the PEL.

Constant threats and intimidation continued until the spring of 1935 when Niemöller was finally arrested but later released. As the Olympic year of 1936 approached, the Reich wished to avoid further negative publicity from the many international eyes trained on Germany. Niemöller was not rearrested.

Of course by 1936 Niemöller's days of supporting the Nazis were long past. He now realized that Hitler's goal had never been a traditional cooperation between church and state but was a hijacking of the church for a religious nationalism seeking to resurrect a Germanic/pagan dream from the ashes of Versailles. This was intended to replace the resurrection of Jesus from the tomb on Easter day. At some point in these developments, Niemöller saw with simple clarity that these two beliefs could never be harmonized. For the remainder of his life, Niemöller, like Bonhoeffer, would struggle to live out a new kind of witness by the church toward the state.

Interestingly, during the relative calm of the Olympic year, Niemöller published an article in which he described three possible responses to the current regime. They are reminiscent of Bonhoeffer's 1933 essay. The first response would be to remain a *Volkskirche*, his former preference, but which he now saw would make the church completely subservient, a tool for . . . (fill in the blank, in this case, National Socialism). The second option was to become a Free Church. That is, to cut all financial links and official roles with the state. This was the approach that Bonhoeffer and Franz Hildebrandt seemed to favor following the Prussian Synod's vote to adopt the Aryan clause. But Niemöller believed this was also a false option because

---

50. Quoted in Scholder, *Churches and the Third Reich*, 1:531.

even here the state would refuse to tolerate any genuine independence. This left the church one remaining possibility—a church of martyrs and the catacombs.[51] Niemöller sensed this was the shape his own life would now take.

Wide awake to the consequences, Niemöller continued his central role in the Confessing Church (*Bekennende Kirche*), which had emerged from the PEL. He became a member of its governing Council of Brethren. However, like the PEL before it, the Confessing Church was intimidated and threatened by the Nazi regime from without and compromised by a traditional German and Lutheran loyalty to government from within. For Niemöller, as for Bonhoeffer, its resistance seemed more like a long, confused betrayal of the gospel than a faithful confession. Hitler and his administrators seemed always able to manipulate it and divide its witness. In reading through many thoughtful studies of the Confessing Church, one doesn't have to search hard to find moments of courage—but again and again, the church seemed perpetually torn as to *when to acquiesce* to the state as God's divinely ordained power of law and order and *when to resist* in the name of the gospel. Gradually, as it limped between two opinions and under constant pressure from the state, it wore down and became exhausted.

An example of a gradual vacillation came on August 9, 1934, when the Confessing Church firmly refused the national synod's directive that all pastors take the personal oath of loyalty to Hitler required of civil servants.[52] Here was bold resistance. But by the summer of 1938, with Niemöller in prison and Barth deported, the synod recommended all pastors take the oath.[53] Another example of courage was the decision in June 1936 to send a personal memorandum to Hitler (in which Bonhoeffer had a significant hand), charging the Reich with persecution, disseminating paganism, absurdly glorifying the Aryan race, and forcing Christians to hate Jews in direct conflict with Christ's demand for neighbor love.[54] Once again, clear resistance. But how can one explain the decision not to make the letter public? Bethge interprets it as a final attempt at a pastoral conversation with Hitler in which the church fully expected a response. In the event of his failure to reply, a plan was made to share a modified (weakened) version of the memo which the pastors would read to their congregations. However,

51. Bentley, *Martin Niemöller*, 96.

52. Conway, *Nazi Persecution*, 98.

53. Busch, *Karl Barth: His Life*, 288.

54. Bentley, *Martin Niemöller*, 120–25. In terms of timeline, this memo preceded by almost a year the Catholic Church's decision to break its public refusal to criticize since its Concordat with Hitler of 1933. In April 1937 the pope's encyclical "With Burning Sorrow" (*Mit Brennender Sorge*) was secretly distributed and read aloud in every Roman Catholic Church on Palm Sunday, infuriating Hitler.

in what became a great embarrassment for the pastors, the week prior to the start of the Olympic games, the memo was leaked to the foreign press.[55] Charges of disloyalty and arrests followed.[56] One of the leakers was later tortured and murdered at Sachsenhausen.[57] Such indecisive deliberations and failure to support those arrested by the Nazis reveal how the Confessing Church agonized and stumbled over the questions of political resistance.[58]

Indeed, the church was stuck: should it move beyond private, pastoral intercessions to public resistance and confrontation? When someone like Niemöller boldly dared, he was shipped away to concentration camp. This became the rationale for public silence given by Friedrich von Bodelschwingh Jr., director of the Inner Mission, whose Bethel Institute had an international reputation for its care for people with disabilities. When it became obvious to him that Nazi administrators were practicing euthanasia and covering it up with lies, Bodelschwingh chose to privately lobby for Bethel's patients rather than publically expose the whole system. As he later reasoned to colleagues: if I publically protest, they will arrest me and none of the remaining patients will have any advocate.[59] Yet despite Bodelschwingh's largely successful advocacy for Bethel patients, elsewhere the disabled were not so fortunate.[60] By the end of 1940 over thirty-five thousand patients had been murdered. When someone finally spoke up publicly, it was the Roman Catholic bishop of Munster, Von Galen, in August 1941. Was it just coincidental that something unexpected followed? Within three weeks Hitler closed down the euthanasia program.[61] One can only speculate if other public protests might have been similarly impactful.

As for Niemöller himself, as the Olympics ended and the world's press corps went home, the pressure escalated. On July 1, 1937, the secret police arrested him for "misusing the pulpit for political reasons" along with forty

---

55. As it happened, the leak was by two of Bonhoeffer's students. They were arrested and later released. Hoffman, "Persecution of the Jews as a Motive for Resistance against National Socialism," in Chandler, *Moral Imperative*, 80.

56. Bethge, *Dietrich Bonhoeffer*, 446.

57. Hockenos, *On the Confessing Church's Memorandum to Hitler*. Sadly, there is no record of any attempt by the Confessing Church to advocate on his behalf.

58. Barnett, *For the Soul of the People*, 90.

59. Ibid., 113–15.

60. The official website of the Bethel Institute acknowledges that seven Jewish patients were allowed to be transferred by the government to other institutions and thus were undoubtedly killed. (It also notes that 58 Bethel patients were killed by Allied bombs.) http://www.bethel.eu/about-us/the-bethel-chronicle/1940-to-1960.html.

61. Barnett, *For the Soul of the People*, 118.

counts of treason.[62] He waited eight long months in Berlin's Moabite prison for a trial. At the trial, his lawyers brilliantly exposed the arbitrary and illegal methods of the Ministry of Church Affairs. In a remarkable display of judicial independence, the judge acquitted Niemöller of all charges. Much reported in the international media, Niemöller's trial had been the most serious negative publicity yet for the Nazi regime before the court of world opinion. Expecting to be free before nightfall, Niemöller returned to his cell to collect his personal items. Upon arrival the Gestapo informed him that he was from that day the personal prisoner of the Führer.[63] He would spend the next seven years in concentration camps, first in Sachsenhausen just outside of Berlin and later in Dachau near Munich.[64]

The years in concentration camp took their toll on Niemöller's health and on his spirits. During these years, his youngest daughter, Jutte, died of diphtheria. His oldest son, Hans Jochen, was conscripted away from his theology studies at Marburg to the Eastern front where he was killed by a Russian tank in Pomerania.[65] By the spring of 1945, with the Allies advancing inside Bavaria and only days before his suicide, Hitler issued orders to remove Niemöller from Dachau along with a convoy of some 160 political prisoners, to take them to the Tyrol in Austria for execution.[66] One evening on the road as the SS guards had some drinks before going to sleep, one of Niemöller's fellow prisoners, British officer Payne Best (the British prisoner who had met Bonhoeffer shortly before and had reported to them Bonhoeffer's death earlier that month) discovered orders which revealed they were being taken away to be executed in secret. Niemöller was informed by one of the German officer prisoners that some had acquired arms and were ready to fight. In a letter to Franz Hildebrandt, Niemöller describes what happened next:

> As soon as I learned that the SS had been ordered to bump us all off, I plucked up my courage and approached the storm trooper who was leading the convoy. I informed him that we had weapons and would defend ourselves. That visibly took the wind out of his sails, and he said that he had no evil intentions against us. . . . After a horrible night, during which two of us

62. Schmidt, *Pastor Niemöller*, 99.

63. See the collection of letters Niemöller wrote during this time in *Exile in the Fatherland*.

64. During a student group visit in 2009 to Niemöller's old church, Saint Anne's, in the Berlin suburb of Dahlem, Pastor Marion Gardei told us that from the night of his arrest until his eventual release, prayers were spoken for him in the church every evening.

65. Schmidt, *Pastor Niemöller*, 126.

66. Evans, *Third Reich at War*, 689. Bentley, *Martin Niemöller*, 155.

were posted on guard behind every SS man, German officers and soldiers came, put the execution squad in a truck and sent them on their way, guarded by machine guns. The Germans brought us to a hotel in Bergen, where we were very well fussed over and fed and looked after. That lasted three days, when one morning an American company arrived, disarmed the Germans and took us into their care.[67]

Up till now, Niemöller's lengthy stay in concentration camp had given him a larger-than-life reputation in America. Journalists eager to find (and create) stories of opposition to the Nazis found Niemöller an irresistible candidate. But in Niemöller's case, this went so far as to fabricate stories about his courage amid torture.[68] However, Niemöller's penchant for speaking unguardedly would soon deflate his heroic status. Taken to Italy for interrogation by the Americans and detained for six weeks, it was in Naples that he gave an interview that negatively impacted his reputation, particularly in the United States. Seeking to ameliorate the already strong urge to tar all Germans as collectively guilty of Nazi crimes, Niemöller defended his fellow Germans as the victims of Hitler's deceptions, insisting that most Germans were unaware of the extent of Nazi atrocities. (Of course, the interview was prior to his return visit to Dachau, where he underwent a profound experience of his own moral culpability.) But the damage to his heroic status had been done.[69] Moved on to France and finally to Wiesbaden, Niemöller was kept in military hands even though the war had now been over for well over a month. Exasperated and depressed, he threatened to go on hunger strike unless he was released. Four days later, he was home with his family on June 24, 1945.[70]

Only months later Niemöller would join other Confessing Church leaders in Stuttgart, where he would deliver the most important sermon of his life. His hope was to help launch a new kind of church in Germany, one which would stand in humbling solidarity both with his fellow Germans and with their former enemies. In his own way, Niemöller would now underline themes articulated by Bonhoeffer. But before we proceed to Niemöller's postwar

67. The letter to Hildebrandt is quoted in Bentley, *Martin Niemöller*, 156. Conway calls the escape almost miraculous ("How Shall the Nations Repent?," 600).

68. A particularly egregious example is the book *I Was in Hell with Martin Niemöller*, by Leo Stein (Revell, 1942). Cf. Bentley, *Martin Niemöller*, 153. Even Richard Evans has mistakenly used Stein's memoir to describe Niemöller's treatment. Cf. Evans, *Third Reich in Power*, 232.

69. Bentley, *Martin Niemöller*, 162–64. One of his most outspoken critics was none other than Eleanor Roosevelt, who publically criticized the Federal Council of Churches for inviting Niemöller on his speaking tour. Hockenos, "Martin Niemöller in America."

70. Bentley, *Martin Niemöller*, 157–58.

service, we must consider the final figure who helped prepare the church for a new approach to the state; a way that would prove especially relevant throughout Eastern Europe in the coming years, particularly in East Germany, where the new Soviet-controlled government would soon persecute and marginalize the church in ways that lacked any of the Nazi subtlety.

3

Against the Stream
How Karl Barth Reframed Church-State Relations

According to the Scriptures the office of the State is that of the servant of God who does not carry the sword to no purpose, but for rewarding the good and punishing the evil, for the rescue of the poor and oppressed, and to make room externally for the free proclamation of the Gospel. And National Socialism in its deeds has fundamentally and absolutely denied and disowned this office.

—KARL BARTH[1]

FROM WORLD WAR I TO THE BARMEN DECLARATION

DEFENDERS OF THE BARMEN Declaration's apolitical tone remind us that it was never intended to establish a program of political protest, that Karl Barth and the others were pastors not politicians; that the goal was to reassert the integrity of the gospel in the face of the attempted subversion by the German Christians.[2] On the one hand, the soundness of this interpretation is self-evident. And yet it should surprise no one that an apolitical strategy would have little political impact on the German state. It is also true that Barth's views on church and state relations changed after Barmen; that afterward he expressed remorse over his own sins of omission. If we explore Barth's writings over a twenty-year period, the change will become evident

1. *The Church and the Political Problem of Our Day*, 52.
2. Cf. Conway, *Nazi Persecution of the Church*, 84.

44

and so also his impact on the emerging political theology in Eastern Europe. The next two chapters will chronicle this development.

Despite the intentionally apolitical tone, it is also true that the high-water mark of the church's political resistance to Nazism was the synod held at Barmen, May 29–31, 1934, in which Barth played the role of principle author. It is also fair to say that this document, though theological to the core, had an implicit political message that would eventually become fully articulated. Before we consider Barmen in detail, we should take a closer look at this Swiss Reformed pastor who came to exercise such influence in Germany's Confessing Church. In particular, what were the sources of his resistance to the Protestant Christianity which was so amenable to supporting National Socialism? To answer, we must begin with a brief consideration of World War I and its shattering impact on Barth.

A Double Insanity

Not long before the Great War, Barth returned from his pastoral education in Germany to become a curate in a Reformed parish in Geneva. Two years later he followed his father's footsteps as a pastor in the Aargau region of Switzerland, in Safenwil, a small industrial town near his native Basel. There he served from 1911–21. During the years in Safenwil Barth became known throughout Protestant circles in Europe and North America for his provocative restatement of Christian theology in conversation with Western culture as it had evolved from the Reformation to the Enlightenment era. Barth has testified that what was decisive for him in his new approach to theology was the outbreak of World War I. Why the outbreak and not the German defeat? Barth answers: "Ninety-three German intellectuals issued a terrible manifesto, identifying themselves before all the world with the war policy of Kaiser Wilhelm II. . . . And to my dismay, among the signatories I discovered the names of almost all my German teachers."[3] This was the theological half of a "double insanity" that shook Barth to his core. The other half was learning that his own political party, the German Social Democrats, endorsed the war as well. This deflated Barth's youthful confidence that the emergence of socialism signaled the coming kingdom of God.[4] How was it possible that his politi-

3. Barth, *Theology of Schleiermacher*, 263–64. The "Manifesto of the 93" included the following prominent theologians in order of signature: Adolf Deissman, Adolf von Harnack, Wilhelm Herrmann (one of Barth's favorite teachers), Adolf von Schlatter, and Reinhold Seeberg (who later supervised Bonhoeffer's doctoral thesis). Cf. *Wikipedia*, s.v. "Manifesto of the Ninety-Three," 2.1. List of Signatories, https://en.wikipedia.org/wiki/Manifesto_of_the_Ninety-Three#List_of_signatories.

4. Jehle, *Ever Against the Stream*, 37.

cal party had joined his theological mentors to endorse this infernal European war? For Barth, there was no need for further evidence to demonstrate that his once revered cultural Protestant synthesis had reached its ignoble end. In both theology and in politics, his teachers were now "hopelessly compromised by what I regarded as their ethical failure in the face of the ideology of war."[5] In a letter to his friend and fellow pastor Eduard Thurneysen, he described this event as amounting to an exchange of the Christian gospel for a "German war-theology," whose Christianity was reduced to "trimmings" and "surface varnish" composed "of a lot of talk about sacrifice and the like."[6] An ethical failure of such magnitude exposed the entire edifice of Barth's biblical interpretation, doctrinal theology and political expression as fundamentally flawed. It must be all rethought from scratch.

But where to begin? Certainly Barth continued to be haunted by the powerful messages of the Russian novelists, challenged by the melancholic Kierkegaard, and inspired with hope by father and son Blumhardt.[7] All these teachers would remain his fellow pilgrims. But after several philosophical false starts, he took the risk of reading Paul's Letter to the Romans as though he had never read it before. The result was at the tender age (theologically speaking) of thirty-two he published his landmark *Der Romerbrief* (The Epistle to the Romans), which the Catholic writer Karl Adam later described as a theological bomb dropped on the playground of the theologians.[8] In retrospect, it may have been the most significant theological book of the century. Eventually, it would lead Barth into political matters but from an entirely new direction.

The Failed Foundations of Cultural Protestantism

To describe the variety of ways in which a church may relate to culture, H. R. Niebuhr's *Christ and Culture* remains invaluable. Using Niebuhr's categories, we could say Barth now set his formidable intellectual ability to articulate a paradigm of *Christ transforming culture*. In light of the "Manifesto of the Ninety-Three," Germany (and no doubt Switzerland), had settled into a *Christ of culture* approach, that is, Christianity had adapted itself rather too comfortably to local culture, and hence had become domesticated by

5. Busch, *Karl Barth*, 81.

6. Barth, *Revolutionary Theology*, 26.

7. Readers unfamiliar with the Blumhardts may consult Roger Newell, "Blumhardt, Johann Christoph (1805–1880) and Christoph Friedrich (1842–1919)," 76–77, in Hart, *Dictionary of Historical Theology*, 76–77. The classic biography of the elder Blumhardt is Züngel, *Pastor Johann Christoph Blumhardt*. A comprehensive new biography is Ising, *Johann Christoph Blumhardt*.

8. Quoted in Torrance, *Karl Barth*, 17.

other cultural values, some far from neutral. The German adaptation was all the stronger because it was woven together by two reinforcing threads, one conservative, one liberal.

The Conservative Thread: Pietism

Among the various movements within the Swiss church, Pietism was Barth's next of kin. Many of his family were Pietists. Throughout his life, he remained their troublesome friend.[9] As a movement, Pietism emerged from a series of spiritual awakenings in various regions of Germany throughout the end of the seventeenth century. Key guides of the movement included Philip Spener (whose classic devotional, *Pia Desideria* [1675], remains in print), his colleague August Franke, and later Count Nicholas von Zinzendorf and the Herrnhut community to which he gave refuge at his family estate, including the Moravian Brethren. The spiritual legacy emerging from this German stream of witness is immense. It includes John and Charles Wesley as well as legions of later revivalist and charismatic renewal groups.

Perhaps the defining form of Pietism's way of being Christian in the world, is that while it *assumes* Luther's teaching on *justification* by faith, its focus has shifted to *sanctification*, the living awareness of Christ's interior presence in the believer.[10] Despite or perhaps due to this emphasis on the inner life, Pietism soon became a familiar supporting feature of what might be termed Germany's military/spiritual complex. For example, Otto Von Bismarck, the architect of German unification in 1871, was much admired in his lifetime for both his personal devotion to Christ and his "blood and iron" approach to the settling of political disputes. To say the least, Pietism's proximity to power politics demands we recalibrate our normal views about the spiritual life. Furthermore, the focus on the inward side of faith also stressed the link between personal (individual) *conversion* and *separation* from the world with its carnal values and temptations. Yet as a matter of historical record, the seeming opposites of personal conversion and power politics were connected. What is the best way to make sense of this paradox?

Consider the saying attributed to Bismarck: "You can't rule a nation by the Sermon on the Mount." How does an inward piety connect to a style of politics famous for its preference for military over diplomatic solutions? In a talk given after the Second World War, Barth suggested several links. First, Bismarck's strategy ought to be mentioned in the same breath as Hitler's because the former had neglected the basic contribution of Christianity to

9. According to his biographer, Eberhard Busch (*Karl Barth and the Pietists*, 316).
10. Sheldrake, *Pietism*, 491–92.

political community, which, to put it simply, is to serve, not to rule. "Bismarck—not to mention Hitler—was (in spite of the *Daily Bible Readings* on his bedside table) no model statesman because he wanted to establish and develop his work on naked power" that is, *potentia*, the kind of power that "masters and bends and breaks the law."[11] Interestingly, Bonhoeffer also spotted this lack of congruence between private faith and public policy as a recurrent failure of the German church in the Third Reich. The result was to make church a narrow place, where "there have been many cases of pastors refusing to assume the public responsibility of speaking out on the affliction of their colleagues and those suffering persecution of all kinds precisely because their own congregations had not yet been affected."[12] The failure here is the notion that any intervention by the church oversteps its calling and interferes with the state's God-ordained duties.

For Barth, the ethical irrelevance of Pietism manifested itself for all to see when many of its adherents among German leadership in church and academy publically supported the Kaiser's war. Perhaps one might argue this was simply business as usual for all stripes of Lutherans with their "two kingdom" tradition whereby one was taught to obey the state as a Christian duty. However, after Hitler ordered German soldiers into Europe for a second time in twenty years, how did the Pietists respond? Busch records that when revelations of Hitler's brutality came to light, Pietist leaders typically pleaded ignorance of Hitler's true nature. "Had we known, we wouldn't have supported him." Busch, however, presents a collage of Pietist comments from one of their primary magazines during Hitler's rise to power which gives ample evidence to the contrary. For example, while the Pietist theme of separation from the world mandated an aversion to movie theatres, dancing, opera and alcohol, there is no sliver of caution about separation from the war effort.[13] Other articles lament the demise of the death penalty; some reject pacifism as ignoble. The broadside against pacifism is particularly revealing for it shows the extent to which Pietism had aligned itself with the military and *Volk* mentality that permeated Nazism.

> We are all human beings only through the medium of a particular nation. . . . We are not human beings in and of ourselves, we are Germans. Loyalty to our nation and loyalty to our faith go hand in hand. Those who cannot sacrifice for the nation cannot make sacrifices for God.[14]

11. Barth, *Against the Stream*, 40.
12. Bonhoeffer, *Ethics*, 296.
13. Busch, *Karl Barth and the Pietists*, 232.
14. Ibid., 233.

Busch includes other examples of Pietism's Christ of culture align-
ment, including:

1. A critique of parliamentary democracy as a kind of hypnosis, with a
   preference for an authoritarian state.

2. A lack of concern for labor issues at the heart of the workers movements and trade unions. ("Selfishness is the great engine . . . in the
   economic life" which is irreplaceable).

3. Open anti-Semitism. "Generally speaking, we too consider the Jews to
   be a detrimental influence, and we are convinced that a curse rests on
   the Jewish people . . . and they also carry this curse into the host nation
   in which they have settled. . . . A Jew remains a Jew, and his blood is
   not changed by baptism's washing with water."

4. A fierce attack on the treaty of Versailles as shameful, including the
   "lie" about German war guilt.[15]

If we take these various pronouncements as representative of German
Pietism between the wars, it seems disingenuous to argue that the Pietists
who supported the Third Reich were gullible innocents. Despite the strong
claim to have separated themselves from the world with its dance halls and
alcohol, their political-social record reflects an unequal yoke between the
kingdom of God and the toxic myth of the German *Volk*. The result was to
encourage a corporate narcissism, one that not only tolerated but encouraged the loss of civil rights to minorities of race or politics. Thus Pietism,
judged by the fruit of its reflections on political ethics, particularly its enthusiasm for the *Volkish* revival, "dug a riverbed for the things that were to
come." As Barth put it at Barmen: "What was not good about Pietism has
woken up with the German Christians."[16]

Christianity Without Solidarity

If we leap ahead to Leipzig and Pastor Führer's theme of radical welcome
(*ofen für alles*) for atheists and dissidents, Pietism's attack on various outsid-
ers contrasts starkly. It exposes the extent to which Pietism severed itself
from any sense of solidarity with the world. From the very first edition of *Der
Romerbrief*, Barth challenged the church-centric style that enabled Pietism
to remain indifferent to the earthly distress of the working classes.[17] The

15. Ibid., 232–34.
16. Quoted in ibid., 236.
17. Ibid., 20.

sheer contrast between the Pietist focus on individual salvation, individual sanctification, and individual happiness, was in large part why Barth was completely won over by J. C. and C. F. Blumhardt. Father and Son Blumhardt's ministry in the Baden-Württemberg region (1840–1919) expressed quite prophetically an awareness of a kingdom that was "comprehensive" and "holistic." Blumhardt wrote: "Yes, dear Christian, make sure that you die saved! But the Lord Jesus wants more. He wants not only my redemption and yours, but the redemption of all the world."[18] As Barth saw it, a self-preoccupied frame of mind was very near the darkness at the core of a fallen world. How could a temperamentally *individualistic* approach to human life ever stand in solidarity with the poor, the hungry, the persecuted of the world? Indeed to withdraw was to separate oneself from the world, but not in a Christ-like way! It was a separation that walked by on the other side. Moreover, to walk by on the other side was the severest form of worldliness, for it only reinforced the curvature inward pattern that turns away from the other, which epitomizes the deformity at the heart of a fallen world. Barth was convinced that though Pietism imagined it had separated itself from the world, in fact it had only hid its complacent connection.[19] That the Pietists gave their spiritual *imprimatur* to Germany's "thoroughly sinful, godless" march to war provoked an angry Barth to assert that "it was time to become an atheist against this would-be god of German nationalism and militarism precisely for the sake of the real God's honor!"[20]

Conversion Without Transformation

Barth's evolving approach to eschatology was another source of turbulence in his relationship with Pietism. Though Barth would always see personal conversion as central to discipleship, he grew increasingly skeptical that we either can or should draw a distinction between two tangible groups of humans, those converted and those unconverted.[21] Augustine had already warned centuries before that in the visible church there are wolves within and sheep without. Besides, can one identify a single, visible difference between believer and worldling that cannot collapse into a new form of Pharisaism? As if, mused Barth, we can confidently lay hold of God "by performing our negative works of repentance, humility and self denial."[22]

18. Quoted in Barth, *Protestant Theology*, 650.
19. Busch, *Karl Barth and the Pietists*, 42–45.
20. Ibid., 295.
21. Ibid., 101.
22. Ibid., 110–11.

Here Barth put his finger on the way Pietism unequally yoked creature and Creator, that is, culture (specifically German) and the crucified Lord of culture. What was now clear for Barth was that the church can and must be *against* Germany when Germany wanted the church to confirm its endemic racism and cultural imperialism. The church could only truly serve the German people by faithfully declaring and living out of the gospel. True service to the German people was by no means the same as doing whatever it takes for Germans to come back to church again.[23] As the church is intended to be *for* the world *against* the world, so the church must be *for* the German people *against* the German people.[24] Though the church holds out the gospel to all worldly kingdoms, including that of the Germans, she must preach it *in* the Third Reich, not *under* it, nor in *its* spirit.[25] With such expressions, we can see that already in 1933 Barth's theology was moving toward some kind of political embodiment. "If the German Evangelical Church excludes Jewish-Christians, or treats them as of a lower grade, she ceases to be a Christian church."[26] Barth never retreated from the awareness that the church must always swim against the stream and that Pietism, despite its rhetoric, had become unequally yoked to a people's (*Volk*) religiosity that, given certain conditions, could become toxic, indeed demonic.

Cultural Protestantism's Other Thread: Liberalism

Pietism was not the only stream flowing into the swelling river of German war theology. Barth was never shy about naming the other. He declared that the theology exposed in Kaiser Wilhelm's war manifesto was "grounded, determined and influenced decisively" by Friedrich Schleiermacher.[27] Schleiermacher, the father of liberal theology, was the crucial figure in moving theology from a study of Christian doctrine to the study of "conceptions of states of mind of Christian piety."[28] That is, doctrines derive from an inner state of experience. Hence the real subject matter of theology is a human state of consciousness. Whereas sixteenth-century theology said "the gospel," the "Word of God" or "Christ," Schleiermacher said "religion"

23. Barth, *Theological Existence Today!*, 51.

24. A phrase used by Newbigin, *Word in Season*, 54. Newbigin may well have Barth's own words from *Rectfertigung und Recht* in the background. Cf. Barth, *Community, State and Church*, 140.

25. Barth, *Theological Existence Today!*, 52.

26. Ibid.

27. Barth, *Theology of Schleiermacher*, 264.

28. Barth, *Protestant Theology*, 454.

or "piety." In this way, Barth was convinced that theology's center had been transferred from God to human action in regard to God. Hence Barth posed the disturbing question: had theology lost its proper theme?[29] Of course, the focus on human interiority was not original with Schleiermacher: it was the legacy of being raised in a Pietist home.

But was there a more intimate link between Schleiermacher and theologians who endorsed the Kaiser's war? If so, it had to do with the relation between individual and group awareness. No one, said Schleiermacher, can be a person apart from a living community. All personal awareness of God occurs within the living community which is the church.[30] Moreover for Schleiermacher, individual self-awareness is so naturally linked together with group awareness that he fatefully named the church the *Volkskirche*, the People's Church. National Socialism arose within a society permeated by the awareness that Christianity was at the core of what it meant to be German *Volk*.[31] Nazi iconography constantly drew on the themes of sacrifice and redemption—themes borrowed directly from the gospel.[32] It will be no surprise then, to find that the theologians who most ardently supported the Nazi movement were enthusiastic about coupling church and *Volk*. They were the ones to provide a sense of authority in church and in academy for a theology of *Volk* that undergirded the *German Christian* merger of Christianity with Nazism.

Theologians of the Volk

Robert Ericksen's *Theologians under Hitler* tells the story of three professors who exemplified why Barth rejected the joining together of *Volk* and Christian faith. Ericksen begins with the story of Gerhard Kittel, famous for his scholarship as editor of the *Theological Dictionary of the New Testament*, who described Nazism as a "*volkish* renewal movement on a Christian, moral foundation."[33] After seventeen months in an Allied prison following Germany's defeat, Kittel claimed he had been deceived; that the *Volk* was "falsified into a system of imperialistic and megalomaniacal politics of

---

29. Ibid., 460.

30. Barth, "Schleiermacher's Celebration of Christmas," in *Theology and Church*, 153.

31. Interestingly, Bismarck, the architect of Germany unification, was confirmed on his 16th birthday in Berlin by Schleiermacher. Cf. Hesekiel, *Bismarck*, 111.

32. Bergen, *Twisted Cross*, 9, 10.

33. Quoted in Ericksen, *Theologians under Hitler*, 35.

brutality."[34] Nonetheless he still valued "Volkish ideas" as a proper German alternative to Western liberalism.

Ericksen also relates the story of "moderate" Lutheran theologian Paul Althaus. At the time of World War I, Althaus had a self-described "epiphany" in which he experienced the *Volk* as a religious reality. As a result he longed for this awareness to be felt by the entire church in Germany. When the first war ended in defeat, he was convinced the new Weimar Republic was a disaster, lacking moral integrity. If only Germany could find a way to recover moral discipline, even a totalitarian state would be acceptable—as long as it embodied the needs and desires of the *Volk*.[35] So it came to pass that when Althaus read the very same Aryan paragraph which so appalled Bonhoeffer and Barth, he saw simple missional common sense. Yes, there is unity in Christ, but when admitting people to ministry the church has always recognized restrictions based on age, gender, and physical ability. The Aryan paragraph was more of the same.[36] The bottom line for Althaus was that Nazism was not just another political party; it was a movement of the *Volk*. He wrote in 1935, "We Christians know ourselves bound by God's will to the promotion of National Socialism, so that all members and ranks of the *Volk* will be ready for service and sacrifice to one another."[37] Moreover, Althaus reckoned that "living history" and the "law of conflict" made war more or less inevitable. Thus service and sacrifice *in war* were simply part of one's duty to the *Volk*.[38] Not surprisingly, when the Confessing Church proclaimed its faith at Barmen, Althaus was unsympathetic. He not only refused to sign Barmen but endorsed an alternative, the Ansbach Counsel (*Ansbacher Ratschlag*), which included the following endorsement of Hitler: "We thank God our father that he has given to our *Volk* in its time of need the Führer as a pious and faithful sovereign . . . who wants to prepare a government of good rule . . . with discipline and honor."[39]

At the height of denazification after the war, Allied authorities required Althaus to present letters of endorsement in order to apply for exoneration for his Nazi affiliation. On behalf of his old teacher, Helmut Thielicke defended Althaus on the grounds that his enthusiasm for the Nazis was basically an expression of nationalism.[40] To his credit, after the war Althaus roundly con-

34. Ibid., 44.
35. Ibid., 106.
36. Ibid., 108.
37. Quoted in ibid., 86.
38. Quoted by Barth, *Doctrine of Creation*, CD, III/4, 457.
39. Quoted in Ericksen, *Theologians under Hitler*, 87.
40. Ibid., 111.

demned the Nazi years, interpreting Germany's defeat as the clearest evidence that God had withdrawn his blessing. Nevertheless, as Ericksen insists, his commitment to the ideology of *Volk* had led him to ally himself to the Nazis for far too long.[41] Meanwhile, Althaus was unrepentant in his deference to the verdict of history as the natural criterion of God's curse or blessing.

Ericksen's final study examines Emmanuel Hirsch, professor of theology at Göttingen, who, like Althaus, was convinced the Weimar democracy had led to Germany's moral failures. Yet he believed war could become a heroic prayer uttered as "a question to God" in which nations that deserve strength and honor may win these because of their inner strength.[42] Through war Germany could be restored by will, unity, discipline, purpose and sacrifice as the *Volk* acted within history to accomplish God's purposes. Like Althaus, Hirsch happily applied the Aryan paragraph to the church, since he was convinced that evangelism works best through identification, common blood and culture.[43]

In the end, Hirsch's central theme virtually became the core argument of the German Christian movement, viz. the belief in a *Volk* in which religion and racial self-awareness reinforced each other in a decisive historical meeting point determined and designed by God to bring a further maturation of the world toward its destiny. With prestigious figures like Kittel, Althaus and Hirsch promoting these ideas both in church and academy, the *German Christian* movement flourished. It gave explicit voice to what everywhere was implicit in German culture: the mystical link between nationalism, spirituality, and militarism which energized the German *Volk*. It was not a big step to link this with race. If the spirituality of Germans was embedded in its racial DNA, church was the natural place where soldiers could feel at home, where pastors would not obsess about doctrine. Instead, familiar and supportive religious rituals would bring strength and solace to the *Volk*.[44]

There is a further complication: to be fair to the Nazi apologists, the use of *Volk* as a missiological category had a resume that reached to the center of international missionary strategy, including that of American evangelicals. It began with Gustav Warnack (1834–1910), perhaps the greatest German mission theorist of his era, who advocated an ethnic strategy for

41. Ibid., 119.

42. Ibid., 135.

43. Ibid., 147.

44. Bergen, *Twisted Cross*, 8–11. The failure of postwar Allied justice was never more evident than with Hirsch. No theologian of stature gave greater allegiance to the Nazis and yet he not only avoided imprisonment through early retirement, but was not required to undergo the rigors of the denazification program. Hirsch never acknowledged his embrace of Nazism as an error. Ericksen, *Theologians under Hitler*, 176.

all missionary efforts. Later Afrikaner theologians in the Dutch Reformed tradition referenced Warnack to legitimize separate ethnic, economic and church development in South Africa. It became the grounds for rejecting mixed-race congregations. Even Donald McGavran, the American founder of the church growth movement, shared this approach. With his "homogenous unit principle" he virtually elevated ethnicity above catholicity in the church's witness to the nations.[45]

For Barth this strategy erred in elevating a particular human community or *Volk* as a revelation of God within the historical process. Nationality became an organizing principle of human life *revealed from nature*, not from Scripture.[46] In contrast to Barth, Ericksen identifies Hirsch's error *not* as his belief in historical process as revelation, but rather in his "bold act" to align himself with German nationalism, thus undervaluing the liberal, democratic tradition within history.[47] Ericksen even accuses Barth of lacking any sense that God has a role in the historical process.[48] But surely the life, death and resurrection of Jesus is sufficient sign that God has indeed engaged fully in human history? For Barth, in the light of God's engagement, the imperial aspirations of Germany were idolatrous identifications of one nation's historical journey as divine revelation. In his critique of Barth, Ericksen finds the source of what he calls Barth's "lack of engagement in history" (lack, that is, compared to Hirsch?) as due to "irrational premises." What Ericksen censures as "irrational" is that Barth had the audacity to reject the Enlightenment definition of "reason."[49] However, rather than use "reason" and "irrational" in such a polemical way, historical theology is better advised to remain as descriptive as possible. The fact is Barth refused to allow the plausibility structures of the Enlightenment to dictate what can or cannot be considered a rational approach to theology. Barth's insight has recently been forcefully corroborated by the philosopher Alasdair MacIntyre, in *Whose Justice? Which Rationality?* where he argues that it is illusory to suppose that a pure kind of rationality is available in a tradition-free, disembodied

---

45. The repudiation of this racist missiological strategy became a central conviction of the leading South African missiologist, David Bosch. Cf. Yates, "David Bosch," 72–78. In fairness to McGavren, he never justified post-conversion segregation. Nevertheless in Bosch's opinion, an "obsession" with numbers led him to endorse Warneck's *Volk* strategy.

46. Quoted in Bergen, *Twisted Cross*, 21.

47. Ericksen, *Theologians under Hitler*, 191.

48. Ibid., 191, 183.

49. Ibid., 16.

form, capable of passing judgment on all the various ways of grasping truth developed in particular socially embodied traditions of rational discourse.[50]

Barth found one other German Christian agenda malevolent: their brusque rejection of most of the historical doctrinal debates between Calvinists, Lutherans and Roman Catholics as simply unnecessary. Doctrines, they claimed, divided Germans; ritual and ethnicity united Germans. However, the emphasis on *national* identity apart from the worldwide Christian community, in fact was divorcing Christians in Germany from Christians everywhere else. It even lent a kind of pious credibility for Germany's preparation for war.

Barth's Early Response: The Barmen Declaration

The decisive moment for a clear theological protest against the German Christian (*Deutsche Christen*) movement came on May 29–31, 1934. But with three-quarters of Protestants already "coordinated" into the new Reich Church, the possibility of any serious challenge to the German Christians was already improbable.[51] Nevertheless, 139 delegates of the Protestant church from eighteen different *Landeskirchen* (regional churches) gathered at the Barmen-Gemarke Reformed Church in Westphalia, in the suburb of Wuppertal in the Rhineland, and issued their famous declaration.[52] While others took a well-deserved Saturday afternoon nap, Barth has testified that "fortified by strong coffee and one or two Brazilian cigars," he drafted the now famous six points of the document.[53] The main order of business was simple: to discuss and formulate an appeal to the Protestant churches of Germany to resist the German Christian marriage of Christianity to National Socialism which now threatened its very existence. The declaration's format was also simple. It consisted of six positive theses, with each thesis introduced by a text of Scripture and ending with the rejection of a competing German Christian teaching. It is worth considering each briefly in turn.[54]

Article 1 begins by quoting John 14:6 ("I am the way, truth and life") and John 10:1, 9 ("He who does not enter the sheepfold by the door but

50. Cf. Newbigin, *Gospel in a Pluralist Society*, 84.

51. Scholder, "Crisis of the 1930s," in *Requiem for Hitler*, 85.

52. Cochrane, *Church's Confession*, 148. Cochrane notes the average age of attendees was a surprisingly youthful forty-one. For a detailed study of the events, see Scholder, *Churches and the Third Reich*, vol. 2.

53. Busch, *Karl Barth*, 245. For more details, cf. Scholder, *Churches and the Third Reich*, 2:137–38.

54. The summaries which follow are indebted to Niesel, *The Gospel and the Churches*.

climbs in by another way, that man is a thief and a robber. . . . I am the door; if anyone enters by me, he will be saved.") The positive affirmation follows: "Jesus Christ as he is attested for us in Holy Scripture, is the one Word of God which we have to hear and which we have to trust and obey in life and in death." Having spoken a clear yes, there follows an equally clear no. "We reject the false doctrine as though the church can and must acknowledge as sources of her proclamation, except and beside this one Word of God, other events and powers, forms and truths, as God's revelation." Instead of Hirsch's devotion to the *Volk*, the first article begins with devotion to a person: "Jesus Christ, as he is attested for us in Holy Scripture." Article 1 rejects as "false doctrine" the idea that history or nature reveals a decisive role for the *Volk* beside and apart from "this one Word of God." To welcome the events of 1933 politically is one thing; to welcome them as part of the church's proclamation, as if God had raised up Hitler for the redemption of the German people, is false doctrine.[55] Simply put, this article asserts that the church does not have several different sources of revelation which it must somehow coordinate. It has one source of knowledge and proclamation, namely, Jesus Christ as he is witnessed to in Scripture.[56] If the church adds the voice of the German nation as another source of revelation alongside Jesus Christ, a false god is introduced into the church's proclamation. The corruption of the *entire* church follows.[57]

Article 2 details the nature of the one Word's authority: it is that of one who grants forgiveness and whose rule over us is a gracious, joyful sovereignty. It is the opposite of a totalitarian claim that demands the whole person without first granting wholeness.[58] It also rejects the notion that there are spheres of life that do not belong to this gracious authority. The reference here is to the German Christian distortion of Luther's two kingdoms, by which the sphere of God's left hand, the state, aspires to an autonomy that effectively annuls and usurps Christ's kingship. When preachers are accused of "meddling in politics" it is frequently a sign that the church has dared to speak outside the box of "personal spirituality" assigned to it by a political system seeking total power.[59]

The third article describes the church as a communion in which Jesus is present as Lord in Word and sacrament by the Spirit. Moreover, it recalls the church to its profound connection to the world, which is the opposite

---

55. Cobham, "Significance of the Barmen Declaration," 36.

56. Jüngel, *Christ, Justice and Peace*, 20–21.

57. Busch, *Barmen Theses*, 31.

58. Jüngel, *Christ, Justice and Peace*, 34–35.

59. Littell, "From Barmen (1934) to Stuttgart (1945)," 46.

of a false solidarity that assimilates itself to the teachings of current ideologies and politics (such as the Aryan paragraph). The church's true solidarity shares with the world a *solidarity in sin* as it also witnesses to the world that sin does not have the last word. The last word is the strength of the church's life and message.

Article 4 set a clear boundary against Hitler's authority in the church by applying the third article to ministry as the *serving* rule of Jesus in contrast to the domineering, secular *Führerprinzip* (leader principle). A year earlier Barth had already rejected the idea of applying the pattern of Hitler's leadership to the church. "Let it be clear that the German church has the 'leader' it needs in Jesus."[60]

The fifth article begins with an affirmation of the positive task of the state. "The state has the responsibility to provide for justice and peace in the as yet unredeemed world . . . by the threat and use of force." However the church is called to remind the state "of God's kingdom, God's commandment and righteousness, and thereby the responsibility of rulers and ruled." In the light of the fourth article, the fifth article declares that the state's authority is not autonomous, but stands within the rule of Christ and creates a proper responsibility for both citizens and elected officials (rulers and ruled). By reminding the state of God's justice, the church reminds the state that there are criteria for its actions which are not set by itself, but which are set by God's word.[61] Barth would later develop this theme elsewhere but here is the beginning of what has been described as a "distinct advance" (Cochrane) or "a redefinition" (Scholder) of church/state relations from the confessions of the sixteenth century. With Barmen, Barth is moving toward a mutual interaction in which the state is neither an "order of creation" (Brunner) nor an event or power which the church must hear as revelation. The state exists by God's divine appointment to serve the church but also the church serves the state, helping it achieve its true calling, which is to provide for justice and peace.[62] Here is a final, definitive *no* to the state's attempt to control or coordinate the church.[63] And yet here is also a divine permission for the state to attend to its appointed responsibility.[64]

The sixth and final thesis further defines the church's task: to proclaim to the world the "free grace of God." But the church is misused and perverted

---

60. Barth, *Theological Existence Today!*, 45.

61. Scholder, *Churches and the Third Reich*, 2:153.

62. Cochrane, *Church's Confession*, 284–85.

63. Scholder, *Churches and the Third Reich*, 2:154.

64. But what if the state misuses or abuses its power to serve justice and maintain peace? This is not directly addressed by Barmen. Cf. Busch, *Barmen Theses*, 80.

when it is used to buttress the state. The church has but one mission which cannot be abandoned to serve other tasks.

The declaration was debated and adopted without amendment by the participants. As deliberations ended, the assembly spontaneously rose and sang together the third verse of Martin Rinckart's hymn:

> All praise and thanks to God, the Father now be given,
>
> The Son, and him who reigns with them in highest heaven.
>
> The One Eternal God, whom heaven and earth adore,
>
> For thus it was, is now, and shall be evermore.[65]

Many ink cartridges could be used up reviewing all the literature that has poured forth on Barmen. Since our concern is its relevance for the events of 1989 leading to German reunification, we should note that Barmen provided direction and invigorated the church to face the increasingly difficult challenges in the years which followed. We should also remember for better and for worse, that Barmen was not a political document; it was a church document that recorded "a struggle for the church against itself for itself."[66] The logic here is that before the church can address other spheres, it must know its own identity. And this is where our survey of Pietism and Liberalism has revealed an absence. Hence the German Christian merger of Nazism and Christianity was the culmination of a long process of accommodating the gospel to German and European culture. The core of the message that emerged with such energy in the German Christians was not original. When its platform announced that they saw in "race, folk and nation natural orders by which God was revealing his will to the German people"[67] they were voicing a sentiment that had been implicit in the church for some time.

To no one's surprise, the German Christians counterattacked. Kittel remonstrated there was never a gospel apart from a historical moment, guided and shaped according to the soil God prepared in particular cultures for it to take root. This pattern was God's plan.[68] As already noted, Althaus signed a counter-document, the *Almsbacher Ratschlag*, which endorsed Hitler. More disturbing to Barth was the pamphlet published later that year by his fellow Swiss, Emil Brunner. The article, "Nature and Grace," criticized Barth for rejecting all forms of natural theology, which Brunner argued was tantamount to dismissing all evidence of God's nature and purposes apart from Scripture. That Brunner's tract was loudly applauded by the German Christians no

---

65. Scholder, *Churches and the Third Reich*, 2:146–47.

66. Cochrane, *Church's Confession*, 11.

67. Quoted in Cochrane, *Church's Confession*, 71.

68. Bentley, *Martin Niemöller*, 102.

doubt influenced Barth's "angry no" in response.[69] In Barth's view, Brunner's essay was an appeasement position at the very moment the church faced a crisis. It was another chapter in the three-centuries-long story of European Protestants blending Christ with culture, nature with grace. Again and again, the church's biblical foundation had been compromised by cultural, *Volk/* ethnic and nationalist agendas. With Barmen, Barth sought a fresh start; an intentional rejection of such mergers, grounding everything in the Reformation principle of *sola Scriptura*. The time was urgent for the church to refuse any attachments to mystical Christs fashioned from personal experiences, national experiences and historical trends. No! The church's life depended on grounding itself simply on Christ "as attested in Scripture."

In the coming years, Barth would add both detail and scope to the Barmen theses. But as the Nazi years marched into a second world war in twenty years, followed by a Cold War of iron curtains and nuclear threats, Barmen remains the most significant refashioning of church and state relations since the Reformation.[70] Essentially, Barmen declared that the state did not have the right to prescribe the meaning of Christianity.[71] The power of Barmen lay in the sheer simplicity with which it refocused the church on its sole foundation: Jesus the Christ. Cochrane was correct: Barmen confined itself to the religious realm. And Barnett is also correct in saying, "its words contained the theological seeds of broader resistance."[72] Certainly Cochrane's description of Barmen as essentially a church document may be used as a ploy to head off criticism that Barmen's apolitical tone was erroneous. However, it was commonly understood from the beginning that Barmen was a different kind of theological document, one with a political edge. When Barmen says, "We repudiate the false teaching that there are areas of life which do not belong to Jesus Christ but to other lords, areas in which we do not need justification and sanctification through him," there were few readers so uninformed that they failed to discern the challenge being put to the current regime.

As Cochrane put it, whenever the church concerns itself only with itself, it forgets that Christ died for the world "and the church has been called to serve the world with its message of God's grace for all peoples."[73] This was of course the ongoing temptation for the Confessing Church. At Barmen the Confessing Church wrestled with the paradox that at the core of its message

69. Cochrane, *Church's Confession*, 71.

70. So Scholder, quoted in Barnett, *For the Soul of the People*, 56.

71. Bettis, "Barmen," 151, 156.

72. Barnett, *For the Soul of the People*, 55.

73. Cochrane, *Church's Confession*, 206.

was a Word that *in its essence was for others*, not simply a private possession of the devout. It remains true that Barmen as a church document did not seize the wheel of the Third Reich. Neither did it build an autobahn leading inevitably to the Leipzig prayer meetings and the dismantling of the Berlin Wall. When after the war Niemöller began to speak of the church's guilt, Barmen was included in his rebuke. Barmen was a flawed first step toward faithful witness, but it was a genuine step nevertheless. It insisted that the Word of God declared by the church was not a private word reserved for likeminded church folk. The Word it declared could not be silent in the face of other powers or principalities which claimed a final independence or authority apart from this Word. But there is yet something more precise to say about the flaw in Barmen.

A Time to Speak, a Time to Be Silent

Barmen was not the last time the Confessing Church spoke forthrightly about the crisis facing Christianity in Germany. At its next synod, meeting at Niemöller's parish in Dahlem (October 30, 31, 1934), it declared that, given the role of the German Christians in the Reich Church, the Confessing Church had become the sole legitimate church in Germany. As such, they were now entitled to educate and ordain their own pastors, and govern their parishes under *Notrecht* (emergency laws).[74] Later, on June 4, 1936, its governing council sent a private memorandum personally to Hitler, which directly challenged the pagan notions of the Nazi state, condemned its record, naming in particular anti-Semitism, racism, concentration camps, secret police methods, ballot violations, the destruction of justice in the civil courts, and the corruption of public morals.[75] One can debate the wisdom of voicing this only in a private correspondence but we should not fault the intention. In this way the Confessing Church urged Hitler to change course and did so without the complicating ingredient of public censure. Publicity, they reckoned, might provoke unnecessary public posturing in order to save face. However, once the contents of the document were leaked to the press, a follow-up pastoral letter to church constituencies softened their protest considerably. All mention of concentration camps or anti-Semitic behavior vanished. It is hard to defend such public reticence. Was it not a failure of nerve?[76]

In a reflection published in 1944, Julius Rieger, Bonhoeffer's colleague at the German Protestant Church in London, distinguished the silence of the

74. Barnett, *For the Soul of the People*, 65.

75. Cochrane, *Church's Confession*, 208.

76. Conway calls it politically naïve (*Nazi Persecution*, 163–64).

church caused by unbelief and fear from the silence due to being muzzled as the state took draconian measures against it. Persecution renders a victim mute. When the Gestapo whisked away a local pastor who is not heard from again, when concentration camps locked away pastors such as Niemöller, the resulting silence bears testimony not to fear but to fidelity to the gospel.[77] But how should we interpret the silence of the vast number of pastors who refused to follow Niemöller's example and publically challenge the corrupt practices and abuse of state power? Moreover, how should we interpret Barmen's own silence regarding the Jews or the Confessing Church's public reticence concerning the incident surrounding the Hitler memo?

In recent years another silence has been broken by Jewish scholars. Drawing on the evidence compiled by Raul Hilberg, Hannah Arendt brought to light the extent to which Jewish leaders were complicit in cooperating with the Nazis, even down to the details of arranging deportation, transportation and confiscation of the property of fellow Jews.

> Without Jewish help in administrative and police work—the final rounding up of Jews in Berlin was, as I have mentioned, done entirely by Jewish police—there would have been either complete chaos or an impossibly severe drain on German manpower. . . . In Amsterdam as in Warsaw, in Berlin as in Budapest, Jewish officials could be trusted to compile the lists of persons and of their property, to secure money from the deportees to defray the expenses of their deportation and extermination, to keep track of vacated apartments, to supply police forces to help seize Jews and get them on trains, until, as a last gesture, they handed over the assets of the Jewish community in good order for final confiscation. They distributed the Yellow Star badges, and sometimes, as in Warsaw . . . the sale of armbands became a regular business; there were ordinary armbands of cloth and fancy plastic armbands which were washable. . . . To a Jew this role of the Jewish leaders in the destruction of their own people is undoubtedly the darkest chapter of the whole dark story.[78]

Not surprisingly, many in the Jewish community have not welcomed the attention to its failures cast by the reports of Hilberg and Arendt. But Arendt's refusal to remain silent is a sign of hope. Denial repeats the past; it cannot heal it. It is better to pay careful attention to moments when

---

77. Rieger, *Silent Church*, 43–45.

78. Arendt, *Eichmann in Jerusalem*, 116–17. Evans seeks to mollify Arendt's criticism, noting that Jewish room for maneuver was minimal. However, he confirms that Jewish councils were recruited by the Nazis to police themselves and in fact largely complied. Evans, *Third Reich at War*, 774.

unexpectedly the truth was spoken. For example, out of a fearful silence, in March 1937, the Roman Catholic Church smuggled into Germany the papal encyclical *Mit Brennender Sorge* (*With Burning Concern*). It was read from every Catholic pulpit on Palm Sunday before a single copy fell into Nazi hands. In it Pius XI called on the church to resist the idolatry of race or people, state or constitution, and to resist the perversion of doctrine and morality. Hitler was furious at this public act of defiance.[79]

Even at Barmen there was an uneasy sense that the Confessing Church was silent about something that needed to be spoken publically. We have already noted Barth's letter to Bethge, in response to his gift of the Bonhoeffer biography, in which he praised Bonhoeffer for facing and tackling the Jewish question "so centrally and energetically" as early as 1933. The same letter also tells Bethge that had Barmen attempted this it would not have been acceptable to his fellow delegates. Indeed, Barth blamed himself for not making this question "a decisive issue." There was no excuse for not trying.[80] Much earlier in June 1945, with the carnage of war displayed on all fronts, Barth lamented how partial was the church's resistance. Yet even this limited resistance must be set against a backdrop of the cultural surrender of both the liberal and the conservative church. Regarding the Confessing Church's limited resistance, Barth wrote this assessment:

> In 1933 and the years immediately following—at the time the National Socialists "seized power"—there was no struggle of the German universities and schools, of the German legal profession, of German business, of the German theater and German art in general, of the German Army, or of the German trade-unions. Many individuals, it is true, went down to an honorable defeat. But in no time at all, those large groups and institutions were subdued and made to conform. On the other hand, from the very first months on there was a German Church struggle. Even it was not a total resistance against totalitarian National Socialism. It restricted itself to repelling the encroachment of National Socialism. It confined itself to the Church's Confession, to the Church service, and to Church order as such. It was only a partial resistance. And for this it has been properly and improperly reproached: properly—in so far as a strong Christian Church, that is, a Church sure of its own cause in the face of National Socialism should not have remained on the defensive and should not have fought on its own

79. Conway, *Nazi Persecution*, 165. However, Lewy points out that even though the pagan teachings of blood and soil were specifically mentioned as contrary to Christian faith, the letter was silent about anti-Semitism *per se*. Lewy, *Catholic Church*, 296.

80. Barth, *Karl Barth Letters, 1961–1968*, 250.

narrow front alone; improperly—in so far as on this admittedly all too narrow front a serious battle was waged, at least in part and not without some success. At any rate, the substance of the Church was rescued and with a better understanding of it than it had had before. If at least as much had been done in other areas as was done at that time in the Church, National Socialism would have had a hard time of it in Germany right from the start. In proportion to its task, the Church has sufficient reason to be ashamed that it did not do more; yet in comparison with those other groups and institutions it has no reason to be ashamed; it accomplished far more than all the rest.[81]

In this context we should recall the unexpected commendation of the church's resistance by Albert Einstein, hardly a church insider.

Having always been an ardent partisan of freedom, I turned to the universities, as soon as the revolution broke out in Germany, to find there the defenders of freedom. I did not find them. Very soon the universities took refuge in silence. I then turned to the editors of powerful newspapers, who, but lately in flowing articles, had claimed to be the faithful champions of liberty. These men, as well as the universities, were reduced to silence in a few weeks. I then addressed myself to the authors individually, to those who passed themselves off as the intellectual guides of Germany, and among whom many had frequently discussed the question of freedom and its place in modern life. They are in their turn very dumb. Only the Church opposed the fight which Hitler was waging against liberty. Till then I had no interest in the Church, but now I feel great admiration and am truly attracted to the Church which had the persistent courage to fight for spiritual truth and moral freedom. I feel obliged to confess that I now admire what I used to consider of little value.[82]

As Conway notes, when Barmen was unanimously endorsed by its 139 delegates in May of 1934, no one wanted a political resistance movement led by the churches—especially the churches themselves! The church much preferred to ride along with the recovery of German national pride. A majority of the church welcomed Hitler and hoped his rise would restore its special role in society, which had been tottering since the failure of the Kaiser's war. Given this cultural background, it is all the more remarkable

81. Quoted in Cochrane, *Church's Confession*, 41.

82. Quoted in Rieger, *Silent Church*, 90. Also quoted with a condensed and slightly different translation in Cochrane, *Church's Confession*, 40. Cochrane cites Wilhelm Niemöller, *Kamp und Zeugnis der Bekennenden Kirche*, 526

that with Hitler's popularity only rising, the Confessing Church at Barmen steeled itself to resist the German Christian marriage between church and the National Socialist Party.[83] Barth's task at Barmen was not that of a political theorist writing a political manifesto to mobilize the people of Germany. He wrote as a theologian to his family of faith, the body of Christ, in the context of a family dispute among his brother and sister Pietists, Liberals and their traitorous offspring, the German Christians.

In a family crisis, one's tone and intent matter as much as one's actual words. "As a Christian I can criticize other Christians only if I am also in solidarity with them. . . . Further when I do criticize I do so not in a tone of harsh indignation but in a tone of sad dismay at a threat that somehow turned into a temptation for me as well."[84] Despite his irenic intentions, this did not keep Barth from asking the family if the time for a separation had come. As we have noted, what first evoked Barth's theological change of course was not Hitler's rise to power nor the German Christian heresy; it was twenty years earlier when the German Church endorsed the Kaiser's war. To give divine sanction to the "thoroughly sinful, godless enterprise" of the German war efforts in WWI, that is what made Barth wonder aloud if the time had come to be an atheist![85]

The tipping point in Barth's resistance to the war theologians also contains the source of his opposition to the German Christians: *it had to do with the church's task in the world.* That is, the church had a special service to render which was essential to its identity in bearing witness to the gospel. But only later did Barth see clearly that to render properly to God what belonged to God, one must also render to Caesar a service which the church alone can and must render to the state. Given its occurrence amid the Hitler years, the Barmen Declaration was an "astounding" affirmation of the state in God's purposes.[86] Existing within the polarity between Romans 13 and Revelations 13 the state exists not as an "order of creation" which the church *must* hear as revelatory by divine appointment, but by divine appointment the state is a body granted the *gracious* calling to provide for justice and peace. Moreover, the state as a body includes not just the rulers but also the ruled! Hence for the church to simply "keep out of politics" would fundamentally abrogate the church's witness to the gospel.[87]

---

83. Conway, "German Church Struggle," 98.
84. Quoted in Busch, *Karl Barth and the Pietists*, 289.
85. Ibid., 295.
86. Cochrane, *Church's Confession*, 284–85.
87. Ibid.

When we read Barmen today, its silence about the Jews is no doubt its most disturbing feature. Yet at the time, its author was hardly viewed by the government as a soft opponent or an irrelevance. A secret report of the Gestapo in May 1934 documents that for the Nazis, Barth and friends such as Niemöller were a serious threat.

> Barth's following must be regarded as a real danger. With his theology he is creating islands on which men can isolate themselves, and so evade the demands of the new state on religious grounds.[88]

Would that these little islands had made a further connection and become a landmass sufficient to unite dissent against the Nazis! But for Barth and those influenced by his initiative, Barmen was a beginning. In the face of extraordinary Nazi intimidation, the church's one foundation had been clearly declared; the implications would be worked out in the travail that would follow.

88. Quoted in Conway, "Political Theology," 529.

4

Barth beyond Barmen

Just as the church is constantly asked if she is what her name signifies, the same question must be put to the state.

—KARL BARTH[1]

DESPITE RUDOLF BULTMANN'S PLEA to reconsider, and only six months after Barmen, Karl Barth refused to take the personal oath of loyalty to Hitler, newly required of all government employees, including all university faculty. As it happened, Barth wrote to the government to say he was willing to sign the oath if he could include the stipulation that his loyalty to the Führer could be only within "my responsibilities as an Evangelical Christian."[2] This proviso was rejected and Barth was immediately suspended from the faculty of the University of Bonn. However, he continued to live in Bonn and work for the church until in March of 1935 he was served with a ban on speaking in public.[3] Even so, it was Barth's hope to stay in Germany to teach and preach. But by this time the Confessing Church was deeply conflicted over whether or not to support Barth's attitude to the state.[4] By the end of June his suspension was finalized, all appeals exhausted.

As he prepared for his deportation, Barth prepared a farewell paper that wrestled further with the believer's responsibility to the state. As its title

1. Barth, *Knowledge of God*, 223.
2. Busch, *Karl Barth*, 255, 257.
3. Ibid., 259.
4. Ibid., 261, 266.

announces ("Gospel and Law"), Barth reversed the traditional Lutheran sequence of "law and gospel." He argued that if God's will is decisively revealed in Christ, then to speak of any notion of law today, including a "people's law" that speaks of an event in history (for example, the coming of Hitler to power) as a law for the *Volk*, it exalts a law that does not spring from the gospel. Moreover, it is not only hazardous and dangerous but perverse to read a law of God out of some event other than the event in which God's will has been definitively manifested both in form and content in the grace of Jesus Christ. As he was no longer permitted to speak in public, the pastor of the Barmen church read the text while Barth sat in the assembly. That same evening his train was accompanied by the Gestapo to the Swiss border. He would not set foot again in Germany for ten years. But as his thinking continued to evolve, Barth only became more, not less outspoken about the German situation.

Return to Switzerland

Upon returning to his native Switzerland, Barth urged the Confessing Church to address not only church policy, but also politics.[5] Every year from 1935–39 he wrote an annual reflection on the German situation. The tone was one of penitence and lament, never of congratulation. In his first annual letter he described the Confessing Church story as "no glorious chronicle." Yes, she had fought hard for her freedom to proclaim the gospel, but "she has, for instance, remained silent on the actions against the Jews, on the amazing treatment of political opponents and the suppression of the freedom of the press in the new Germany and on so much else against which the Old Testament prophets would certainly have spoken out."[6] He also began publically to reproach himself for failing to offer any *political* resistance alongside a theological resistance to National Socialism.[7]

In 1937 Barth traveled to Scotland to give the prestigious Gifford Lectures, endowed by Lord Gifford with the express purpose of the study of natural theology "in the widest sense of the term" as a science of God and morality. Gifford's will specifically required that its presentations be constructed independently of all historical religions and "without reference to or reliance upon any supposed special exceptional or so-called miraculous revelation."[8] Having already rejected the *Deutsche Christen* merger with National Socialism based in natural theology, Barth took this Scottish

5. Ibid., 273.

6. Barth, *German Church Conflict*, 45–46.

7. Busch, *Karl Barth*, 274.

8. Barth, *Knowledge of God*, 3.

opportunity to articulate a *post* natural theology framework for Christian theology. His intention in accepting this invitation was to render all future natural theology the "service" of articulating the fullest opposition against such a methodology. In support of his effort, Barth chose to comment upon the old Scots Confession of 1560. This would form the Reformation background beyond which he now deliberately sought to move.

Barth's first crucial move was to distinguish between the Lutheran and Reformed approach to the state. The Lutheran, he claimed, prefers a "certain independence" of the state from Christ's kingdom. In contrast, though Barth *distinguished* the two kingdoms, he rejected the idea of *separation*. Instead, the Reformed Church "claims the order governing the world as an order for the service of God."[9] In other words, the state has a task to render God and it is always a proper question to ask the state if it is being faithful to its task: does it violate or safeguard justice, peace and freedom?[10] Under Hitler, Barth claimed the state in Germany had obscured this question because it made its own aims absolute. In the process, the state had made itself a church. Therefore the church was bound to ask the state: are you on the way to becoming what Romans 13 calls God's representative and priest or are you on the way to becoming the beast rising up out of the sea depicted in Revelation 13? All states are on the way either to one or the other.[11] But when, he warned, the church confronts a government "of liars, murderers and incendiaries, a government which wished to usurp the place of God, to fetter the conscience, to suppress the church and become itself the church of antichrist" then the church not only prays for the conversion and salvation of such people, it also prays that "as political rulers they may be set aside."[12]

Barth was not finished. He asked: ought the church's resistance to such regimes take the form of active, forcible resistance? His answer: this question cannot be determined in advance. However, since Jesus is Lord of the world as well as the church, the church cannot pray to be spared "the political service of God as such."[13]

In his annual report on the German church written the same year, Barth brought attention to a change in Nazi strategy from the days of Barmen. Earlier the Nazis used indirect means through an internal movement (the German Christians), to take over the church from within. But by 1937 the church had been banished from the public life of the nation into an "allegedly freely

---

9. Ibid., 220, 221.

10. Ibid., 224.

11. Ibid., 226.

12. Ibid., 231.

13. Ibid., 232. Bush, *Karl Barth*, 280.

bestowed inner room of private devotion and ceremony."[14] This *inner room strategy* explains how it came to pass that the German Free Church representatives (Methodists and Baptists) dared to claim at a recent Oxford ecumenical conference that the gospel was freely proclaimed in their nation![15] But as the Nazi strategy had changed, so must the tactics of resistance. For if the church has no public voice, its resistance cannot take a public approach. Here Barth's words remind us of Niemöller's prediction about a church of catacombs and martyrs. By July of that year, Niemöller was in prison.

As Europe moved closer to war, Barth's thinking moved as well. The year before the war commenced, Barth traveled in July to the Netherlands (Utrecht) to meet with Confessing Church leaders. This seems to have been the meeting in which he first proposed a fundamental reframing of the relation of church and state. Barth reported that in searching the Reformation for guidance, he found little evidence that either Calvin or Luther had much curiosity regarding the relationship between human justice (including politics and law) and their grand theme of justification by grace. Yet as a result of his recent study of Scripture, Barth was convinced that *a more positive relationship inhered within* these two themes. He chose to announce this link by his paper's title, *Rechtfertigung und Recht* (Justification and Justice).[16]

The first new positive theme Barth expounded was that Scripture called believers to pray for those wielding political power—even when the church suffered persecution. In the conflict Scripture narrates between Christ and Pilate, the state failed its duty to protect someone whom the head of state, Pilate, called both just and innocent. In other words, the state had not overstepped its boundaries; *it had done too little.* Had Pilate taken his responsibility more seriously, he would have interrupted this gross miscarriage of justice. Yet such is God's mighty hand, that even in his failure of duty, Pilate became the involuntary agent of divine justification.[17] This key text also revealed that the state as a power ordained by God never exists for itself or belongs to itself. Like all principalities and powers, the state belongs to Christ its true head. Moreover, like all principalities and powers, the state will not be destroyed, but will be led into the service of Christ.[18]

So what does this mean for the church? It means the church should neither deify the state nor demonize it (as Augustine nearly did when he

---

14. Barth, *German Church Conflict*, 56.

15. Ibid., 69.

16. "Church and State" is the English title given to this essay. Barth, *Community, State and Church*, 106–7.

17. Ibid., 113.

18. Ibid., 116.

identified the earthly city with the city of Cain). When the church proclaims the kingdom of God through declaring God's justification, it actually "founds, here and now, the true system of law, the true State."[19] This doesn't mean the church should set itself up as an alternative earthly state, nor be a state within the state, nor conceive of itself above the state. But it affirms its hope *in the city and the law that is coming*. Meanwhile the church rightly must show loyalty to the state even when the state honors evildoers and punishes the good. But when such tragic failures occur, the church shows its *proper* loyalty by summoning the state to its true mission and its true possibility—*which is coming*.[20] Until Christ's kingdom comes, the church's task will be to hold the state accountable to its mission by expecting the best of it.[21]

But suppose the state goes to the extreme of perverting its God-given vocation? Then the church will truly honor the state by criticizing it and holding it accountable.[22] In this way, whenever the state is tempted to view itself as autonomous or necessary *apart from its function as God's servant*, then the church will defend the state from the state. The church performs this task out of loyalty to the state whether the state wishes to know about or receive this service or not.[23] But when the state demands an inner claim, a certain *Weltanschauung* (worldview), we are approaching the "beast out of the abyss" of Revelation 13. When the state demands "love" it makes itself into a church; a church of a false god and thus an unjust state.[24] For Barth, the "higher powers" of Romans 13 are linked to angelic powers, which are ever in danger of falling and turning satanic. This is what has happened in Germany. This is why the state attacked the church.

In summing up, Barth says the Christian's obligation to the state is not to love it, but to fulfill one's duty as a responsible citizen. This duty is not exhausted by passive forms of legality such as obeying rules or paying taxes. It involves "responsible choices" about the validity of laws and hence inevitably will entail "political action, which may and must also mean political struggle."[25] We cannot pray for the state unless we are willing to engage in

19. Ibid., 126.

20. Ibid., 127, 131.

21. Ibid., 137.

22. Ibid., 139.

23. Ibid., 141. Barth includes military service as a self-evident duty owed the state because to refuse this is a fundamental rejection of the state itself (142).

24. Ibid., 143. The tell-tale sign that the state has become a false church is when its devotees speak insistently about "loving my country."

25. Ibid., 144.

this struggle. For when the church seriously prays for the state, it becomes "the force which founds and maintains the state."[26]

Throughout this entire explanation, Barth avoided any grounding of the state upon "some Romantic or Liberalistic idea of natural law." Whenever the West claims that freedom of religion is granted by the state, Barth declared it to be upside-down thinking. Religious freedom precedes all political organization. To say otherwise grants the state untenable divine authority.[27]

The Brink of War

As war approached, the church's situation in Germany only worsened. In Barth's next annual assessment, he used the word *extermination* to describe the policy of the German government toward the church.[28] Of course, extermination Nazi-style would not be the Bolshevik or Russian "line up Christians and shoot them." No, the Nazis, he predicted, would instead change the meaning of historic Christian doctrines, destroy the church's possibility to govern itself, and impose a "neutral" administrative machinery which would serve its own totalitarian efforts by forbidding ordinations, publications, cancelling meetings, and stirring up young people against the church.[29]

This was the apocalyptic atmosphere—the threat of extermination—in which the Confessing Church now convinced itself to require its clergy to make a personal oath of loyalty to Hitler by the end of May 1938.[30] This was also the context in which Barth addressed the persecution of Jews; its growing intensification only made it more lamentable that the church had shut its eyes to the truth that the Jewish question had always been a question of faith.[31] In such a moment, the church's worst enemies were those who watered down the witness of the church, the "army of neutrals in that non-confessing church which is yet prepared for any compromise."[32]

Also in this report (1938–39) Barth addressed the critics of Martin Niemöller. Niemöller had been in prison since July 1937, yet his critics insisted that his incarceration was the result of his engagement in politics instead of proclaiming the pure gospel. Barth asked, are these critics suggesting that a "pure" gospel would have no visible bodily expression? If so, then

26. Ibid., 146–47.
27. Bettis, "Barmen," 157.
28. Barth, *German Church Conflict*, 71.
29. Ibid., 72.
30. Ibid., 68.
31. Ibid., 75.
32. Ibid.

such a gospel would "remain completely invisible to the world!" How ironic that what Niemoller's critics wanted—a church that is only inward and not at all outward—was identical with what National Socialism demanded.[33]

Now came the moment when all of Europe listened as Hitler threatened to invade Czechoslovakia. In September Barth wrote his Czech friend, Pastor Josef Hromadka, to speak to the practical implications of his essay *Rectfertigung und Recht* for the Czech situation. His words were blunt. Stand up with arms to Hitler's threat of arms! When this advice became public knowledge, the Confessing Church council issued Barth a formal letter of censure.[34] By contrast, during this same month the greatest contrast to Barth's advice became public policy: England and France sanctioned Hitler's annexation of half of Czechoslovakia, the *Sudentenland*. Upon returning from meetings with Hitler in Munich, Britain's prime minister, Neville Chamberlain, famously held aloft a document, calling it "peace in our time." Barth records that when he heard of this news, he felt utterly alone as even the Swiss churches were holding services of thanksgiving that peace had been preserved. "Of course, six months later Hitler broke even that shameful treaty."[35] As Britain negotiated the handover of the *Sudentenland*, Barth responded bluntly again. Christians had a political task to perform. An attitude of avoidance toward Hitler's threat to the political order and freedom of Europe was simply irresponsible. So at this crucial historical moment, the Confessing Church's preference to avoid confrontation with Hitler was the mirror image of the French and the British negotiators at Munich.

Despite his growing sense of isolation, in July of 1939, Barth proceeded to publish a tract in England with the uncompromising subtitle: *The Church and the Political Problem of Our Day: The Church Ceases to Be the Church if It Shirks the Political Problems of Totalitarianism*. In this essay Barth argued that German National Socialism now threatened to become the form of society for all Europe, a form of society in which the government expropriated both the political and religious responsibility of the people. About such a society, a church that confessed Jesus Christ could not be neutral. Unfortunately the decision of the Confessing Church to take an oath of loyalty to Hitler pretended such neutrality was possible. But by appropriating both political and religious authority, the German government had dissolved a just society. It had created a National Socialist deity impossible to reconcile to the Christian God. Barth's most compelling evidence of this grasping for religious authority? The strident anti-Semitism of the regime and Hitler's

33. Ibid., 72.
34. Busch, *Karl Barth*, 289.
35. Ibid.

resolve to physically exterminate the Jews.[36] We should recall these words were written prior to the invasion of Poland and the construction of the web of concentration camps in the East. But those who persecute the Jews, said Barth, persecute him who died for the sins of the Jews. Barth's tract ended with further grim evidence of the dissolution of the just state in Germany: the fraudulent burning of the Reichstag, the fraud of false elections, the use of terror on its own citizens, and the loss of personal rights as arrest, torture and prison were imposed on citizens without any government accountability.

Only days before the invasion of Poland, Barth reminded his readers that in all these sorry happenings, the hands of Germany's neighbors were not clean. Hadn't the peace of Versailles given a semblance of legitimacy to Nazi aspirations? If the church in Germany had been what it ought to have been, if its form of life honestly reflected its Master, it is "inconceivable" that a Nazi form of political life would have been sought.[37] "Christian Europe" richly deserved to be threatened with ruin. The only prayer appropriate now was "deliver us from evil" and "restore a just state."[38]

With war now imminent, we can summarize Barth's development since Barmen as follows: the time had come for political action to resist the German government as a false state that had become a false church. Before Poland was invaded, Barth wrote W. A. Visser't Hooft, General Secretary of the Provisional Committee of the World Council of Churches, urging him to use his office to broadcast to Christians throughout Germany that the growing threat of war must be named and that Christians should do everything in their power to prevent the war or a victory either by refusing to take part in military service, by sabotage or by other actions. However, his ecumenical colleague rejected this counsel as "too unusual, too novel, too bold."[39]

Clearly, such an urgent request indicates that for Barth, political resistance to National Socialism now included military resistance. He considered it as wrong for the church to embrace pacifism in response to Hitler as it had been wrong to be thoughtlessly nationalistic and militaristic in previous wars.[40] The democratic states of Europe must now defend themselves against this onslaught of "manifest inhumanity" and the church must not be afraid to say so. In April 1940 a fifty-six-year-old Barth duly reported for Swiss military service. As the war progressed, he became active in any

36. Barth, *The Church and the Political Problem*, 50–51.

37. Ibid., 69.

38. Ibid., 64.

39. Busch, *Karl Barth*, 298. Cf. Visser't Hooft, *Memoirs*, 114.

40. Busch, *Karl Barth*, 303.

number of organizations, some highly secretive, committed to Swiss defense against invasion.[41] Such was the outspokenness of his political resistance to the German regime, that he was seen as a threat to the Swiss government's official neutrality. In 1942 he was banned from speaking concerning political matters. His telephone was (illegally) tapped.[42]

Are the Germans Uniquely Wicked?

In a letter to French Protestants (1940) Barth repeated his *Rechtfertigung und Recht* argument: because the church knows about justification it cannot remain silent when justice is at stake. The church has a duty to tell the German people, "You are mistaken. Your cause is not just. Change your course while there is still time."[43] But Barth rebuked Germany's neighbors as well. As victors in WWI, France and England "are responsible for the state of affairs which arose in Europe after 1919" and thus for making Hitler possible.[44] He asked: does the current crisis reveal that Germany is uniquely wicked? No, he said. Every people has a heritage which twists and confuses various natural paganisms with Christianity. Hitler is but the present evil dream of the German pagan wearing a Christian camouflage as it regressed into paganism. At the moment, the German adversary was a "sick man" who when the war ends will need to be treated "as a sick man is treated" with firm but compassionate hands.[45] With the war now raging, Barth warned the Allies that the only way to have a good conscience about this war would be if it is carried on *for the sake of* the Germans![46] After the war, compassion toward Germans would be essential.[47] Such warnings to the Allies were part and parcel of Barth's political response as a witness of the gospel. He was declaring an even-handed solidarity in which the justification of the sinner is the foundation for all earthly justice. If the future justice of the Allies isolated itself from mercy, he said, the result would be a foolish return to Versailles, throwing Germany back into a crisis in which something worse than Hitler could emerge.[48] But as we will see shortly, Allied postwar strategy was in grave danger of doing exactly what Barth warned against.

41. Ibid., 307. Busch provides details.

42. Jehle, *Ever Against the Stream*, 70.

43. Barth, *Letter to Great Britain*, 34.

44. Ibid., 33.

45. Ibid., 37.

46. Busch, *Karl Barth*, 318.

47. Ibid., 322.

48. Barth, *Letter to Great Britain*, 38.

As the war dragged on, so did Barth's isolation. By the time his "Open Letter from Switzerland to Great Britain" was published (1941), censors had already banned it in Switzerland. In this essay Barth insisted that armed resistance to Germany should not be viewed as some kind of necessary evil; it was rather a large-scale police measure, necessary because Hitler was attempting to impose an arbitrary, anarchic order on Europe, whose essence would be the sovereignty of the German race and state. About such a state, Christians could be neither neutral nor passive.[49] He also addressed his fellow Swiss regarding the urgency of helping Jewish refugees. "The Rhine will not wash away our guilt of having turned away 10,000 refugees and having treated unworthily those whom we did accept."[50]

War's End: Forgiveness and the Future

By war's end Bonhoeffer was dead, executed by personal order of Hitler only days before Allied soldiers reached the Flossenburg prison. Niemöller had escaped during his own execution journey to the Tirol and was in the hands of American soldiers. Barth was isolated in Basel, his phone tapped, banned from speaking about politics by the Swiss government. To think the primary contribution of the church to the 1989 reunification and the end of the Cold War would be intimately joined to this circle of witness seems one of the most unlikely of historical contingencies. And yet this is the trajectory we are examining. How then, after Hitler's barbaric reign, would grace *and* costly discipleship ever walk together again in Germany? How would the little flock inspired by this group of pastors create a narrow path of reconciliation that would bring an end to the Cold War?

With Europe now exhausted after a second war in less than twenty years, two questions will direct the next phase of inquiry into the peculiar service which the church would now render to Caesar.

1. Would it be possible for the world (ecumenical) church to be reconciled with the church in Germany, a church that had either embraced Hitler's crusade or had been too submissive, failing to offer true service to the state?

---

49. Ibid., 4, 21.

50. Busch, *Karl Barth*, 318. A relevant story in this regard is that of Paul Grüninger, the Swiss border guard whose merciful behavior toward hundreds of Jewish refugees cost him his career in the Swiss police. Grüninger's merciful side-stepping of orders from his superiors is told in Press, *Beautiful Souls*.

2. How could a church so compromised contribute toward rebuilding a humiliated nation, one that had caused suffering on such an enormous scale both among its neighbors and within its own borders?

The tasks facing the church were made all the more awkward because its own membership contained the full diversity of German life, from the fiercest critics of the Nazis to its most strident German Christian defenders and all shades in between. Our next station on the road to 1989 will consider the gathering at Stuttgart, where after his dramatic escape from seven years in concentration camp, Martin Niemöller returned to the Confessing Church Council of Brethren. The document composed by the council would become the Confessing Church's most controversial and most important contribution to Germany's postwar restoration.

5

Guilt, Forgiveness and Foreign Policy
The Stuttgart Declaration of 1945

The Allied armies are in occupation of the whole of Germany and the German people have begun to atone for the terrible crimes committed under the leadership of those whom in the hour of their success they openly approved and blindly obeyed.

—POTSDAM DECLARATION[1]

I have just heard the news. . . . Russians 60 miles from Berlin. It does look as if something decisive might happen soon. The appalling destruction and misery of this war mount hourly: destruction of what should be (indeed is) the common wealth of Europe, and the world, if mankind were not so besotted, wealth the loss of which will affect us all, victors or not. Yet people gloat to hear of the endless lines, forty miles long, of miserable refugees, women and children pouring West, dying on the way. There seem no bowels of mercy or compassion, no imagination, left in this dark diabolic hour. By which I do not mean that it may not all, in the present situation, mainly (not solely) created by Germany, be necessary and inevitable. But why gloat! We were supposed to have reached a stage of civilization in which it might still be necessary to execute a criminal, but not to gloat, or to hang his wife and child by him while the orc-crowd hooted. The destruction of Germany, be it a hundred times merited, is one of

1. Potsdam Declaration, August 3, 1945, from Morgenthau, *Germany Is Our Problem*, 216.

the most appalling world-catastrophes. Well, well—you and I can do nothing about it. And that should be a measure of the amount of guilt that can justly be assumed to attach to any member of a country who is not a member of its actual Government.

—J. R. R. TOLKIEN,
LETTER TO HIS SON CHRISTOPHER,
SERVING IN THE R.A.F. [2]

There is no such thing as the guilt or innocence of an entire nation. Like innocence, guilt is not collective, but personal.

—RICHARD VON WEIZSÄCKER,
PRESIDENT OF THE FEDERAL REPUBLIC OF GERMANY
FROM 1984 TO 1994 [3]

Free confession of guilt is not something that one can take or leave; it is the form of Jesus Christ breaking through in the church. The church can let this happen to itself, or it will cease to be the church of Christ.

—DIETRICH BONHOEFFER [4]

The artistry of the preacher is to disclose the power of guilt and of healing and to lead the congregation through the delicate transaction whereby healing overcomes and overrides guilt.

—WALTER BRUEGGEMANN [5]

ON OCTOBER 17–19, 1945, in Stuttgart, a Declaration of Guilt (*Stuttgarter Schuldbekenntnis*) was authored by the newly reconstituted Council of the Protestant Church in Germany. It became the most significant postwar document written by the Confessing Church.[6] It was also controversial for several reasons. However, a reason rarely noted is that the document was the initia-

---

2. Tolkien, *Letters*, 111.
3. Weizsäcker, *From Weimar to the Wall*, 385.
4. Bonhoeffer, *Ethics*, 142.
5. Brueggemann, *Finally Comes the Poet*, 13.
6. Oestreicher, introduction to Gollwitzer, *Demands of Freedom*, 17.

tive of an ecumenical church that did not passively wait for their governments to establish postwar Allied policies. Today we have forgotten that as the dust settled on the war in Europe, there was mounting pressure at the highest levels to teach defeated Germany a lesson that would make the Versailles treaty look generous. In the teeth of this vengeful mood, Bonhoeffer's friends in the nascent ecumenical movement strove to reset the church's relationship to Germany along a very different path. By taking this initiative, the events of Stuttgart put a direct question to the Allied governments: would they pursue a victor's spirit of vengeance or the irenic example of their nations' churches?

The hurdles for attempting a gathering to restore ecumenical relations with the Germans were many. How does one reestablish relations between churches whose members have spent the past five years trying to obliterate the other in a total war? The end of hostilities raised perhaps the fundamental challenge of Christian faith, namely, how to practice the difficult love of forgiving one's enemy? Moreover, how does forgiveness function within the complexity of international relations? Is it possible for governments to enact policies of a "victor's justice" or "collective punishment" when their churches choose the path of forgiveness?

Recent studies have suggested the gathering at Stuttgart was further complicated by a deep disagreement between the Lutheran and Reformed parts of Protestantism, with "acrimonious debates" about preconditions to forgiveness in regard to the question of German guilt.[7] But the testimony of those most closely involved suggests the notion of acrimonious debates is overstated. Nevertheless, as Bonhoeffer's ecumenical colleagues gathered at Stuttgart, a stubborn human reality remained that was less to do with *theological* preconditions, than with something more prosaic: how do Christians with a shared history of violent estrangement actually go about practicing the "delicate tension" whereby healing overcomes guilt?

The ecumenical gathering was painfully aware of the implications should their meeting for reconciliation fail. The memory of the failed peace after the 1919 Versailles treaty hung over everyone. Under the famous Article 231 (known as the War Guilt clause), Germany was forced to be liable, both morally and financially, for total responsibility for the war. The toxic consequences of this policy were many, including futile debates about guilt and blame in which ecumenical relations languished for seven long years after WWI, years of bitter resentment toward Europe which helped Hitler get his start.[8] For if the church could not practice what they had been called by Je-

---

7. Hockenos, *Church Divided*, 74. Conway, "How Shall the Nations Repent?," 603.

8. Herman, *Rebirth of the German Church*, 21. Shortly after the treaty was announced in 1919, a youthful British treasury representative, J. M. Keynes, would write a devastating economic critique of the treaty that unfortunately was decades ahead of

sus to preach to the nations, how could they expect their governments to do anything but double down on the punitive Versailles policies that followed World War I? The representatives at Stuttgart hoped by God's mercy to guide postwar history along quite a different path. It was this hope that led them to take a risk—to arrange, as soon as humanly possible, a meeting for reconciliation between themselves and representatives of the German church.

Willam Visser't Hooft of the Netherlands was the *de facto* leader of what was to become the World Council of Churches. His memoir describes the actions which now commenced. Through contacts he discovered that the council of the Evangelical Church of Germany (renamed and reconstituted after the war) was to meet in Stuttgart in mid-October. He knew this council was chosen for their faithful witness during the church conflict. He wondered: would it be possible for a gathering of church leaders to actually implement the vision for reconciliation which inspired Bonhoeffer and his friends: "that they might be one, Father, just as you and I are one" (John 17:21).[9] Before his arrest, Bonhoeffer had met both with Anglican bishop George Bell in Stockholm and Visser't Hooft in Geneva. To each Bonhoeffer spoke of how the only road open to the Christians of Germany was the road of repentance.[10] In July Visser't Hooft wrote to Otto Dibelius, bishop of Berlin-Brandenburg, to say that while there was no wish to adopt a pharisaic attitude, future conversations should include frank discussions about both Nazi crimes *as well as* the sins of omission of the German people.[11]

A Surprise Visit

Through something of a miracle, just four months after hostilities had ceased, a group of eight ecumenical visitors managed to assemble the various permits from military authorities to travel to Stuttgart on October 17, 1945. Due to shortness of time and woeful communications, it had not even been possible to let the council know they were coming. "So our arrival caused considerable surprise and also much joy."[12]

Only weeks before the Stuttgart meeting, Karl Barth had written Martin Niemöller to encourage his old friend that in its dark hour of defeat, Christians of many nations wanted to help Germany. But it was *necessary*,

---

Allied thinking. Cf. Keynes, *Economic Consequences of the Peace*.

9. Visser't Hooft, *Memoirs*, 189.

10. Ibid. For details of Bonhoeffer's conversation with Bell, see Chandler, *George Bell*, 97.

11. Ibid., 190.

12. Ibid., 191.

said Barth, for Germans to say frankly and clearly, "We Germans have erred—hence the chaos of today—and we Christians in Germany are also Germans!"[13] Barth knew only too well that the hands of the Confessing Church were not clean in regards to the German infection. To present herself as untainted by the illness manifest in Nazism was not only "nonsense" but if maintained, would set Germans against each another, the faithful remnant versus the guilty masses, making their lives even more unbearable than they already were.[14] Somehow the church must act in a way that would join in solidarity with the entire people, even though any action would take place amid chaotic circumstances.

Chaos is not too strong a word to describe Germany at war's end. The word *Zusammenbruch*, disastrous collapse, was frequently used to describe the shambles that was now Germany.[15] Seven million Germans had perished in the war, half of them civilians. One million soldiers languished in POW camps awaiting their fate at the hands of their conquerors. At least another million were missing, scattered along the roads stretching east of Berlin as far away as Russia. Deported, despised, and doomed to resettle within a shrinking land space, Germans languished in helplessness as the Allies debated how much German land should be pruned and apportioned to their neighbors in the east (Poland and Czechoslovakia) and in the west (France).

Throughout the country, food, fuel, housing, and transport were scarce or nonexistent. Industrial machinery that had not been destroyed by bombing was being dismantled and sent away daily by the four Allied nations occupying Germany.[16] Niemöller reported that due to the shocking conditions which prevailed during the first days of Berlin's occupation by the Russian army, over two hundred persons had committed suicide in his former parish of Dahlem, a wealthy suburb. Such were the conditions in greater Berlin, twenty pastors had committed suicide.[17] Niemöller reported these dark facts not to blame anyone but simply to illustrate how Germany "has reached the brink of the precipice."[18] Daily new reports arrived detailing atrocities perpetrated by the occupying armies, particularly the Russians, as they took revenge for Hitler's devastating invasion of their homeland in

---

13. Quoted in Bentley, *Martin Niemoller*, 175.
14. Barth, *Only Way*, 12.
15. Conway, "How Shall the Nations Repent?," 603.
16. Hockenos, *Church Divided*, 90.
17. Bentley, *Martin Niemöller*, 175.
18. Niemöller, *Of Guilt and Hope*, 22.

which more than twenty-six million Soviet citizens had perished, including nearly three million Soviet POWs.[19]

An eyewitness to Germany's chaos was Stewart Herman, pastor of the American Church in Berlin prior to the war. On behalf of the nascent World Council of Churches, Herman spent six months from August 1945, traveling the country and gathering information. His report describes scenes of countless homeless people milling around in despair, sleeping along the roadsides. How could a nation be reconciled to its neighbors while it was simultaneously being ravaged by chaos? Moreover, with the war over and Hitler dead, who was responsible for the current crisis? One could argue it was all Hitler's fault. But unlike so many things he did, this chaos was now within the power of others to change.[20] Regarding the current shambles, many Germans blamed the Russians; others blamed the Americans, the British, the French. Herman's stories of revenge visited upon German non-combatants deported and driven out of Poland make for disturbing reading. Staring at the collapse of all social order, Niemöller saw his fellow Germans both numb and full of self-pity. He wondered, could Germans move from being stuck in self-pity and blaming others—Nazis, Russians, Allies, and start to live again by taking responsibility for their own actions and inactions which had enabled this tragedy?[21] He became convinced a new start could only happen if the church took the lead in self-examination. If he and other pastors led the way it might help others take a similar responsibility—despite the chaos.

In the meantime, governance plans for the occupation of Germany were well under way in the Allied corridors of power. In England, Bonhoeffer's friend, Bishop George Bell was alarmed that the tone of public comments thus far, including the Potsdam agreement drafted by Truman, Stalin and the newly elected Clement Atlee, revealed a plan to "humiliate and enslave the German nation."[22] Meanwhile in America, it was not a well-kept secret that President Roosevelt's secretary of the treasury, Henry Morganthau, himself a Jew, had prepared a thoroughgoing punitive plan of reparations, partition, and de-industrialization, returning Germany to a preindustrial, agrarian society.[23] Given such alarming indicators, Bell,

19. According to Daniel Goldhagen. Cf. Evans, *Third Reich at War*, 707.

20. Herman, *Rebirth of the German Church*, 242, 271.

21. Schmidt, *Pastor Niemöller*, 146.

22. Conway is especially helpful in setting the political context as well as the complex logistics of the ecumenical visit to Stuttgart. Conway, "How Shall the Nations Repent?," 610ff.

23. Morgenthau, *Germany Is Our Problem*, 16, 79–80. Morganthau, writes Beschloss, was a firm believer in collective guilt for German war crimes (*Conquerors*, 52).

Visser't Hooft and other ecumenical friends of Bonhoeffer had resolved not to wait for their governments' intentions simply to play themselves out.

As already noted, Visser't Hooft's *Memoir* is clear: there was no question of seeking to extract a confession of guilt as some kind of precondition. On the other hand (as Barth had put it to Niemöller), it seemed necessary somehow for Germans, *including the German church*, to acknowledge their failure. How might this acknowledgment take place without it becoming a kind of precondition?

Let us recall Bonhoeffer's 1937 diagnosis at the height of the Nazi era: the church in Germany had been living in a false dream of cheap grace, that is, grace without discipleship, grace as a presumption due to its privileged Lutheran theological heritage. There could be only one remedy from such a disorder: repentance. The question arises in the exigency of the postwar environment, should repentance now be framed as a necessary prerequisite for restoration to fellowship?

Evangelical or Legal Repentance?

In a series of writings J. B. Torrance has described how, to its profound detriment, the Western church frequently confused the relation between repentance and forgiveness. Nowhere was this confusion more virulent than during the medieval era, with its penitential scheme by which forgiveness was framed within a schema of meritorious transaction, conditional upon confession, contrition and satisfaction.[24] To understand the representatives who gathered at Stuttgart, it is important to be clear that *both* Luther and Calvin had broken decisively with the conditionality of the medieval scheme on the grounds that it had turned a personal relation of forgiveness into a legal transaction. Luther himself had written:

> Rome maintains that justification and forgiveness depend on the conditions of penance. Therefore we are not justified by faith alone. We maintain that contrition does not merit the forgiveness of sins. It is indeed *necessary* but not the cause. The cause is the Holy Spirit.[25]

Regarding the same topic, John Calvin left no space between his view and Luther's. He wrote:

> But we added that repentance is not the cause of forgiveness of sins. Moreover we have done away with those torments of souls

24. Torrance, "Covenant and Contract," 51–76.
25. Luther, "Disputation Concerning Justification," 171–72 (italics added).

which they would have us perform as a duty. We have taught
that the sinner does not dwell upon his own compunction or
tears, but fixes both eyes upon the Lord's mercy alone. . . . Over
against these lies I put freely given remission of sins . . . what is
forgiveness but a gift of sheer liberality! When can he at length
be certain of the measure of that satisfaction? Then he will always doubt whether he has a merciful God; he will always be
troubled, and always tremble.[26]

In this moment of crisis when the Protestant churches of Europe
sought to model for their nations the way of reconciliation, did they engage
in "acrimonious debates" about the necessity of repentance as a prerequisite
to forgiveness? In effect, were the heirs of the Protestant tradition on the
verge of repudiating a shared foundation from the heart of the Reformation? If not, how can we understand both Barth and Bonhoeffer's emphasis
on the necessity of repentance?

Much of the confusion lies with the word "necessary." Four centuries
earlier Luther said that repentance is "necessary but not the cause." Only
weeks earlier Barth had written Niemöller that it was "necessary" for the
German church to say "we have erred." But as we have been reminded by
the words of Luther and Calvin, both traditions were united in the hope
that God's mercy was not the prisoner of preconditions. The kind of necessity Barth, Luther and Calvin all acknowledged was that of *response* to
God's unconditional grace, not a precondition. As Torrance puts it, implicit
in receiving the forgiving message of the cross "there must be on our part,
a humble submission to the verdict of guilt."[27] That is, repentance was a
necessary response to the life-giving power of God's grace. But it is grace
alone that releases in the sinner the freedom to confess, to cease making
excuses or covering up. It is the same logic of grace which freed Augustine
to write his famous *Confessions*—not in order to effect God's pardon, but as
a result of having been gripped by God's sheer mercy. As grace had released
in Augustine an extraordinary autobiographical honesty, so in Niemöller's
mind, grace was the sole grounds upon which the German church could
confess its guilt after its long and conflicted tale of resistance, yes indeed, but
also of compromise and collusion.

Torrance has further noted that to require repentance as a precondition of forgiveness severs repentance from gratitude.[28] For when repentance
springs from fear of punishment instead of gratitude, notions of bargaining

26. Calvin, *Institutes*, 3.4.3., 134.
27. Torrance, *Worship, Community*, 55.
28. From a remembered conversation with J. B. Torrance.

and merit rush in to disfigure the true necessity of repentance into what the legal mind of Tertullian, the second-century Latin theologian, unfortunately described as the price of which the Lord awards pardon.[29] Such a framework deforms repentance from the only proper response to grace into a causally necessary act of merit.

Guilt and Hope

On the evening they arrived, the visitors joined in a public service of worship at which Niemöller, Bishop Dibelius and chair of the Protestant Church Council, Theophil Wurm, all spoke. Niemöller preached on Jeremiah 14:7–11. "Though our iniquities testify against us, act, O Lord, for Thy name's sake." In an unforgettable message, Niemöller said it was not enough to blame the Nazis. The church must face its own guilt. "Would the Nazis have been able to do what they had done if church members had been truly faithful Christians?"[30] Hearing Niemöller's message, Visser't Hooft grew hopeful that the sterile debates and mutual recriminations concerning guilt after the first world war would not be repeated.

At their meeting the following day, Visser't Hooft describes their preparations thus:

> On the one hand we could not make a confession of guilt the condition for a restoration of fellowship for such a confession could only have value as a spontaneous gesture; on the other hand, the obstacles to fellowship could only be removed if a clear word were spoken. Pierre Maury gave us the right phrase. He suggested that we should say: "We have come to ask you to help us to help you."[31]

Visser't Hooft is clear: the conversations launched that day had nothing to do with negotiations. They began by his expressing the ecumenical delegations's desire to reestablish fraternal relations, and to express gratitude for the Confessing Church's witness. He spoke in particular of the sacrifice rendered by Bonhoeffer. He then picked up the phrase of Pierre Maury (quoted above). Hans Asmussen spoke decisively in reply. He said he determined years ago that at the first opportunity he would say to brothers from other churches, "I have sinned against you as a member of my nation, because I have not shown more courage." Niemöller spoke plainly as always:

29. Tertullian, "On Repentance," 661.
30. Quoted in Visser't Hooft, *Memoirs*, 191.
31. Visser't Hooft, *Memoirs*, 191–92.

as a church we share in the guilt of our nation and pray that God may forgive that guilt. From the Netherlands, Dr. Hendrik Kraemer responded with deep emotion. These words, he said, contained within them a call to his own church as well, that it could only live by the forgiveness of sins. "It could not be a matter of bartering."[32] As the session came to a close, Asmussen proposed the Germans meet alone to decide about a public declaration in light of their conversation. The following day, Bishop Wurm read aloud the text the council had agreed upon. Below is the crucial passage:

> We are all the more grateful for this [ecumenical] visit, as we not only know that we are with our people in a large community of suffering, but also in a solidarity of guilt. With great anguish we state: through us infinite wrong was brought to many peoples and countries. That which we often testified to in our communities, we express now in the name of the whole Church: We did fight for long years in the name of Jesus Christ against the mentality that found its awful expression in the National Socialist regime of violence; but we accuse ourselves for not standing to our beliefs more courageously, for not praying more faithfully, for not believing more joyously, and for not loving more ardently.[33]

These words were a *personal* confession of guilt offered by the representatives of the Confessing Church in response to the initiative launched by their ecumenical brothers. Despite the fact that each member of the council had shown great courage in resisting the Nazis, there was a gnawing personal awareness that their own hands were not clean. In the coming months, Niemöller's many speeches and sermons described a visit he made with his wife, Else, to the concentration camp at Dachau soon after they were reunited.[34] There he read a notice fixed to a tree: "Here between the years 1933 and 1945, 238,756 human beings were incinerated." He sensed God asking him, "Martin, where were you when these people were being slaughtered?"[35] Of course being incarcerated in a concentration camp was an undisputable alibi from 1937 to 1945. But what about 1933–37? Through the text of Matthew 25, Niemöller sensed God speaking to him personally. To gatherings up and down Germany he confessed that when the communists, the trade unionists and the Jews were thrown into concentration

---

32. Ibid., 192.

33. See Appendix II, "Stuttgart Declaration of Guilt."

34. The Dachau visit occurred after Niemöller's undiplomatic interview in Naples while still in Allied custody.

35. Schmidt, *Pastor Niemöller*, 150–51.

camps, he did not recognize Christ in them, suffering and persecuted. He remained silent.

> Here the question of guilt reveals for us Christians in Germany its horrible face. The Lord Jesus Christ asks his disciples, his Church, he asks you and me, whether we are really without guilt in regard to the horrors which came to pass in our midst. I cannot reply with a clear conscience: "Yea, Lord, I am without guilt. Thou wast in prison and I came unto Thee." Indeed I have said: "I do not know this man."[36]

In another sermon, Niemöller asked his listeners: when the communists were thrown in the concentration camps or murdered, who cared about them? "We knew about it; it was in all the papers." It happened again later with the Jews and also with "the incurables. Can we say it was not our fault? We preferred to keep quiet."[37] But Niemöller's relentless self-examination was not over. Imagine what might have happened, he asked, if fourteen thousand evangelical ministers had defended the truth with their lives in 1933? Perhaps they would have died, but such an act might have kept alive thirty or forty million people.[38]

In sermon after sermon Niemöller summoned his listeners to make a personal response to the Stuttgart Declaration. He asked his listeners whether the Christians of Germany might carry a greater responsibility before God than the Nazis? "Because we ought to have recognized the Lord Jesus in the brother who suffered and was persecuted, regardless of whether he was a communist or a Jew. And we did not recognize him!"[39] It was a devastating indictment. But with countless communities in a state of collapse, what could ordinary people do now? First and foremost, he pled, do not wait for a pastor or some official to come along to aid those in need, but go oneself, and do not pass by Christ yet again as had been done in 1933. "During these days let us keep our eyes wide open for the misery of our neighbor. If this can happen, then Christianity still has a task to perform in Europe."[40] As expressed in the title of a series of sermons, Niemöller's post-

---

36. Niemöller, "The Need and the Task," 210.

37. Niemöller, *Of Guilt and Hope*, 14.

38. Ibid., 16.

39. Ibid. Reinhold Niebuhr echoes Niemöller's argument when he writes that what was lacking in the Stuttgart Declaration was any acknowledgment of the special contribution of the church to the moral confusion out of which Nazism emerged. Niebuhr, "Reunion of the Church through the Renewal of the Churches," in *Essays in Applied Christianity*, 279.

40. Ibid.

war ministry was a compound message of guilt and hope, not one without the other. To meet Christ in one's suffering neighbor and to offer mercy was solely premised upon hope in God's mercy; in showing mercy to the sufferer, the believer participated in God's own merciful coming.

The Legacy of Stuttgart

Sixty years later, it remains difficult to read the Stuttgart Declaration with indifference. In an interview conducted in the 1980s, Victoria Barnett recorded the comments of a wife of a Confessing Church pastor who was herself also a member of the Nazi party:

> The Stuttgart Declaration of Guilt impressed me deeply, and I passed it on, even to people who didn't want to accept that guilt. . . . I was simultaneously a party member and a victim of fascism. I think it was much easier to be one or the other.[41]

If you are simply a victim, you are caught up in your own suffering. But such simplicity was not possible in Germany. In the autumn of 1945 Germany was in shock, devastated in every way by the allied bombing campaign, its civil and industrial infrastructure destroyed, an occupied country under martial law, with no self-government, incapable of any initiative in recovery. But Germany was not simply a nation of victims. Hitler's ruthless invasion of neighboring countries both to the east and the west had inflicted untold brutality and suffering on others. As news of the atrocities in Nazi concentration camps spread worldwide, Germany also became a nation in disgrace, almost a pariah nation. With winter approaching, they faced a final catastrophe—starvation. In response, the occupying powers set rations varying from 950 to 1150 calories per day. To put this number in context, the rations at the *Belsen* concentration camp had been 900 calories.[42] These number differentials created a worrisome reality in the competition for German loyalties as the Cold War began to emerge. As military governor of occupied Germany (1947–49), General Lucius Clay bluntly warned Washington, "There is no choice between becoming a Communist on 1500 calories and a believer in democracy on 1000 calories."[43] To make matters worse, the severe winter of 1945 was followed by one even worse. As a result, most Germans were far more conscious of their own sufferings than the sufferings they had recently inflicted on the rest of Europe.

41. Quoted in Barnett, *For the Soul of the People*, 213.

42. Bacque, *Crimes and Mercies*, 90.

43. Quoted in Beschloss, *Conquerors*, 273.

Such was the case for ten-year-old Martin Rumscheidt, the future theologian, who describes the mood of his own family circle.

> Until well into my twenties, I did what all too many Germans did: I focused on the suffering of my people, and specifically, of my family and relatives during the War and during the occupation of Germany afterwards by the Allies. What my country, my people—some of them as close as my father—had inflicted on "the others" was secondary to what had been "inflicted" on us. It was not until after my ordination and post-graduate studies that I began to ask about and research the horrific history of Nazi Germany and its legacy to my people, my church, my family and-most urgently-Christian theology.[44]

At this *Zusammenbruch* moment, many Germans felt they had been pried loose from the Nazi hands of terror only to be placed in the vice-grip of a victor's justice; that as a nation they were being punished collectively for Nazi crimes. Certainly, anyone aware of the Morganthau Plan or who had read the Potsdam Declaration would not find this an unwarranted conclusion. Thus as news about the Stuttgart Declaration was reported in the Allied controlled press, many feared their pastors' words would be used to further justify the endless collective punishment to which Germans now were powerless to escape. Niemöller, the most famous living survivor of the concentration camps, was a heroic figure, a symbol of those who stood up to Hitler, a reminder that not all Germans were indiscriminately to be lumped together. But now here he was, traveling the country for the next two years telling his story of personal guilt, hoping by his own honest acknowledgment to release in people the willingness to face their own responsibility, hoping that an experience of forgiveness and a fresh start might also be theirs. But instead he frequently heard people respond: "I was just a little man; I only obeyed orders." Others blamed the Gestapo, and finally everyone blamed Himmler and Hitler. A grieving Niemöller asked: "Does our guilt thus disappear into thin air? No, the guilt exists without any doubt. Even if there were no other guilt than that of the six million clay urns, containing the ashes of burnt Jews from all over Europe."[45] For many Niemoller's personal vulnerability in acknowledging his own guilt was not easy to imitate. For some, it was not admirable; it was treasonous.[46]

---

44. Rumscheidt, "Europe Between Wars," 11.

45. Niemöller, *Of Guilt and Hope*, 13–14.

46. According to Hockenos what angered many people about Niemöller was his refusal to play the victim. Hockenos, *Church Divided*, 97.

In its final paragraph Stuttgart ended with a concern at the back of most German minds: was the punitive spiral that began with the Versailles treaty simply to repeat itself? A spiral of revenge had been the poisonous context for Hitler's successful campaign of vengeance against Allied injustice. What might happen this time round? Stuttgart spoke clearly:

> We hope in God that through the common service of the churches *the spirit of violence and revenge, which today again wants to become powerful* [italics added], may be brought under control in the whole world, and that the spirit of peace and love may gain the mastery, in which alone tortured humanity can find healing. So in an hour in which the whole world needs a new beginning we pray: "*Veni Creator Spiritus*."

The pastors had not intended for the declaration to be published in Germany for an obvious reason: it might lend the appearance that the church had foolishly or even treasonously provided legal cover for the enemy to justify a fresh round of collective punishment.[47] Already in 1942 Asmussen had noted there was anxiety that some kind of legally binding declaration of guilt by German church leaders could become in the hands of vengeful victors a legal validation for "violence and revenge" by the occupiers. When the Allied controlled press leaked news of the Stuttgart Declaration, its choice of headline, "Protestant Churches Acknowledge Germany's War Guilt," seemed to confirm that a group of naïve pastors had foolishly colluded with Allied strategy.[48] Ever since Versailles, one of the more disastrous consequences of the policy of collective punishment was that Germans were prone to focus on their seemingly perpetual sufferings. Now despite Niemöller's hopes, the acknowledgment of personal responsibility was being eclipsed by a bitter sense of Germans again being the victims of victor's justice.

From his post just across the border in Basel, Switzerland, Barth had foreseen the delicacy of the postwar situation. Already in his *Letter to Great Britain from Switzerland* (1941), he had warned that winning the war would be but the first step in helping Germany make a permanent change. A victor's justice, he warned, would be a grave mistake. History should have made this lesson obvious! For after WWI, Germany was not granted "freedom to live by her own labor. . . . It is for this reason that every nation has its share in the responsibility for the rise of Hitlerism."[49] With the war now over, Barth pled with the Allied nations: your task now is to succeed in the very thing the Germans had not succeeded in doing in the territories they now occupied: "to

47. Hockenos, *Church Divided*, 90.
48. Visser't Hooft, *Memoirs*, 193.
49. Barth, *Letter to Great Britain*, 38.

show how gentlemen behave when they have power."[50] Would the Allies be up to the task or would what Niemöller called a "perplexing mixture of warmth and vengeance" collude with Germany in a spiral of isolation, resentment and revenge?[51] For those in the Allied camp searching for reasons to double down on punitive justice, the Stuttgart Declaration provided both welcome proof of Germany's "collective guilt" as well as providential legitimation for collective punishment and the accompanying rigor of denazification.[52]

Denazification

The purpose of denazification was eminently sensible: to rehabilitate German political and moral life by eradicating all traces of Nazi influence over public institutions. Its strategy was to remove Nazis from all public life and influence. How? By removing from their jobs any teachers, civil servants, pastors, journalists, etc., who had any links with the party. Though each occupying power set up its own procedures, without a doubt denazification was most rigorously applied in the American zone, where the intelligence officers in charge were often ex-Germans, that is, Jewish refugees who spoke the language fluently and were unprepared to accept any excuses.[53]

But there was a problem with such severity. As Helmut Thielicke recollects in his autobiography, every official in his Württemberg region whose job ended in "rat" (a German ending for "office" or "council") was dismissed, including veterinarians and schoolmasters. To recover their jobs, one had to persuade proven anti-Nazis to provide written testimonials on your behalf. In the meantime, whole families were made destitute because the head of house had been made compulsorily idle unless and until he was cleared of any serious criminal behavior.[54] In 1945 there were eight million Nazi party members and millions more in various party organizations. By the end of September, 120,000 people had been removed from their jobs; seven hundred people a day were being arrested. How long could this go on?[55] The sheer numbers involved probably doomed the program to failure.

The primary unintended consequence of denazification was that it succeeded in uniting the Germans as nothing else during this time period. One

50. Barth, *Only Way*, 6.

51. Bentley, *Martin Niemöller*, 194.

52. Schmidt, *Pastor Niemöller*, 150. Cf. Hockenos, *Church Divided*, 99.

53. Barnett, *For the Soul of the People*, 218. Conway, personal correspondence with the author, July 18, 2014.

54. Bentley, *Martin Niemöller*, 194. Thielicke, *Notes from a Wayfarer*, 231.

55. Barnett, *For the Soul of the People*, 218.

of Barnett's interviewees noted that requiring a court-like trial for each and every party member to justify oneself was psychologically counterproductive since motivations for joining the party were so varied that a trial could hardly tease out the nuances.[56] Moreover, as Evans has made clear, for quite some time most of the German population had been cowed by coercion and fear into at least publically towing to the party line. Though the youth were particularly targeted and impacted by propaganda, many adults simply retreated into the private sphere. By the time Hitler announced the invasion of Russia in June 1941, the number of people still enthusiastic about the war was *very* small. By the time of the British bombing of Hamburg (1943), popular anger was directed, not at the British, but against Göring and the German air force for failing to defend the homeland and against the Nazi party for bringing such devastation on Germany.[57] Thielicke lamented that the strategy of having to prove one's anti-Nazi credentials actually nipped in the bud any real remorse or sorrow and replaced it with various moral gymnastics as Germans tried to convince themselves and others through pathetic written excuses how they had tried in their own way to resist. "What a noble portrait gazes out at me from my denazification certificate! There thus arose the 'incapacity to mourn.'"[58] In effect, instead of helping cleanse the nation of Nazi ideology, denazification perversely encouraged cover-up and self-justification.

In concert with denazification, the Allies embarked on a program to dismantle all German industries perceived as potentially useful in a future war. Deeply troubled at the implications, Bishop George Bell made a bold speech in Britain's House of Lords in which he argued that the policy of de-industrialization promised a future of mass unemployment and lead to a total lack of confidence in Allied governance and intentions. Such policies, he argued, would create the danger of re-nazifying Germany.[59] Immediately after reading this speech, Niemöller wrote on behalf of the EKD Council to

---

56. Ibid., 219.

57. Evans, *Third Reich at War*, 190, 447, 708–9.

58. Thielicke, *Notes from a Wayfarer*, 231. Fully two decades later a remarkable best seller was written by Alexander and Margarete Mitscherlich with the title *Inability to Mourn*. The book explored why many Germans were emotionally distanced from their recent past due to the unresolved and denied guilt and how this had postponed a proper reckoning with the recent Nazi past until the 1960s generation. Cf. Barnett, *For the Soul of the People*, 239.

59. Bentley reports these words from a speech given by Bishop Bell in the House of Lords, which Niemöller had obtained and underlined (*Martin Niemöller*, 193). Cf. also Thielicke, *Notes from a Wayfarer*, 28. "The punitive measures taken by the military government were more likely to give rise to renazification than to prevent it."

express deep gratitude.[60] Meanwhile Germans could only watch helplessly as the Allies' official orders of occupation (JCS 1067), heavily influenced by the Morganthau Plan, and enforced by the US Army, dictated that nothing be done in any way to rehabilitate the destroyed German economy.[61] As a result, it became widely believed within Germany (as Stewart Herman's visits to Germany document), that two consecutive postwar winters of increasing starvation were largely due to deliberate Allied policy. Though Niemöller was deeply grateful for Bishop Bell's advocacy in Britain, Germany itself lacked a government to speak on behalf of the people. Could the church play any role in this deteriorating situation?

The Guilt of the Others?

Out of this affliction some pastors felt compelled to challenge the twin measures of denazification and deindustrialization as dangerously foolish. To be silent before the Allies would be a new cowardice. "Had we not already kept silent long enough in the Third Reich? Were we now once again to make ourselves guilty through not speaking out?"[62] Only a month after the Stuttgart gathering, Bishop Theophil Wurm wrote a robust public letter in response to Geoffrey Fisher, Archbishop of Canterbury, declaring that Fisher's appeal for Germans to lift themselves up sounded like mockery "when the last raw materials and machines are taken away even from branches of German industry which had nothing to do with the production of armaments."[63] The next two years brought further deterioration. What could be done? All public criticism of Allied occupation was strictly forbidden under the laws of occupation.

In this context Helmut Thielicke preached his controversial sermon, "The Passion Without Grace," on Good Friday 1947. Before he left his house to deliver the sermon, Thielicke packed a toothbrush and a small bag, fully expecting to be arrested because the sermon was a devastating public warning of the unintended consequences of Allied policy. In perhaps the most blistering passage, he said:

> All of us must one day face the Last Judgment—that is, all of us who helped by our silence and complicity to release the hound of hell, *and* also those who now allow it to continue to rampage, despite their claim to come in the name of Christianity. . . . I think

60. Jasper, *George Bell*, 305.

61. Beschloss, *Conquerors*, 169.

62. Thielicke, *Notes from a Wayfarer*, 231–32.

63. See appendix 1, "Broadcast of the Archbishop of Canterbury with Response by Bishop Wurm," in Herman, *Rebirth of the German Church*, 277.

of the many refugees who are dying in the ice cold cattle trucks in which they are being transported, and who perish more merci-lessly than cattle in an abattoir. I think of the prisoners-of-war and the many thousands that have been allowed to die of starvation by those who came in the name of humanity. . . . I see how in the name of denazification it is not the guilty that are punished and not justice that is helped to victory, but injustice and arbitrari-ness. . . . Perhaps I might have remained silent about all this if those who are doing it, together with their German henchmen, had said that they had come in the name of vengeance. Then our young people would have seen just where lawlessness and god-lessness and the awful law of response and retaliation lead. Then we would have to submit silently to God's dreadful rod.

But of course, they did not say that they had come in the name of vengeance, but solemnly announced that they had come in the spirit of Christianity and humanity. At least our former rulers were honest enough not to use the image of the crucified Christ but the "blond beast" as their emblem. For this reason we, as a community of Jesus, must stand before the des-ecrated image of Our Lord, as some of us also at least tried to do in the Third Reich. We must *also* stand before the youth of our nation whose disappointed faith in the justice of the vic-tors is destroying their faith in the Christianity in whose name the victors claimed to have come. And whoever has heard the voices that whisper in secret, whoever has traveled by night in the darkened trains where people converse without fear of recognition, that person knows that on top of all this there is the danger of a *large-scale renazification* taking the place of the denazification we have all been hoping for.[64]

To his surprise, Thielicke wasn't arrested. But the sermon was confis-cated and not allowed to be reprinted. Mimeographed copies soon widely circulated, however, and Thielicke reported that he received several hun-dred letters in response. Some thanked him for freeing their conscience and enabling them to begin the path of repentance; others chided him for being an opportunist riding a new wave of German nationalism. The largest num-ber thanked him in a way which shocked him: they were not interested in his religious content, they had "merely heard aggressive statements against the allies."[65] It made him pause: in declaring the guilt of the others had he hardened the attitudes of some people? "Once again, I realized how dubious all human undertakings are, how dubious too the understanding of theol-

64. Thielicke, *Notes from a Wayfarer*, 232–33.
65. Ibid., 234.

ogy is. It again became clear to me how little we know our own hearts and how little we can control the hearts of others, and that we consequently have to entrust everything to the judgment and grace of One who is higher than we."[66] Not surprisingly, his scheduled preaching tour of the United States was cancelled—purportedly due to lack of finances.[67]

Thielicke's struggle here is complex. On the one hand, his mature verdict on the Stuttgart Declaration was to name it "a thoroughly moderate and level-headed document." However, at the time he was convinced that by not mentioning "the guilt of others," the church had betrayed the German people one more time.[68] Stuttgart was "unable to prevent the Allies from constantly expecting the admission of a wholesale and highly indiscriminate collective guilt from the Germans."[69] When visiting other countries during this period, Thielicke sensed that "the others" enjoyed rather too much their focus on German guilt because it reinforced a pleasant sense of moral superiority. The Allied tendency to wholesale condemnations of Germany "caused them to overlook the beam in their own eyes." In turn, defensive reaction was aroused in Germans to such an extent they were in jeopardy of refusing to face their own very real guilt in any serious way. Useless comparisons between the Allied sins of the Dresden carpet bombings or cruelties of occupation were played off against Nazi atrocities. The net result was that denazification policies reinforced the danger of Germans relieving themselves of their own need for penitence.

As it happened, Thielicke rejected Niemöller's post-Stuttgart strategy, accusing him of "grossly indiscriminate self-accusations" and "slanderous statements about the German nation."[70] Many pastoral conversations had convinced him that Niemöller's preaching aroused defensive reactions rather than repentance. Instead Thielicke sought to make the case for a *discriminating* diagnosis of German guilt. On the one hand he sought with Niemöller to encourage personal repentance, not the making of excuses.[71] Yet in clear disagreement with Niemöller, Thielicke joined with German grievance against "the others" rather than confront and break down their excuses.

---

66. Ibid., 235.

67. Ibid., 235–36. Thielicke tells of a US general who privately visited to tell him the reason behind the cancelled visit.

68. Barnett, *For the Soul of the People*, 226.

69. Thielicke, *Notes from a Wayfarer*, 218. Interestingly, Thielicke's views are similar to the Roman Catholic reaction to Stuttgart as reported by Spotts. Cf. Spotts, *Churches and Politics*, 30, 92.

70. Ibid. Cf. also 241.

71. Thielicke, *Notes from a Wayfarer*, 219, 221.

How shall we interpret Thielicke's "discriminating" support of Stuttgart and rejection of Niemöller's preaching? Thielicke accused Niemöller of validating the Occupying powers and their media headlines in regards to Germany's collective guilt. But to be fair, Niemöller never advocated the political concept of collective guilt. "This is, rather, a question of the individual's guilt, and the individual's responsibility."[72] In a public exchange of letters with Thielicke following his Good Friday sermon, Hermann Diem argued that Thielicke had reinforced the German propensity to self-pity and gave unfortunate comfort to the nationalistically inclined. By giving moral support to German self-pity, Thielicke was enabling them to avoid engaging at any depth with Niemöller's message.[73] As we have noted, Thielicke himself acknowledged to his horror, that many anti-Allied letters of thanks confirmed the weight of this unfortunate tendency. Perhaps Thielicke's main failing was to interpret Stuttgart in so discriminating a way that he neglected to remind his listeners that they were not *simply* victims of the Nazis. Perhaps it is always easier for a preacher to join with the people's resentment at their mistreatment by others than to raise the awkward question of one's own sins and need for redemption. Certainly from his prison writings, Bonhoeffer's reflections on guilt offer a rebuke to Thielicke: Confession of guilt happens without a sidelong glance at the others who are also guilty.[74]

There remains one perfectly valid point in Thielicke's argument, which is how hard it was for Germans to seriously encounter their own guilt while Allied policy seemed intent on inflicting perpetual punishment. German industry was daily dismantled. Whole families were descending into deeper poverty as the head of house, compulsorily idle, awaited his day in court for denazification certification. In fact Thielicke and Niemöller were in total agreement about denazification. Already in 1945 Niemöller had written a memorandum stating that the entire denazification project was felt most severely by those "small people" who had become Nazis in order to secure their jobs, while more serious players had found ways to avoid punishment.[75] In 1946 Niemöller had told Bishop Bell that it was likely to be twelve years before everyone in Hamburg had been denazified and eight years before Ba-

---

72. Quoted in Schmidt, *Pastor Niemöller*, 149. For a completely opposite view of Stuttgart, which reads Niemöller as an advocate of collective guilt (despite his clear rejection of this notion), see Lang, "Imposed German Guilt," 1.

73. Not long after these public disputes, Thielicke visited Barth in Basel where Barth admitted to being sometimes "annoyed at the rashness and exaggerated aggressiveness" of which Niemöller was capable. However Barth charged Thielicke with being condescending toward Niemöller. Thielicke, *Notes from a Wayfarer*, 242.

74. Bonhoeffer, *Ethics*, 136.

75. Bentley, *Martin Niemöller*, 198.

varia would be cleansed.[76] In 1948 he used his new responsibility as president of the Hessen and Nausau province to launch a fierce attack on the entire denazification project. Read from every pulpit in the region, his statement declared denazification to be a spirit of revenge, that it inspired Germans to take vengeance on each other, that it encouraged people in their hundreds of thousands to tell lies, that entire families were being arrested, interned, and unable to earn a living while they awaited release or sentence. "In these circumstances every Christian must ask whether it is his responsibility to go along with these judicial processes or not."[77] His advice as always was clear: Christians should no longer participate in denazification trials, whether as judges, prosecutors or witnesses. The entire project was unfair, unjust, corrupt and corrupting. Hence no less than Thielicke, Niemöller was never shy in challenging denazification. Each in his own way reinforced a growing understanding among the Evangelical Church of Germany (EKD) that the church can and must perform a public and yes, a political role in society.

One other point seems clear: Thielicke's willingness to risk arrest for public criticism of Allied policy shows how difficult it was for Germans to hear Niemöller's astringent message of "guilt and hope" while living under a military occupation based on collective guilt with no end in sight. We must remember that Thielicke's (and indeed much of Germany's) response to Niemöller's message occurred prior to George Marshall's tenure as secretary of state. It was Marshall and his justly famous plan that signaled the crucial turn in US policy toward Germany. However, Marshall's appointment did not come until the summer of 1947, several months after Thielicke's sermon. Moreover, his plan had first to endure vigorous debate in Congress and only became American policy in March 1948, nearly three years after the war had ended.[78]

The Legacy of Stuttgart

Given the context of chaos and collective punishment, we should not be surprised that Stuttgart met with conflicted responses. In retrospect, Niemöller considered his efforts a failure; his personal acknowledgment of guilt more than most Germans were willing to imitate.[79] Yet despite all the difficulties

76. Ibid., 195.

77. Ibid., 196.

78. Bacque, *Crimes and Mercies*, 162–63.

79. Sybil Niemöller von Sell, "Who Was Martin Niemoller?," in Locke and Littell, *Remembrance and Recollection*, 21. Conway says for the most part the German people refused to accept the challenge which Stuttgart put before them—to take personal

and resistances, Stuttgart was more than a lightning rod for debates about how to measure guilt. In the end, the initiative of the ecumenical church to seek reconciliation and the humble, personal response of the German church to confess and lament—*not the sins of the others, but its own*—was stronger than the denials of the defeated, stronger than the victor's justice demanded by certain Allied politicians.

In fact, it took decades for Germany to come to terms with the Stuttgart declaration. At the time, perhaps it is true that most Germans preferred not to acknowledge their complicity. Ehrhart Neubert has noted that part of what fueled the later student uprisings of the 1960s was the nation's repression of past complicity with the Nazis. The hypocrisy of sweeping the guilt under the carpet led to a critical loss of confidence in institutions of government and business.[80] Donald Shriver Jr. has argued that Germany's coming to terms with its Nazi past was a three-generation struggle in which minority voices such as Niemöller blazed the trail for the historical honesty that was later demanded by the student movement. During the late 1960s young people began to inquire of their parents, "What did you do?" Then together they began to ask, "What have we to do now?"[81] But only in the 1980s and '90s did large numbers of Germans begin to answer the question, "Who was responsible for the debacle of Nazism?" with the answer: "A lot of people like us." Despite its roller-coaster journey and its violent fringe, the student movement helped teach postwar Germany how to participate in a democracy instead of being spectators watching the traditional oligarchy perform.[82]

Why then did Germany eventually come to change (repent) and embrace Stuttgart's confession as personally relevant? Klaus Scholder traces the beginning of the answer all the way back to the Barmen Declaration. Barmen's spirit of resistance that said a clear no to certain errors for the sake of a clear yes to distinct beliefs also motivated the authors of the Declaration of Stuttgart. In the end, Stuttgart was both theologically and psychologically simply more convincing than self-justification and blaming others.[83] Up and down Germany, Niemöller declared in a steady drumbeat of preaching: If you are going to travel the path of reconciliation with God and with our neighbors, you must step out personally. You cannot wait for it to be popular. You cannot wait to see if your repentance will be reciprocated in some advantageous way. If you do not take personal responsibility, how can you

responsibility for their nation's tragic course ("How Shall the Nations Repent?," 619).

80. Burgess, *East German Church*, 118. So also Barnett, *For the Soul of the People*, 239.

81. Shriver, *Honest Patriots*, 21–24, 39–40.

82. Thomas, *Protest Movements*, 248.

83. Scholder, "Fate and Guilt in History," in *Requiem for Hitler*, 32ff.

receive personally a new start and personal forgiveness? Confession sets us free. When we face our own culpability, we shall cease blaming others and never again repeat our mistake.

Over the next decades, Niemöller's argument increasingly won reluctant respect.

Responses Outside Germany

In an interview shortly after the escape from his death convoy, Niemöller was asked by an American chaplain if the world should simply say, "We forgive Germany" and start all over? Niemöller replied that the world would not be able to say, "We forgive you, but the Christians all over the world should say that, and they will start all over again with us. Measures of punishment against the people will not help."[84] Niemöller's words proved prophetic for Christians did respond to Stuttgart's message as Niemöller anticipated. Many months before any change in Allied policy, food parcels and supplies from foreign churches began arriving, many of whom had made personal sacrifices in sending them.[85]

The generous ecumenical response to Stuttgart was also noted by Otto Dibelius. The controversial bishop records in his autobiography that though it was very painful to write words of confession of guilt with no mention of "the guilt of the others," that was not the German church's role. Indeed, the stream of assistance which poured into Germany from their ecumenical partners convinced Dibelius that their confession had been heard in the spirit it was intended.[86]

Niemöller's contribution to the sparking of postwar Allied generosity is not something he is usually credited with, but it is a consequence of the Stuttgart initiative not to be ignored. Nor should we forget that the ecumenical church's initiative for reconciliation was not immediately followed by an Allied change of policy. But over time Stuttgart's confession of guilt opened the hearts of those tempted to seek revenge. Visser't Hooft reports that wherever he relayed the events of Stuttgart to Protestant assemblies, whether in France, Holland, Britain or the United States, many spoke of how this declaration made it possible for them to acknowledge how their own struggle with the Nazis had not been sufficiently faithful and courageous.

---

84. Niemöller, *Of Guilt and Hope*, 77.

85. Schmidt, *Pastor Niemöller*, 152.

86. Dibelius, *In the Service of the Lord*, 260. Thielicke has also testified that the first helping hands from abroad which Germans received after the war were those of Christians. Thielicke, "Religion in Germany," 154.

Stuttgart made a more honest Allied response possible. Visser't Hooft insists the launching of the World Council of Churches itself in 1948 would have been impossible without Stuttgart.[87]

Stuttgart as Crisis for the Allies

We can summarize the situation following Stuttgart thus: it was a period in which hope inside Germany was quite fragile and emotion regarding guilt highly conflicted. The Allied (Morganthau) policy of collective punishment ("until Germany had learned its lesson") made Niemöller's nuanced message of hope amid guilt very hard for Germans to hear. Despite the various food and aid parcels from foreign church groups, all duly acknowledged, Germany remained stuck in a near starvation state for three long years after the war, unable to sufficiently repent of its misdeeds to satisfy its conquerors, unable to feed itself, unable to repair its economy, unable to escape from self-pity. Such a quagmire was precisely what the ecumenical visitors and the Evangelical Council of Brethren hoped to interrupt when they gathered on October 17, 1945. That day the ecumenical church had sounded a different message, in retrospect one incompatible with Allied policy prior to Marshall. Allied governments and their churches could not limp between two different opinions forever; sooner or later, one or the other would have to change (repent).

In other words, the church's initiative at Stuttgart and the declaration which resulted created a crisis for the Allies as well as the Germans. The Allied governments and the ecumenical church were in no doubt they had rescued Europe and indeed, Germany, from a wicked, anti-Christian regime. But what were the implications of Christ's gospel for how one treats a defeated enemy? Should the triumph of a "Christian civilization" over its "pagan" enemies entail policies amounting to the permanent degradation of the defeated, including *de facto* the starvation of the most vulnerable—elderly, women and children?

Nowhere is the Christian message of forgiveness and reconciliation more relevant than when a nation state with a large Christian population must decide how to treat a defeated enemy. The issue reduces to basic questions, such as whether or not to allow a defeated enemy to starve. In the aftermath of the previous war in Europe, future president Herbert Hoover organized the mission of the American Relief Administration to feed millions of starving Europeans. In his memoirs, Hoover records a confrontation with British Admiral Sir Rosslyn Wemyss, the head of the British delegation. Wemyss saw Hoover outside of the official meetings one day and said brusquely, "Young

---

87. Visser't Hooft, *Memoirs*, 193–94.

man, I don't see why you Americans want to feed these Germans." Hoover, a lifelong Quaker, immediately replied, "Old man, I don't see why you British want to starve women and children after they are licked."[88]

Though it is not possible here to explore the full story behind the motivations of General Marshall or why President Truman and his cabinet set aside the punitive approach of the Roosevelt/Morganthau Plan, two pieces of evidence are relevant to our story and deserve mention. First, as Beschloss recounts, while preparing his plan, Marshall accessed Secretary of War Henry Stimson's private memos to Roosevelt for inspiration. Of all the war cabinet, it was Stimson who argued most strongly against Morganthau, insisting that the only way to solve the German problem was "through Christianity and kindness."[89] Second, developmental economists have singled out Herbert Hoover's visit to Germany in 1947 as the catalyst for Truman's abandonment of Morganthau. At Truman's request, Hoover reprised his earlier visit to investigate solutions for Europe's new hunger emergency. Upon his return, Hoover reported to the White House that Morganthau's Plan was "illusory"; it could only work if the Allies were prepared either to relocate or exterminate twenty-five million Germans. Within four months of this warning, the United States announced General Marshall's plan to reindustrialize Germany, bringing its industrial capacity back to its 1938 levels.[90] There is little doubt that Hoover's report helped convince Truman of the folly of perpetuating the Morganthau Plan.

The voices of Stimson and Hoover are linked to the initiative launched by the ecumenical church at Stuttgart, that is, to increase the moral pressure upon the victorious Allies to formulate a postwar policy congruent with the teachings of Christian faith, of whom the majority of their citizens were at least nominally committed. In the end, the Marshall Plan signaled both a transformation in Allied policy and an Allied change of heart. Remarkably, the US government decided the way to increase her own security was not to hoard jealously half of world production, but to share it out in order to generate more wealth for all. What followed was the decision from 1948 and 1951 to channel thirteen billion dollars (equivalent to $130 billion today) to rebuild a war-torn Europe. In other words, America devoted "an unheard of" 3 percent of gross national product and 10 percent of the federal budget to rebuild Europe, including former enemy, Germany, into a formidable economic rival

---

88. Quoted in Bacque, *Crimes and Mercies*, 13–14.

89. Beschloss, *Conquerors*, 278. Stimson is quoted in ibid., 105.

90. Erik S. Reinert, "Increasing Poverty in a Globalized World," in Chang, *Rethinking Development Economics*, 455.

and partner.[91] Cambridge economist Ha-Joon Chang identifies the abandoning of the Morganthau Plan in favor of the Marshall Plan as what kick-started the recovery of postwar Europe. With it, America signaled that it was in everyone's best interest to see that its former enemies prospered. Economically speaking, the result of this strategy was "spectacular."[92]

America's new strategy enabled Germany to emerge from its chaotic economic situation. It also served as political confirmation of the Reformers' theological insistence which informed the ecumenical gathering at Stuttgart: true repentance is the result of mercy, rather than its cause. The same point has been expressed in a highly personal way by Melita Maschmann in her memoir, *Account Rendered*. A committed and unrepentant Nazi journalist, Maschmann spent time in a prison camp for Nazi leaders after the war, always refusing to accept any guilt for her conduct. Though she avoided Jews carefully, in her loneliness, she allowed herself to make friends with a chaplain, whose thoughtful conversation made his visits eagerly anticipated. On one such visit, he brought along a teacher whose parents had both died in concentration camps. When they met, the teacher already knew of Maschmann's past role as a Nazi activist.

> I will never forget the glow of spontaneous kindness in this person's eyes when she first held out her hand to me. It bridged all the gulfs, without denying them. At that moment I jumped free from the devil's wheel. I was no longer in danger of converting feelings of guilt into fresh hatred. The forgiving love which I had encountered gave me the strength to accept our guilt and my own. Only now did I cease to be a National Socialist.[93]

The Lasting Legacy of Stuttgart

As the Marshall Plan took effect, and German society began its first steps toward what became known as the German "economic miracle," both the Stuttgart Declaration and Niemöller's preaching tour can be seen as turning points in facing the truth for both Germans and Allies. Though controversial, Stuttgart led the way for Germans to take unprecedented personal responsibility for their moral failure, and in the decades since they have done so with a vast social consensus that has helped Germany proceed on a trajectory that makes it unimaginable that she will ever again be seduced by the militarism

91. Pond, *Beyond the Wall*, 249.

92. Chang, *Bad Samaritans*, 62–64.

93. Maschmann, *Account Rendered*, 213.

and nationalism that had formerly permeated society and made it so vulnerable to Hitler's message of vengeance masquerading as justice.

A crucial example of Stuttgart's seed bearing later fruit was West German Chancellor Willy Brandt's visit to the Warsaw Memorial in Poland, on December 7, 1970.

The memorial commemorates the thousands killed by the Nazis in the Warsaw ghetto. When Brandt, filled with emotion, dropped silently to his knees before the monument in a spontaneous act of apology and repentance, this humble act deeply impacted the entire nations of Poland and Germany alike.[94]

As for whether Stuttgart has had a lasting impact upon the "guilt of the others," that is, the Allies, the evidence is complex. On the negative side, there is but scattered evidence of a shift in the willingness of American churches to confess their own past errors. For example, American churches always have been slow to confess and apologize their past support of slavery.[95] Nor does the American church seem much interested in asking questions about the history of Native Americans since the founding of

94. Brandt, *My Life in Politics*, 200. Twenty years later, Brandt records the comment of a reporter at the scene to help explain why he knelt in silence: "Then he who does not need to kneel knelt, on behalf of all who do need to kneel but do not—because they dare not, or cannot, or cannot dare to kneel." Spotts confirms the link between Stuttgart and Brandt. Spotts, *Churches and Politics*, 267.

95. For example, only in 1995 did the Southern Baptist convention formally apologize for its support of slavery in 1845 and its later failure to support the civil rights movement. Cf. Ludden, "Southern Baptists Apologize."

this country.[96] Moreover, as we shall see in the next chapter, there is little evidence that American churches have publically acknowledged complicity with politicians in demonizing the new enemy which emerged during the Cold War era. Three decades later, President Jimmy Carter, who more than any American president of the modern era, sought to govern conscientiously as a Christian believer, was unable to acknowledge past wrongdoing toward Iran, thus contributing both to the prolongation of the hostage crisis, and mortally damaging his own possibility for reelection.[97] As for the post 9/11 war in Iraq, it is now common knowledge that the official reasons for the war (the presence of WMDs and the activity of Al Queda), have not held up to serious scrutiny. As no doubt intended, this misrepresentation of evidence was a key reason why the war met with strong popular support when first launched (over 65 percent of the general public in support according to a Gallup poll). But in a survey conducted by Pew Charitable Trust shortly after the war began, a full 87 percent of those identifying as evangelical Christians supported the war. Such a high number provokes one to ask why were evangelical Christians ahead of the curve?[98] In the light of Stuttgart, one must ask why have pastors and churches who were once vocal supporters of the war remained silent when it comes to confessing responsibility for having been caught up in a rush to war, a war whose negative consequences have not yet run their full destructive course? Pastors in America have much to learn from the pastors who gathered at Stuttgart.

If we look farther afield to trace the impact of Stuttgart, we can detect an echo of Stuttgart's narrow path between collective punishment on the one hand and the cheap grace of collective amnesty on the other in the work of the Truth and Reconciliation Commission launched by the new non-apartheid South Africa. Chaired by Bishop Desmond Tutu, the TRC did not focus on determining guilt or innocence in a Nuremberg Trial approach. The goal of TRC hearings (held from 1996–2003) was neither to punish or sentence the guilty. Nevertheless without personal confession of wrongdoing (truth), reconciliation would be impossible. Thus confessing one's past deeds of murder or torture against other human beings was not

96. An encouraging exception is NAIITS (North American Institute for Indigenous Theological Studies), which has partnered with several seminaries in America, including George Fox Evangelical Seminary and Tyndale Evangelical University, to develop ways of studying theology which seeks to listen to this history.

97. Stassen, *Just Peacemaking*, 109.

98. Marsh, *Wayward Christian Soldiers*, 42. Marsh's main point is that all this took place in the face of unanimous urgings of Christians worldwide not to go to war. "Why did American evangelicals not pause to consider the near-unanimous disapproval of the global Christian community? The worldwide Christian opposition seems to me the most neglected story related to the religious debate about Iraq" (182).

an end, but the hopeful spark to ignite a personal liberation. Once publically acknowledged and no longer hidden, who would think of repeating?[99]

As for ongoing positive lessons from Stuttgart, the nonpunitive Marshall Plan stands out both for its economic success in leading Europe toward a new cooperative mentality, and as an economic confirmation of the merciful initiative launched by the ecumenical church at Stuttgart. It is upon the astonishing success of the Marshall Plan that the economist Ha-Joon Chang grounds his hope that today's rich countries will eventually recalibrate their current policies toward developing countries and indeed, have a moral duty to do so.[100] In this regard, it is worth noting that the ecumenical church has repeatedly advocated debt forgiveness in programs like the Jubilee Debt Campaign.[101]

Last, these words are being written in the wake of two significant European events: the Greek referendum over its debt crisis, and the British referendum to leave the European Union. The implications of these events are yet to be fully known but it appears that Germany today faces a new challenge in coming to terms with its past. To paraphrase economists such as Thomas Piketty and Yanis Varoufakis, how in the days of its economic strength shall Germany remember the extent to which its own unpayable debts were forgiven after the war and how will that memory express itself?[102]

In conclusion, we return to where we began: before the Marshall Plan was ever conceived, the ecumenical church determined to meet with representatives of the Evangelical Church in Germany in Stuttgart, not to assign blame nor to extract a confession of guilt, but to take the risk that in spite of everything that had transpired, to seek reconciliation, in accord with Jesus' prayer "that they might be one."[103]

Perhaps the most realistic and most hopeful commentary on Stuttgart's legacy is one written in a prison cell even before the war had finished, as Bonhoeffer expressed his own vision for the future of Europe after the war's end.

> The nations bear the heritage of their guilt. Yet by God's gracious rule in history it can happen that what began as a curse can finally become a blessing on the nations, that out of usurped power can come justice, out of rebellion order, and out of bloodshed peace.[104]

99. Cf. Chapman and Spong, *Religion and Reconciliation in South Africa*, 148. Cf. also De Gruchy, *Church Struggle in South Africa*, 224–26.

100. Chang, *Bad Samaritans*, 221–22.

101. Jones, "Six Key Points about Greece's Debt."

102. See the interview with French economist Thomas Piketty in *Die Zeit*. Cf. also Varoufakis, *And the Weak Suffer What They Must?*, 10, 54ff.

103. John 17:11.

104. Bonhoeffer, *Ethics*, 143.

6

The Church and the Cold War
In Search of a Third Way

Thus the Christian approach surpasses both individualism and collectivism. The Church knows and recognizes the "interest" of the individual and of the "whole," but it resists them both when they want to have the last word.

—KARL BARTH[1]

But the greatest menace to our civilization today is the conflict between giant organized systems of self-righteousness—each system only too delighted to find that the other is wicked—each only too glad that the sins give it the pretext for still deeper hatred and animosity.

—HERBERT BUTTERFIELD[2]

The struggle against war is not only directed against the bellicosity of the Communist powers, but against our own violence, fanaticism and greed. Of course, this kind of thinking will not be popular in the tensions of a cold war. No one is encouraged to be too clear-sighted, because conscience can make cowards, by diluting the strong conviction that our side is fully right and the other side is fully wrong.

—THOMAS MERTON[3]

1. Barth, "Christian Community and the Civil Community," in *Against the Stream*, 37.
2. Butterfield, *Christianity, Diplomacy and War*, 43.
3. Merton, *Peace in a Post-Christian Era*, 11.

PRIOR TO THE STUTTGART Declaration, the Protestant church in Germany had always identified itself with the state and its authority. Thus Luther backed German princes over German peasants, Pietists and Liberals supported Bismarck and later supported the Kaiser. This trajectory reached its nadir when the German Christians (*Deutsche Christen*) sanctioned a marriage between Christianity and the nationalism, racism and militarism of the National Socialist government. Stuttgart rang the change on these repeated variations on the union of throne and altar. Stuttgart also shifted Christians in Germany from a singular and exclusionary sense of *Volk* consciousness to a dual kind of solidarity: a solidarity in guilt with the Nazis and their fellow travelers and a solidarity of empathy for the suffering Germany had inflicted on Europe.

Almost immediately, however, this repentant solidarity, and its theological basis, came under relentless partisan pressure to join with one or the other of the newly emergent superpowers dividing the country. Remarkably, a small but influential group of pastors and theologians resisted. Over the following months and years, the most radical opponents of the Nazis refused to ally themselves with the Western fervor for fighting (and winning) what soon became known as the Cold War. No one better expressed the pursuit of reconciliation over victory than the author of the Barmen declaration, Karl Barth. Over the next decade Barth became the theologian of a nonpartisan response to the Cold War. While doing this caused considerable upset among colleagues and former supporters, it also opened a third way for a church that lived within a communist society such as the German Democratic Republic (GDR). Meanwhile the impact of Bonhoeffer's life and witness continued to brood upon the church in the Eastern sector. Bonhoeffer's personal legacy of courage combined with his ability to articulate a way of engaging the world instead of withdrawing from it, continued to inspire his friends and former students to find an approach to the state beyond the "throne and altar" paradigm. Some of his former students would take on crucial pastoral responsibilities. They would explicitly name Bonhoeffer as central for their ongoing theological engagement in public life.

Against the Stream

Banished since the Nazis deported him in 1936, Barth returned to Germany in August 1945, joining Niemöller as a delegate at the Treysa conference to relaunch the postwar church.[4] The following year he went on a speaking tour that included Berlin and Stuttgart. During these visits Barth soon made it clear he had no intention of identifying the cause of the gospel with

4. Bentley, *Martin Niemöller*, 168.

the political agenda of the West, rejecting the paradigm of mortal conflict between Eastern communism and Western capitalism. On one hand Barth acknowledged a *prima facie* "tendency" for the church to line up with the Western-style democratic state. However, eyebrows were raised when he also asserted it is "certainly not necessarily the form of state closest to the Christian view."[5] The church, he insisted, was free; free to labor in other governmental forms, including monarchy, aristocracy and occasionally "even that of a dictatorship." Perhaps anticipating the founding of the Christian Democratic Union Party under Konrad Adenauer in 1949, Barth expressed opposition to any specifically *Christian* political party. In fact, he referred to political parties in general as "one of the most questionable phenomena in political life" bordering on the pathological![6]

In the years that followed, Barth consistently responded to invitations from churches on both sides of the East/West ideological and physical divide that Winston Churchill famously dubbed "the iron curtain." In his talks and conversations, he never ceased exploring an alternative to partisanship. Thus on a visit to Hungary in 1948, Barth urged Christians to tread a narrow path between Eastern and Western *subservience*. In particular, he mentioned *three false roads* which the church should reject: to set itself up in opposition to the new order in principle by keeping to the old; to identify with the new in an equally partisan fashion; and finally to retreat into a false neutrality along an apolitical "inner" line.[7] One could always identify false paths, he said, by how language was used. For instance, the use of language to demonize the opponent instead of engaging in dialogue; to exaggerate and make slogans, and thus kill all thought in speaker and listener alike.[8] Instead Barth pled for a way that kept an independent yet sympathetic attitude; which invited advocates of both old and new orders to humility and to the praise of God. This was the narrow path, one that encouraged people to trust *the one great change*, far more significant for history than the recent political changes in Europe, namely, the death and resurrection of Jesus.[9]

Freedom for the Western and Eastern Zones

In a talk to young people in Budapest, Barth urged a refusal to glibly identify the biblical notion of freedom with Enlightenment freedom. To those

5. Ibid., 181.

6. Ibid., 182.

7. Busch, *Karl Barth: His Life*, 355.

8. Barth, "Christian Community," in *Against the Stream*, 77.

9. Ibid.

who defined freedom essentially in terms of personal choice, he alerted his audience of some awkward realities. First, given that the Enlightenment project of freedom had recently collapsed into the choices of godlessness and inhumanity, Europe had bought a bogus product. By contrast, biblical freedom would never bear such rotten fruit because its freedom was always freedom *for* God *and* one's neighbor.[10] All across Europe the foundations of this degenerative freedom now lay in rubble. Europe now had the opportunity to turn toward a better freedom. In the conversation that followed, Barth said something that Western Europeans and Americans still have a hard time hearing: a state which only validates individual freedom is a state that is sliding into anarchy.[11] All nations function best with a balance of order, freedom, community, power and responsibility and where none of these elements dominates the others.[12]

Pointedly, Barth was asked what role should the church play in the postwar political conflict between East and West? His reply: cut through all partisanship, because the church must first and foremost remember that Scripture tells us God loves the world, *not the church!* That is, by divine intention, the church is never an end in itself, but "serves God by serving all" because God is not against the world but for the world. Thus if and when a *no* must be spoken against human error, "it will be most audible when the church concerns itself with washing feet and nothing else."[13]

Barth ended his Hungarian visit by urging the church to find a narrow path between an *opposition* which clings to the past (epitomized by Cardinal Mindsenty, the Catholic defender of the regime upended by the communists) and *collaboration* that overly identifies with the new regime. By over identification, Barth had in mind especially his fellow Reformed pastor and friend, Josef Hromadka. Barth was alarmed that Hromadka was falling into the opposite error from Mindsentzy. Yet he never criticized Hromadka publically. Barth's biographer, Eberhard Busch, suggests the reason for his public silence was that Barth did not wish to add "grist to the mill of anticommunism, which was busy enough as it was."[14] That is, he did not wish to feed the partisan frenzy that had become virulent in politicians, such as the American Senator Joseph McCarthy, who gained international attention (and disdain) by sounding high decibel alarms of fear about communism.

10. Barth, "Modern Youth: Its Inheritance and Its Responsibility," in *Against the Stream*, 61.

11. Barth, "From the Discussion in Budapest on the Morning of April 1st, 1948," in *Against the Stream*, 96.

12. Ibid., 95.

13. Barth, "Real Church," in *Against the Stream*, 73.

14. Busch, *Karl Barth*, 355.

Clouds of Fear

During the early postwar years, Barth challenged what he described as a "great cloud of fear" that had settled over the Western nations, impairing thinking. In a report on his Eastern travels to a Swiss journal, Barth remarked that while it might not be easy or pleasant to live behind the "Iron Curtain" he met more calm and serene people there than in his hometown of Basel! People were much less nervous about the Russians, whereas paradoxically such fear had become an epidemic in free Switzerland.[15] It was this constant fear that Barth regarded as the ignoble source of Western misperceptions of the East, especially the anxious refrain that the East posed a deadly threat to the Western church and state. But should the church fear any state? His firm counsel to Western Christians remained "be not afraid."[16] Given the anxiously anti-communist mood, former admirers of Barth the fierce critic of Nazism were both puzzled and alarmed by his warnings against fearmongering in the face of the communist threat. Had Barth lost his courage to resist? Worse, was he a communist sympathizer?

A New Controversy with Emil Brunner

Barth's warnings about partisanship soon erupted into a new conflict with his fellow countryman and Reformed theologian Emil Brunner. Brunner opted to write Barth a public letter of rebuke in which he sharply asked: why do you not issue a call to oppose communism as part of our Christian confession as you did against National Socialism? Were they not both totalitarian systems? In Marxist lands, the individual had no rights *vis-à-vis* the state. Surely communism deserved a denunciation and rejection as anti-Christian! But instead, Barth only complained about Western social injustice. Granted the charge may sadly be all too true, there remained a huge difference, argued Brunner. At least in the West social injustice can be fought and challenged by free people.[17]

> I simply cannot grasp why you, of all people, who condemned
> so severely even a semblance of collaborationism on the part
> of the church under Hitler, should now be making yourself the
> spokesman of those who condemn not merely outward but
> even inward spiritual resistance, and why you should deride as

15. Barth, "Reformed Church behind the 'Iron Curtain,'" in *Against the Stream*, 102.

16. Barth, "From the Discussion in Budapest," in *Against the Stream*, 99.

17. Brunner, "Open Letter to Karl Barth," in *Against the Stream*, 107, 110.

"nervousness" what is really a horror-struck revulsion from a truly diabolical system of injustice and inhumanity.[18]

Brunner's language of "horror-struck revulsion" and "diabolical system" epitomized the prevailing mood of the West. How did Barth reply? Against the stream as ever, Barth urged the church in *both* East and West to find a path in which they were subservient to neither system, but servants of the Word of God in both. Declining Brunner's insistence on a principled condemnation of communism, Barth called such an ideological approach a surrender of the church's freedom to judge afresh in each new historical moment.[19] Truly in 1933 National Socialism had been a very real seduction for the church but in 1948 where were the non-communists in the West tempted to join the Marxist way? Whence came this great worry about communist influence sweeping the West? In the Western nations communism lacked any serious appeal. It did not meet even at a minimal level the West's standards of justice and freedom. So honestly, it was not a live option in the West, hardly a temptation. As for communism itself, "Anyone who would like from me a political disclaimer of its system and its methods may have it at once. However, what is given cheaply can be had cheaply."[20] To proclaim ideological resistance to all things totalitarian was, he argued, simply to echo what could be heard already from both the pope and Mr. Truman! Why should the church join this chorus? "No, when the church witnesses it moves in fear and trembling, not with the stream but against it."[21] Certainly the church would never go with the stream of communism because it was unworthy of advocacy. In closing, Barth reminded Brunner that when the first article of Barmen insisted the church has "no other word to proclaim than the one Word of God, no other events and powers, figures and truths, as God's revelation," democratic capitalism was not an exception.

In effect, Barth's reply to Brunner turned the tables. The real seduction facing the church in the West wasn't communism; it was the ideology of anti-communism allied to Western individualism. Together they were quite capable of constructing a new kind of total system, even embedding the church's proclamation within it. Here we should recall Barth's previous argument with Brunner in 1934 when he declared his angry *No!* to Brunner's endorsement of natural theology. In 1934 Barth argued that Brunner's timing couldn't have been worse—at the very moment the German Christians were promoting their marriage of gospel and fascism in the name of

18. Ibid., 113.
19. Barth, "Karl Barth's Reply," in *Against the Stream*, 114.
20. Ibid., 116.
21. Ibid., 117.

natural revelation, Brunner was recommending the wise recovery of natural connections between faith and historical processes. And now once again here was Brunner going with the stream of American anti-communism, not against it, to advocate a church grounded in and professing confessional support for Western political values. Once more Barth insisted he must reply *No* to Emil Brunner. If during the 1930s Barth opposed the German Christians for being politically co-opted, now he charged Western Christians with the same seduction.

Challenge to the Church in the East

Being *nonpartisan*, Barth also had unwelcome words for the church in the East. In the same year of his public exchange of letters with Brunner (1948) Barth wrote an open letter to the Hungarian church at the request of several pastors, in which he sought to describe a non-ideological form of Christian service within the newly formed communist state. The church was currently suffering, he said, from a dual liability. Formerly, the Hungarian church had compromised its freedom *vis-à-vis* the state. Today with the new political situation not yet set in stone, the church could not predict how the new state would use its freedom. Because of its previous compromise, the church *ought not* to adopt the Roman Catholic attitude of resistance to the new (e.g., Cardinal Mindszenty). And yet the newness of the state suggested that the church ought not go beyond *de facto* to *de jure* recognition and identification with a new ideology.[22] Barth's plea to the Hungarian church was to remain free: free to serve hence do not become a state subsidiary. Using military language, Barth admonished the church neither to attack the new state, nor to defend itself against it, nor capitulate to it! Better to *peacefully* tread a parallel path according to the unique path prescribed by the Word of God.[23] If the church allowed the gospel to be its sole guide, it would be free to respond not in a strategic or tactical way, but in a spiritual way. Barth ended with a warning: certain documents of the Hungarian church were already sounding overly deferential to the new regime. "One faces a government best when one does so with a completely straight back!"[24]

Barth followed up his public exchange of letters with Brunner by writing an article in which he bluntly assessed the present conflict of East and West as essentially a power struggle between Russia and the United States.

22. Barth, "To My Friends in the Reformed Church in Hungary," in *Against the Stream*, 119–20.

23. Ibid., 121.

24. Ibid., 123–24.

With Europe having sufficient self-inflicted damage to no longer compete for world dominion, Russia and the United States were now, each in their own way, Mother Europe's grown-up offspring, each desiring "to be teacher, patron, protector, benefactor—or, to put it more frankly, the master of their old mother, Europe, and with that of the rest of the world as well."[25] Barth also suggested several parallels shared by these systems. Each was surrounded by a safety zone of smaller states, formally independent but in many ways vassals, linked up more or less closely in a so-called bloc, while in between the two blocs lay the infamous Iron Curtain.[26] Both sides were fond of words like freedom and peace, yet neither was clear what they meant by such terms. Barth challenged the church in each sphere: the church should defend "social freedom" against the attacks of the West and "personal freedom" against the attacks of the East.[27]

Here Barth developed two themes. First, both sides were caught up in an important common emotion: the feeling of threat and encirclement by the other. What should be the attitude of the Christian in such an environment? Be not afraid! Such conflicts are only a form of the present age's travail as it groans for its redemption which has appeared in Jesus, but has not yet been fully revealed. In the past, many similar quarrels have come and gone. The church has suffered, endured and survived them all and would do so now.[28] Second, and most importantly, the church ought not to become a partisan in this conflict. "As Christians, it is not our concern at all. It is not a genuine, not a necessary, not an interesting conflict. It is a mere power-conflict. We can only warn against the still greater crime of wanting to decide the issue in a third world war." Instead of taking sides, the church has a positive task: to walk on a path between these two giants and pray "deliver us from evil"; to speak in favor and support for the relaxing of tension; to extend sympathy toward all the victims of the conflict. Between these two paths the Christian would have plenty of mission to engage in and should do so pursuing a third way.[29]

Barth also invited the church on both sides to listen to the accusations of the other system. That way the church might discover ways in which both sides could hear the gospel. So, for example, what does the West criticize about the East? It decries its materialist view of being human, as if humans could create a perfect organization through the recipe of a radical

---

25. Barth, "Church between East and West," in *Against the Stream*, 129.

26. Ibid., 128–29.

27. Barth, "Christian Message and the New Humanism," in *Against the Stream*, 188.

28. Barth, "Church between East and West," in *Against the Stream*, 130.

29. Ibid., 131.

socialism. The East pursues this goal so single-mindedly that in the process it destroys human freedom, turns persons into masses, calls its followers to endless fighting, respects no law but socialism, uses propaganda, brutality, inhumanity—all in the service of this strange god of social progress. These challenges from the West are legitimate. "But as Christians it is right that we should hear what the other side has to say as well."[30]

If the West chose to listen to the East, it might hear that many times Western religion and spirituality sound hypocritical. The East would say, "You know very well that economics (production and consumption) is central to humanity but then you criticize our materialism and talk about spiritual values and morality. You hide what is most obvious: *you* are ruled by blind capital. Maybe some of you are the wheels but most of you are under the wheels! You are breeding the real mass-human beings. Your formal democracies which include the occasional visits to the polling stations and your independent newspapers are a sleight of hand. They all owe allegiance, even your courts of law, to the great banks. Meanwhile, your references to heaven are a cover so that life on earth remains the same." That is how the East might speak to us, said Barth, accusing the West of both hypocrisy and inhumanity.[31]

For reasons of history and geography, Barth acknowledged that he identified as a Western Christian, that he was drawn much more to the Western battle-hymn than to the Eastern. "But it does not follow by any means that it pleases Him that we should simply give way to Western prejudices and especially to the pressure of our Western environment."[32] Let us remember our freedom *as Christians*. The West may think it obvious that the church should simply take sides and choose between these quarrelling systems. But for Barth, this could not be the church's way. It must remember that the church is not simply the West (that is, a subdivision of America and her allies and satellites.) Meanwhile, the same pressures can be observed in the East. Thus to both sides, the church should say decisively:

> Away with the knives! No more oil on this fire! For, if we simply go on cursing each other until there is nothing left to do but have another war, then nothing will improve in any case, no one will be helped and no problem solved. The only possible way is a third way. Let the church in the East see to it that it says the same thing there![33]

30. Ibid., 133.
31. Ibid., 134, 135.
32. Ibid., 135.
33. Ibid., 136.

Barth's third way can be summarized as follows: let the church create a conversation and provide opportunity for reconciliation rather than join sides to argue and fight for victory. But with both sides eager to win the Cold War and fearful of losing, Barth's third way project was not welcomed by the partisans.

The Crusade against Communism: "Not Quite Honest"

Let us explore Brunner's question to Barth a little further. Indeed, why did Barth respond to Eastern European communism so differently than he responded to the Nazis? First, because the Nazis never put a serious question to the church. It was "quite simply a mixture of madness and crime in which there was no trace of reason."[34] Why then was it so seductive for the church? Barth's answer: because it had worn Christian clothing. It took a very long time for the church to see that it had been seduced. (Germany, let us remember, was not alone in finding fascism or militarism or racism attractive.) Communism, on the other hand, had never worn Christian garments. But there was more: in 1933 it was costly to say no to Nazism, in 1948 to say no to communism was simply to go with the Western flow. This was a further clue that a different seduction was at work in the West, a seduction coming from somewhere other than communism.

Brunner claimed all totalitarian systems were fundamentally the same and so equally deserved to be repudiated. To this Barth replied: why doesn't the West say no to the fascist movement in Spain? Why doesn't it say no to the military campaigns launched by the Dutch against Indonesia? On closer inspection, the West's resistance to totalitarianism was blatantly equivocal. Its no was only toward Eastern forms of domination, not Western. "It is, in a word, not quite honest. Therefore we must refuse to make it our own."[35]

Barth concluded it was disingenuous for the West to simply condemn the Soviet Union. The West would be far more convincing if it acknowledged at least that the communists had attempted something positive, that they addressed the crisis of social injustice, something the West had yet to really tackle.[36] Yes, the communist methods were inhumane, but what about Western intentions? In other words, the West stood accused by the East of inhumanity at its core, for in its system of economic egoism it had unashamedly based its social relations upon acquisitive self-centeredness; in effect a systemic violation of the tenth commandment. The West had become so

34. Ibid.
35. Ibid., 138.
36. Ibid., 139.

corrupted by its practical materialism it was blind to the global and personal cost of the Western capitalist system. Yes, some profited from the structure, but the system and its apologists were blind to those left along the side of the road; the unemployed, the underemployed, and the worker exploited by the greed of the private owners busy pursuing their own self-advancement.[37] Hence the East challenged both the core beliefs of the West as well as its good conscience. And just to make things more awkward for the West, Barth reminded his Western readers that even the atheism of the East was itself a Western transplant.[38] In conclusion, Barth returned to his main theme: the church must refuse the temptation to engage in a partisan attitude, agitation and propaganda against the East on behalf of the West. The West did not need a crusade against communism; both West and East needed the Word of the Cross.[39] Both East and West needed a free church; free to walk between the two, free to call both back to advocacy for humanity.[40]

Fifty years later, and with the return of economic inequality in America on a scale not seen since before the Great Depression, Barth's candor in unmasking Western double standards makes for compelling reading. However, one comment has not worn as well. Barth claimed that Russia's Josef Stalin merited a different level of consideration from "a charlatan like Hitler."[41] However, Soviet disclosures since the revelations of Krushchev have exposed the extent of Stalin's crimes against his own people, making Barth's 1949 plea for Stalin's dissimilarity from Nazi thuggery sound naive. In fairness, however, the reputations of Western leaders during this period have not been enhanced by recent disclosures. For example, American journalist Norman Cousins has shown that President Truman's decision to drop two atomic bombs without warning on major Japanese cities had more to do with political expediency than military necessity (which remains the public rationale). Cousins has documented the internal opposition to Truman's decision, whose dissenters included Generals Eisenhower, MacArthur and Marshall. Despite Cousins's nonpartisan efforts, such an internal witness of opposition remains largely unknown. My point is this: Cousins's assembled evidence suggests the historical reputations of Truman and his advisors are also in need of painful recalibration.[42] Nor is Truman the only American president whose Cold War behavior merits reassessment.

37. Ibid., 140.
38. Ibid., 141.
39. Ibid., 142.
40. Ibid., 145.
41. Ibid., 139.
42. Cf. Cousins, *Pathology of Power*, chs. 2–5.

All in all, Barth's exposure of Western hypocrisy in the 1950s reveals the extent to which the West inverted the mistakes of the 1930s. That is, an ideology of capitalist individualism became unequally yoked to the gospel in a way analogous to previous Christ and culture syntheses, including most flagrantly the German Christians. With the Cold War twenty years behind us, Barth's warnings may be starting to sound as even handed as they were intended. But at the height of the Cold War how hard it was to hear such words, nearly as hard as it was for the church in Germany in 1934. In 1948 it was hard for Cold Warriors to hear Barth suggest that Christians should seek to play a positive role (which elsewhere Barth called "helpful solidarity"),[43] within a communist society analogous to the way they should do in a capitalist one. Within a Cold Warrior paradigm Barth seemed to have lost his bearings and his earlier credibility.

Given the self-righteous tendencies at work in both ideologies and the cloud of fear hanging over both East and the West, Barth's challenge for the church to go against the stream gained improbable traction. Barth's third-way perspective is evident in the statement of the first assembly of the World Council of Churches, held in Amsterdam in 1948:

> The churches should reject the ideologies of both communism and laissez-faire capitalism and should draw men from the false assumption that these extremes are the only alternatives.[44]

As the founding secretary-general of the World Council of Churches, Willam Visser't Hooft spoke for an emerging sentiment among the churches that the time had come to "get past the old sterile alternatives" between a social gospel which wasn't so much good news as a system of moral laws and an individualistic orthodoxy which lacked the cosmic outlook of the Bible.[45] If Jesus Christ is the Lord of heaven and earth, then the respective powers and principalities embodied in modern economic systems, whether of individual or collective ownership, cannot be granted definitive status in the coming kingdom for which Christians boldly pray. To identify either polarity with the kingdom is idolatry. A far better way for an ecumenical church would be the narrow path of identifying neither with nor against communism nor capitalism as systems but standing eager to serve its Lord in both.

Not surprisingly in the days of acute Cold War tension, the newly formed witness of the World Council of Churches to a third way received mixed reviews. The United States government's response was particularly

43. Barth, *Letters: 1961–1968*, to Josef Hromadka (December 1962), 82.

44. Quoted in Visser't Hooft, *Memoirs*, 214.

45. Ibid., 215. Visser't Hooft has acknowledged his indebtedness to Barth in helping him formulate a nonpartisan approach for the emerging World Council of Churches (37).

scathing. In 1948 President Truman had sent his personal representative, the financial magnate, Myron Taylor, to ask the WCC to invite government representatives to join the WCC at their first assembly "in order to fight communism together." For Truman, it was simply self-evident that fighting communism would be at the core of the ecumenical church's agenda. When Visser't Hooft as council director explained to Taylor that the assembly was meeting to express the unity of the churches, and that it was necessary for it to be independent of all governmental influences, Taylor was astonished. Moreover, he was incredulous that the leaders of Islam had not been invited to participate nor did he see why it was necessary to mention Christ![46] Truman later dispatched Taylor to the two presidents of the WCC, pastor Marc Boegner in Paris and Geoffrey Fisher, the Archbishop of Canterbury in London, to invite the WCC to come to Washington and devise a joint statement concerning peace *and* common resistance to communism. When both leaders independently refused, an exasperated Truman publically rebuked the WCC for its inability to cooperate on such a vital task.[47]

Meanwhile, Barth's even-handed plea for independence from Cold War partisanship was no more welcome on the Eastern side of the political trenches. We have already noted how more than once, he challenged his friend and fellow Reformed pastor Josef Hromadka. As late as 1962 Barth pleaded with Hromadka that his attitude mirrored that of two prominent Western theologians.

> Dear Joseph, do you not realize that Emil Brunner, Reinhold Niebuhr, and other western fathers defend their western outlook with the same method and in the same style, and being able to do this they thus bring on the scene their crusade against communism, so that you and they are waging the cold war in just the same way?[48]

For nearly eighteen years, Barth lamented, he had been accused of being a communist sympathizer because he refused to thump the anti-communist drum. "I have therefore been attacked and calumniated, directly and explicitly so by Niebuhr and Brunner, not to mention countless lesser minds of various calibers."[49] Barth reminded Hromadka that he had "always spoken out loudly and consistently" against Swiss anti-communism, the Cold War,

---

46. Ibid., 207.

47. Ibid., 225. Visser't Hooft generously describes Truman's efforts as a "confused mixing" of church and state (*Memoirs*, 227).

48. Barth, *Karl Barth Letters 1961–1968*, 83.

49. Ibid., 105.

atomic armament, and the remilitarizing of West Germany.[50] Now he urged Hromadka against doing on the left what Niebuhr and Brunner did on the right, viz. to falsely identify the gospel with one side of the Cold War. Cold war partisans surrendered the capacity to witness to a kingdom that derives from neither West nor East. For Barth it was too reminiscent of the problem the church faced in the 1930s in Germany. "This is what I once battled against in Germany; this is what I battle against on both the right and the left today."[51]

What was the long-term effect of Barth's counsel on the churches? I will briefly comment on his influence on Protestants in East Germany to end this chapter. But for any Westerners (especially Americans) who lived through the Cuban missile crisis, it remains sobering to contemplate that antagonists of the gospel were not solely in the Kremlin but also strode the corridors of power in Washington. At least, that is, from Barth's vantage point, the mindset that sought victory over the enemy instead of redemption and reconciliation was an enemy of the gospel. The calling of the church in a war zone mentality should be to tear down walls within the church between capitalist and communist, and hear both communist as well as capitalist complaints rather than dismiss one side as nonsense.[52]

For the rest of his life Barth never ceased pleading for a third way between East and West. Much to the annoyance of the Eastern Bloc, he refused to sign a Moscow peace appeal against the atomic bomb, for which he was denounced as "bourgeois." On the other side, by 1950 he was under scrutiny from the American secret service for having "too many Eastern friends."[53] As we shall see, his search for a third way led him to publically oppose the rearming of West Germany. Sometimes Barth's advocacy of a third way was quite straightforward. For instance, he called the Cold War a war and summoned Christians to work for peace on both sides. This basic theme—to make peace—had been left unspoken in too many previous wars of his own lifetime. But this time Barth would not make the mistake of not even trying, as he later confessed in an important letter to Bethge.[54] Written the year before he died, he acknowledged Bonhoeffer's complaint that at Barmen he failed to give clear "non-religious" guidance by making the treatment of

50. Ibid., 106.

51. Ibid. Interestingly, Barth named Pope John XXIII as representing the same stance as himself, only the pope did it much better.

52. For those unaware how close the Cold War came to nuclear blows, the private correspondence between Kennedy and Krushchev reported by Norman Cousins makes for disturbing reading. Cousins functioned as Kennedy's personal courier during some of the most anxiety-drenched months. Cf. Cousins, *Improbable Triumvirate*.

53. Busch, *Karl Barth*, 382.

54. Cf. ch. 1 of this present work.

the Jews a decisive feature. He also acknowledged how he took for granted and remained too silent on the issues of "ethics, fellow-humanity, a serving church, discipleship, socialism, the peace movement, and in and with all these things, politics."[55] To speak with vigor on these topics, to draw the links between theology and politics—this was Bonhoeffer's contribution which an older and wiser Barth acknowledged to Bethge.

Barth's No to Anti-Communism

Given Barth's growing sense that a political witness to the gospel was essential, we should clarify why he found the politics of anti-communism simply *unacceptable* as a Christian political response. To put it simply, anti-communism was the inverse of the German Christian movement he had faced in the 1930s. Its defining feature as evidenced by its title was its negative approach to the enemy. By contrast, Jesus' relation to the enemy was based on a positive: "But I tell you who hear me: Love your enemies, do good to those who hate you, bless those who curse you, pray for those who mistreat you."[56] Alas, the Western message of anti-communism "only stoked fear and aggression against the enemy." Barth minced no words:

> I believe anti-communism as a matter of principle to be an even greater evil than communism itself. . . . Have we forgotten . . . that only the "Hitler in us" can be an anti-communist on principle? . . . I think . . . that the Christian churches should have considered it their task to influence both public opinion and the leaders who are politically responsible by superior witness to the peace and hope of the kingdom of God. The churches have injured the cause of the gospel by the largely thoughtless manner in which they have identified the gospel . . . with the badly planned and ineptly guided cause of the West.[57]

Barth's *no* to anti-communism was grounded not in tactics or pragmatics, but in his *yes* to the gospel.

> *Anti* means against. God is not against, but *for* men. The communists are men, too. God is also for the communists. So a Christian cannot be against the communists but only *for* them. . . . I

55. Barth, *Letters 1961–1968*, 251.
56. Luke 6:27–28.
57. Busch, *Karl Barth*, 383.

am not for communism. But one can only say what has to be
said against communism if one is for the communists.[58]

In his biography, Busch details how Barth's stance led to his vilification
by the popular press in Switzerland. Various Swiss politicians even sought to
tar him as a "friend of communists" in order to enhance their electoral re-
sumes. But Barth's no to anti-communism was for the sake of the gospel: the
good news for communists is the same as the good news for capitalists. Both
have been claimed by God in Jesus Christ, even if neither thinks as believers
think they ought to think, or even if they are not recognizable as fellow Christians. In obedience to Jesus, we ought not to "think the worst of everyone of
those frightened, miserable, erring, misled and perhaps really godless creatures around us, but rather the best, just as we like to think well of ourselves."[59]

As we will see, Barth's plea to German pastors in the East to proclaim
a gospel *for* communists not against them, became formative for the church
in the lead-up to 1989. By contrast, Franklin Littell has noted that a key
problem with anti-communism was its tactics, in which it frequently imi-
tated the communists with its use of character assassination, guilt by association, insinuation, slander, and attempts to polarize society.[60] Such modes
of speech have ruinous consequences for any government which uses them
as standard communication strategies.

How shall we assess the consequences of anti-communism as a postwar political policy, one that stretched over decades? Any detailed reflection
would take us far away from our present study. But we can note in a very
preliminary way, that this ideology was the crucial influence on the United
States' decision to invade Vietnam. The loss of American life during that war
was over 58,000 dead. Estimates of Vietnamese casualties vary from one to
three million.[61] One of the chief architects of the Vietnam War, Defense Secretary Robert McNamera, has candidly admitted the war was a mistake. Of the
eleven major causes McNamera lists for the disaster of Vietnam, the top reasons he names are closely linked to the fears and confused thinking aroused
by anti-communism, almost as if McNamera had been reading Barth's Cold
War essays. McNamera laments we misjudged the geopolitical intentions of
our adversaries and exaggerated the dangers to the United States.[62] However
Vietnam does not stand alone as the bitter fruit of anti-communist philosophy. The number of military dictatorships supported and trained, particularly

58. Ibid.
59. Barth, "Christian Message in Europe Today," in *Against the Stream*, 179.
60. Littell, "From Barmen (1934) to Stuttgart (1945)," 41–42.
61. Hirschman et al., "Vietnamese Casualties," 809.
62. McNamera, *In Retrospect*, 321.

in South America and in Africa as a result of anti-communism, are too many to list. Democratically elected governments were covertly overthrown by American action. Billions of dollars were invested in military efforts to destroy communism which could have been invested to strengthen education, health and infrastructure around the nation and across the globe. In other words, the destructive consequences of our commitment to this negative ideology have yet to be fully and publically examined by our political and educational institutions, our churches, or our media.

Barth's No to German Remilitarization

In 1952 Barth weighed in on the public issue that led Gustav Heinemann, the primary legal council to the Confessing Church and signatory of the Stuttgart Declaration, to resign from the cabinet of Konrad Adenauer's Christian Democratic government of West Germany. The issue was the remilitarization of Germany by the same Allies who had previously and thoroughly demilitarized it.[63] For Adenauer, as for most Catholics during this period, German rearmament was simply the logical implication of Western defense against communism. Pius XII had declared in his Christmas message of 1948 that a strong Western defense was the best arrangement for peace.[64] But even for someone as boldly critical of communism as the pro-Western bishop of Berlin, Otto Dibelius, the future of Germany was put at risk in the Allied decision to rearm Germany. Despite the politically divisive implications, Dibelius spoke out strongly against rearmament. He was convinced that if the Western sector was rearmed by its occupying powers, the Soviets would follow suit in East Germany. Hence any hope for Germany's reunion would be postponed indefinitely. "It will ever remain memorable that the western powers, after destroying Germany's military potential down to the last pillbox, suddenly arrived at the conclusion that Europe could be defended against the forward march of communism only if Germany contributed half a million soldiers. Germany must therefore rearm as quickly as possible!"[65] On the Western side, Anglican Bishop George Bell also criticized the rearming of Germany, saying it would only damage the prospects for peaceful unification and perpetuate the Cold War, making Russia ever more afraid of Allied intentions.[66]

63. Barth, "Political Decisions in the Unity of the Faith," in *Against the Stream*, 150.

64. Cf. Spotts, *Churches and Politics*, 247, 254–55.

65. Dibelius, *In the Service of the Lord*, 239, 240–43.

66. Jasper, *George Bell*, 340.

Barth was convinced the rearmament decision posed a crisis *for the church*. After only a few years of demilitarization, ought Germany return to its old military tradition? Such a question bore on the inner structure of the life of this deeply wounded nation. In making a public stand against German remilitarization, Barth acknowledged that the church should rarely speak out as an organized body on political issues. Usually, it is best done as the "daring service" of individual members from their own sense of responsibility as Christians.[67] Barth mentioned Bonhoeffer in particular, which suggests Bonhoeffer served as a goad for Barth to speak and not to be silent. Thus in the concrete issue of German rearmament, Barth joined his name to that of Martin Niemöller and Gustav Heinemann as part of his political service to the gospel. It was not coincidental that those who "unswervingly adhered" to the Barmen Declaration also joined together in opposition to German rearmament.[68]

Because of his public stand on the political issue of German rearmament, Barth considered it necessary to clarify his reasons. First, he described his manner of coming to a decision; that it came only after carefully weighing all sides and in faithfulness to the gospel of God's justice. As crucial to this fairness, Barth rehearsed the arguments on both sides in the debate, a discipline he urged all citizens in a democracy to embrace. Christians do this in a unique way, he said, by testing and discerning the spirits that run through each pattern of arguments. As part of a Christian's assessment, Barth stressed the urgency to make a decision of choosing life not death, choosing God not idols. But through the process of careful listening to both sides, Barth laid out what for him became the determinative argument: West German remilitarization would make "practically impossible the one effective defense against Communism, that is, the establishment of a higher degree of social justice."[69] In other words, investments in human resources and taking steps to the amelioration of social disparities between economic groups in society would dwindle and be dwarfed by armament spending. Lastly, during and at the end of this process, Christians must admit they may well end up opposing each other on concrete political matters. This raises the question of the "unity of the faith."[70] By publically opposing remilitarization Barth would be accused of imposing a law on his fellow Christians, binding their consciences, etc. Barth's reply: would this charge

67. Barth, "Political Decisions," in *Against the Stream*, 151.

68. Cochrane, *Church's Confession*, 11. From Adenauer's view, Niemöller's public declaration was virtually treason. Adenauer's authorized biography devotes an entire chapter to the conflict with Niemöller and Heinemann. Cf. Weymar, *Konrad Adenauer*, 358–81.

69. Barth, *Against the Stream*, 153.

70. Ibid., 155

also be made against those in favor of remilitarizing Germany? Lastly, he asked, "Why are there no pro-Adenauer Niemöllers?" By naming his friend and famous pastor who led the resistance to Hitler, Barth was suggesting that those who argued for remilitarization did not argue from the obedience of faith, or take their stance from the Word of God.

As for the charge that taking a political stance would disturb Christian unity, Barth replied that Christian unity is never something guaranteed, never something based on inaction and silence. Where unity takes no risks, it risks no obedience. A proper political decision needs both simple common sense and the urgent love of Christ as revealed in a spark of prophecy.[71] But in the end, a prophetic Christian word can and should be spoken with both Old Testament severity and New Testament joyfulness.[72] Hence at times some in the church must stick their necks out—in courage and in humility. Thus on the specific political decision of German rearmament Barth (hopefully with courage and humility) "stuck his neck out."

It is worth recalling that during his imprisonment Bonhoeffer had complained that Barth, despite his impressive theological framework, offered no clear direction in concrete situations (example: Jewish persecution) but had remained silent.[73] Indeed, as we noted, at Barmen there were no political specifics, no guidance in regards to "non-religious interpretations." However, if one takes a specific stand, the critics will howl. So when it came to the crucial decision to rearm Germany in the interests of the Cold War belligerents, Barth (perhaps inspired by the example of Bonhoeffer), joined with Niemöller and Heinemann in risking a political witness to the gospel.

The howls came quickly. Barth's remarks were met with bewilderment by many in the West and adversely affected his popularity in American theological seminaries for the next two decades.[74] As part of our background study for the church's political engagement in 1989, we must ask: did Barth's public stance regarding rearmament impact the church in Germany toward its singular path to 1989? Barth joined with Niemöller and Heinemann in speaking a clear no to any partisan military build-up. Meanwhile for the next two decades, the ever-increasing militarization of the two Germanys became a flash point of protest in both Eastern and Western zones. In the East, the church would join in nonviolent solidarity with the *Swords into Ploughshares* movement as a positive witness for peace *within* a socialist society, but not against socialism *per se*. The church's support expanded the movement both unex-

---

71. Ibid., 159.

72. Ibid., 162.

73. Cf. Bonhoeffer, *Letters and Papers*, 429.

74. Busch, *Karl Barth*, 405.

pectedly and exponentially, culminating in German reunification. It became a crucial turning point in the church's service to the community *within* social-ism. As Christian Führer would one day testify, this nonpartisan movement prepared the way for events of biblical proportions, as against all expectations, the communist system in the East was brought to an end.

Conclusion

We have been studying the emergence of a new kind of solidarity to which Barth lent his considerable theological support. Despite the nearly over-whelming atmosphere of Cold War partisan fervor, Barth became a primary advocate of a nonpartisan way. Though one cannot measure the extent to which Barth's intervention was crucial to the future transformation of Ger-many, clearly he pointed forward to a third way, a way of solidarity *for* social-ists *and* capitalists. Consistently and insistently Barth remained *nonpartisan* throughout the Cold War because he was convinced that Christians were summoned to be joyful partisans of the God who stood in solidarity with both communists *and* capitalists. Here was a solidarity that did not hold a club (or secretly hide a club behind its back) to thump the communist (or the capitalist). Here was a solidarity willing to speak to political leadership "with its back straight," as the church serving within communism, proclaim-ing good news for socialists. Barth joined with Niemöller and Heinemann to express a nonpartisan political stance against rearmament because he was convinced the church's mission was to foster reconciliation rather than further division.[75] Of course there is no direct link from here to the evening in October 1989, when seventy thousand demonstrators wielded candles and said prayers *for* the people rather than threw rocks *at* communists. Was it sheer coincidence when that same evening comrades of the one-party state did not defend the people by shooting "traitors"? Together such acts of solidarity embodied a lived parable in which the refusal to throw stones at the others (reminiscent of Stuttgart's refusal to blame the Nazis for all of German ills) combined to form the only successful revolution in German history. But how, against the odds, did these seeds of nonpartisan witness become rooted in the hard ground of the German Democratic Republic? To that question we now turn.

75. Spotts, *Churches and Politics*, 241. Despite his repeated criticism of Barth's non-partisan approach, Reinhold Niebuhr acknowledged Barth's ability to inspire a "religious resistance" in East Germany without raising "false hopes and fears in the political realm." Niebuhr, "Why Is Barth Silent on Hungary," in *Essays in Applied Christianity*, 188.

7

The Wilderness Era
A Forty-Year Journey to a Peaceful Revolution

Perhaps the most important contribution the church can make is to bear in mind in the shaping of its own life that, gathered as it is directly and consciously around the common center, it has to represent the inner within the outer circle. The real church must be the model and prototype of the real state. The church must set an example so that by its very existence it may be a source of renewal for the state and the power by which the state is preserved.

—KARL BARTH, 1946[1]

Might it not be your special calling to be a living example for the rest of us of how a church lives that seeks for and perhaps has already entered upon a new way, of a church for not of, the people—the church in "God's beloved (deeply beloved!) East Zone"?

—KARL BARTH, 1958[2]

TWENTY-FIVE YEARS ON, IT is still hard to fathom that a critical mass within the pluralistic and compromised church of the German Democratic Republic became a living parable of Bonhoeffer's church for others. As a result, the

1. Barth, "Christian Community and Civil Community," in *Community, State and Church*, 186.
2. Barth and Hamel, *How to Serve God*, 65.

many voices excluded from full participation in the life of the state, including artists, writers, and young people, were heard not as illegitimate but as essential.[3] Some of the events on the path to 1989 seemed rather unremarkable at the time, but step by step a group of pastors and participants grew mindful about living out a public, and hence political, witness to the gospel. To these developments we now turn.

Robert Goeckel has described eight stages in the church's journey through the German Democratic Republic or East Germany.[4] With some modification, I will use this frame to give context for key events. Along the way I will note the ongoing influence of Barth and Bonhoeffer, especially through the crucial roles played by their former students. In particular, I will focus on the contributions of Albrecht Schönherr, one of Bonhoeffer's student at Finkenwalde, and Heino Falcke, a former research assistant for Barth in Basel. Schönherr was appointed Episcopal administrator of the Evangelical Church in the Berlin-Brandenburg Region in 1967 and in 1972 presiding bishop of the GDR Church after it severed all formal ties with the church in West Germany.[5] Falcke, perhaps the most influential Protestant theologian during the life of the GDR,[6] served as Barth's assistant in preparing volume 3, part 4 (The Doctrine of Creation) of the *Church Dogmatics*. In this way Falcke acquired a firsthand acquaintance with Barth's emergent approach to an ethics centered in the gospel. Falcke's writings and lectures gave invaluable clarity and direction to the GDR Church in the years leading up to 1989. For twenty-one years he served as provost (dean) of Erfurt.[7] Finally we will consider their link to the ministry of the Leipzig pastor of *Nikolaikirche*, Christian Führer, with whom our study began. Führer's autobiography, published in 2009, provides a unique eyewitness interpretation of the events of 1989.

Act 1: 1945–1948, The Darmstadt Meeting and Its Hopeful Legacy

As the war ended, the Eastern quarter of Germany was occupied by Russia, the rest of the country by the French, the British and the Americans. Not surprisingly the Eastern sector came under Marxist governance, with its

---

3. Cf. Lazarus, "Pulling the Curtain Down," 8.

4. Goeckel, *Lutheran Church*.

5. Conway, "Kirche im Sozialismus," 4.

6. According to Stephen Brown. Brown's work in making Falcke's writings available for non-German speakers has made a valuable contribution to ecumenical studies. Brown, *Introduction to Heino Falcke*, 160.

7. Ibid.

security overseen by a large presence of Russian soldiers. This became the GDR, that is, the German Democratic Republic (*Deutsche Demokratische Republik, DDR*). Historically speaking, it is hard to overemphasize the enormous role played by the church in this region of Germany. It was Luther's zone long before it was Russia's. Of its nineteen million citizens, 87 percent were members of the Protestant Church.[8] Internally, the GDR contained eight out of the former twenty-eight basic organizational units (*Landeskirchen*) of the Protestant Church in Germany. Until 1945, five of these were known as the Old Prussian Union (a merger of Lutheran and Reformed churches under the influence of Prussian King Frederick William in 1817). Thus the GDR was the only nation in the entire Soviet bloc whose majority population was Protestant. As we will see shortly, the SED government (*Sozialistische Einheitspartei Deutschlands*) seemed torn between two strategies in dealing with the church within its borders.

For Martin Niemöller, this situation meant that 47 percent of all Protestant Germans now lived behind the Iron Curtain.[9] Despite the pressure for Germans in the Western Zones to see themselves as a people quite distinct from those in the East, Niemöller refused to accept the notion of a permanent split.[10] Much to Chancellor Adenauer's irritation, Niemöller suggested with characteristic invective that Germany's current policy had been conceived in Rome and born in Washington! In saying this, Niemöller was rejecting the strategy of Cold War partisanship. In a more irenic mood, he put it this way: "If Christ said, 'love your enemies' what right did Christians in Germany have to tear up this fundamental command?" In a conflict between lethal rivals, the church had the clearest of duties: to serve the cause of peace.[11]

When the Confessing Church Council of Brethren met in Darmstadt on April 1947, there was already a sense of urgency to counter the escalating Cold War rhetoric. Was it possible to declare a clear call for reconciliation instead? Choosing words built on the Stuttgart Declaration, the Darmstadt Statement named two German sins of the past that now threatened her present and future. Instead of working for reconciliation the church had identified itself with German pride and nationalism, "as if the German character could heal the sickness of the world."[12] Second, the church had allowed itself

8. Goeckel, *Lutheran Church*, 8.

9. Schmidt, *Pastor Niemöller*, 167.

10. As noted in the previous chapter, Niemöller was not alone. Cf. Dibelius, *In the Service of the Lord*, 238.

11. Quoted in Schmidt, *Pastor Niemöller*, 168–69.

12. Darmstadt Statement, April 1947, sect. 2 (Hockenos, *Church Divided*, appendix 6, 193).

to become the chaplain for a nationalism wedded to an anti-communism which had played right into the hands of the Nazis.

> We went astray when we failed to see that the economic materialism of Marxist teaching ought to have reminded the church of its task and its promise for the life and fellowship of men. We have failed to take up the cause of the poor and unprivileged as a Christian cause, in accordance with the message of God's Kingdom.[13]

At Darmstadt, the Council of Brethren alleged that the church's task in postwar Europe could not be to pursue a one-sided victory in a new war between former allies who had combined to defeat the Nazis. Her task rather was to "work for justice and for the welfare, peace and reconciliation of the nations."[14] Darmstadt had applied a distinct theological theme to offer political guidance for the church on both sides of the divided nation. But it was not a theme welcomed by either occupying power.[15] Nevertheless its affirmative tone created an opportunity for the church in the Russian zone to work with the state in a partnership rooted in the church's confession. Moreover, it was rooted in the repentant memory of the church's guilty silence when the Nazis' first victims, the communists, were stripped of their rights and persecuted at the launch of the Third Reich. Darmstadt provided a spirit of openness that offered hope for the church to engage positively with the new regime, together in service for the common good instead of seeking to undermine the government. For its part, the state could not easily dismiss or ignore such service. As late as 1950 the church in the GDR was running over fifty hospitals, eighty homes for the disabled, two hundred nursing homes, twenty-one orphanages, eleven infant homes, three hundred kindergartens, and twenty centers for persons with developmental disabilities.[16]

But was it really possible for the church to serve God and neighbor in a Russian/communist zone as it did in the American/capitalist zone? Were not communists officially atheist? And yet, could a Marxist state simply deny the church's enormous community service as a powerful and historical contribution to the good of the whole society? In the background of this conflict was the Marxist article of faith which held that eventually all religion in a non-capitalist society would die away once the source of religion

---

13. Darmstadt, sect. 5 (Hockenos, *Church Divided*, 193).

14. Darmstadt, sect. 7 (Hockenos, *Church Divided*, 194).

15. Scholder notes that Darmstadt created lively arguments within the Council of Brethren itself, which became incorporated into a commentary that provided further explanation and clarification (*Requiem for Hitler*, 123, 124).

16. Goeckel, *Lutheran Church*, 21.

(viz. exploitation of the working masses) had been eliminated. Thus why worry too much about the presence of a capitalist-era dinosaur if it thrashed about for a few more years? Engels himself had warned that the persecution of religion would only promote martyrdom.[17] Was it not better therefore to cooperate with the church in ways that promoted common values of social welfare rather than create martyrs? Martyrs would only slow down the inevitable maturation of the state.

There was, however, a darker approach brooding within the SED as it faced this dinosaur. Marx had spoken also of *militant* atheism. Lenin once noted that the presence of "disinterested clergy" could keep religion alive and hinder the development of the socialist mind. Hence a dual policy evolved in which active forms of persecution and repression against the church coexisted with cooperation until the party gradually perfected a socialist system that would eliminate the oxygen of worker oppression that kept religion alive.[18]

The events of 1989 have since revealed the militant approach to have been a spectacular failure. Not only did the church survive its planned extinction; it became the mother of the revolution that ended the Marxist government on German soil. But such a result was never destiny. Decisive moves were made by both sides as in a high-stakes game of chess. In the end, Stalin's mocking question, "How many legions does the Pope have?" was turned on its head as the masses took to the streets armed only with the spirit of nonviolence, solidarity and prayer.

Thus from the very beginning of the GDR, the church played a crucial role. It entered the GDR as the only social institution from which the Nazis had received serious resistance. Its moral prestige was only enhanced when it confessed its shortcomings in dealing with the Nazis at Stuttgart in 1945. Then at Darmstadt in 1947 it took a further step by expressing words of reconciliation toward Marxism and respect for some of its fundamental concerns. Having adopted an attitude of service to help the nation recover morale after its devastating collapse and defeat, the church hoped that positive relations with the communist state would indeed be possible. After all, communists and Confessing Church believers had suffered alongside one another in Nazi concentration camps. Unfortunately, those communists who had exiled themselves to Russia were more dogmatic and less sympathetic toward the church. Over time these "hard liners" took control of the party.[19] Their intolerance led to a series of conflicts and eventually a

---

17. Moses, "Church Policy," 231.

18. Ibid. This dual strategy is also discussed in Sollberg, *God and Caesar*, 111.

19. Barnett, *For the Soul of the People*, 260.

dramatic worsening of relations. Yet it should be said, the initial hope for cooperation was evidence that, despite relentless Cold War pressure, Barth's search for a third way was not stillborn in the East German Church.

Act 2: 1949–1953, Relations Dramatically Worsen

By the summer of 1948, relations between the Russians and the Western Allies had deteriorated to the point where the Russians blockaded Berlin and the West responded with the Berlin airlift. Despite hopes of something much different, by 1949 church and state relations were badly deteriorating. Religious belief became grounds for dismissal from the communist party (SED). Dramatic confrontations occurred over youth work. Pastors were arrested. Church holidays were stricken from the school calendars. The financial maintenance of denominational schools ended.[20] The ministry of Otto Dibelius, bishop of Berlin, seemed to epitomize the growing fissure with the regime when he publically declared that with its reliance on force and hostility to the gospel the GDR now showed many characteristics of the Nazis.[21] Dibelius's comments reflected almost a reversal of the conciliatory verdict struck by the Council of Brethren at Darmstadt. Meanwhile, his words also gave notice that the church would never again simply play the role of a compliant partner as it had done too often under the Nazis. On May 11, 1948, Dibelius and the other bishops in the Eastern zone wrote a letter to the Russian military administration, expressing their commitment to respect the laws of the state while at the same time maintaining the freedom to criticize the state, though not with the intention to undermine or destroy its authority.[22] Even so, the church's attitude to the new state was not simply negative. For example, the church launched a new venture in Christian education, the *Kirchentag* (Church Congress), where clergy, laity and politicians met biennially for a week to worship together and discuss the relevance of the gospel to society and social issues, East and West. *Kirchentag* reflected the growing awareness that it was important to speak and teach on these issues, as a correction to the wrongful silence of the previous era.[23] During this time, the church retained its traditional right to give religious instruction in

20. Goeckel, *Lutheran Church*, 45–56.

21. Moses, "Church Policy," 237. Dibelius's uncompromising opposition in these early years of Stalinist rule had many parallels among the churches in Eastern Europe. Cf. Chadwick, *Christian Church in the Cold War*, 91.

22. Sollberg, *God and Caesar*, 58–59.

23. Steele, "At the Front Lines of the Revolution," in Johnston and Sampson, *Religion*, 121–22. Also Barnett, *For the Soul of the People*, 248.

the schools. The universities also retained faculties of theology though they were increasingly staffed with regime-friendly theologians.

Because the church hoped the current separation between East and West was only temporary, it neither pledged loyalty to the state nor advocated political opposition.[24] This phase ended on a confusing and much-debated note when in early March of 1952 Stalin penned his controversial "March Note" in which he proposed German reunification with the proviso that Germany remain neutral. When the Allies abruptly dismissed it as propaganda, hopes for imminent reunification receded. Following Stalin's death, the church hunkered down in an increasingly hostile environment. In the coming months more than seventy pastors and church workers were imprisoned for alleged sabotage and disloyalty toward the state, with attendant show trials full of slanderous accusations regarding the church's agitating role. Thousands of high school students were also expelled for alleged disloyalty just as exams were approaching.[25] Many young people simply had enough and became refugees, some for religious, others for economic reasons. From 1949 an average of fifteen thousand East Germans per month were leaving for the West. As the pressures for Marxist conformity mounted, numbers soared to a peak in March 1953, when over fifty-eight thousand fled, most of them under twenty-five years of age.[26]

Act 3: 1953–1958, Incomplete De-Stalinization

The same month refugees fled in record numbers, Stalin died. The numbers abandoning East Germany suggested that Stalinization had pushed too hard and German disillusionment had reached a danger point. Under pressure from Moscow, on June 10, Prime Minister Otto Grotewohl met with church leaders and to their astonishment, apologized for serious mistakes in the handling of church relations and promised to rectify injustices. He also spoke at a teacher's rally, declaring that the strict imposition of Marxist-Leninism on all teachers would be abandoned.[27] He released thousands of political prisoners. Meanwhile, SED party secretary Walter Ulbricht confessed that the focus on rapid build-up of heavy industry at the expense of consumer goods production had been a grave mistake. Despite such sweeping changes, the government did not rescind its recent imposing of a 10 percent increase in productivity without any increase in state-owned factory

24. Goeckel, *Lutheran Church*, 47.

25. Sollberg, *God and Caesar*, 144–45.

26. Ibid., 156.

27. Ibid., 165.

wages. Sensing the weakness of the government, and encouraged by such public admission of mistakes, on June 17, 1953, workers responded with a general strike. Beginning in Berlin, the strike spread quickly throughout the country. Twenty-five thousand protesters gathered in Berlin. The regime, alarmed at its inability to win back the confidence of the workers, summoned the Russians to rescue it from collapse. Twenty thousand Soviet soldiers supported by tanks ruthlessly crushed the protest. Somewhere between fifty-five and one hundred twenty-five protesters were killed, many more were injured and hundreds were jailed. Others were later executed for participation.[28] It was a devastating blow for any hopes of reforming the system. Almost immediately, there was a spike in interference with the church.

In 1954 the state introduced a ceremony of dedication to the state (*Jugendweihe*) as a secular, atheist alternative to the church's traditional confirmation training for young people. At first the church responded by refusing to grant confirmation to students who participated in this ceremony. But gradually the educational and economic benefits of *Jugendweihe* participation overcome all resistance. This both reflected the rapid secularism of the GDR and also illustrated the party's success in finding ways to marginalize the church.[29] In 1956 the state further sidelined the church by terminating the church tax (*Kirchensteuer*). For Americans and British citizens, the idea of the state collecting taxes for church upkeep sounds odd, but its practice in Germany had roots going back to the nineteenth century at a time when the church retained major responsibility for health care, education and charitable work. Despite the 1919 Weimar Constitution's secular intentions, the church tax had been maintained and until 1956, had never been seriously challenged.[30] The system typically transferred 8 percent of one's taxes to serve the church, which could only be avoided by writing an official letter formally leaving the church. The tax amounted to between 70 and 90 percent of the church's total income.[31] Hence leaving the church to collect its

28. Barnett, *For the Soul of the People*, 261.

29. Althausen, "Churches in the GDR," 6.

30. Cf. Petersen, *Kirchensteuer Übersicht*, www.kirchenfinanzen.de. Spotts gives 1803 as the origin of the *Kirchensteuer*, when the Imperial Reichstag gave monasteries and church lands to the state. In exchange they ordered the state to cover the church's expenses with annual payments. Spotts, *Churches and Politics*, 194. At one time Hitler considered severing all financial linkage with the church but when the Confessing Church welcomed the idea, he changed his mind, reckoning that control of the church's purse strings was a useful way to control the church. Herman, *Rebirth of the German Church*, 157.

31. Christmann, *Germany*, 11.

own contribution from its members was a radical departure from German history. Needless to say, it led to a perilous decline in church revenue.[32]

By the mid-1950s, the formerly imposing church membership numbers were shrinking dramatically. If one looked at numbers only, the state had spectacularly succeeded in marginalizing the church. But as Führer later noted, the large church statistics of the early years of the GDR (as those during the rule of the Kaiser!) were as misleading to the church's real health as the large numbers in state youth organizations later became. That is, the big numbers belied the people's loss of faith in the system. So for Führer, the time of shrinking numbers and the total disapproval of the atheist state had unintended positive consequences: it refined the church, and helped it to focus not on its privileges (or the loss thereof), but only upon the crucified and risen Jesus Christ. In retrospect, these wilderness years were a training camp for faith.[33]

In 1954 West Germany officially became an independent nation. An invitation was received to formally join NATO. In 1955 the United States deployed its first nuclear missiles on German soil. Russia responded with the Warsaw Pact as the separation between the two Germanys looked forebodingly permanent. The final crisis during this period came in 1958 when the United Protestant Church, the EKD (*Evangelische Kirche in Deutschland*), agreed to provide military chaplains for West German troops in NATO. The East German state reckoned that the EKD had now partnered itself with an enemy state, whose missiles were pointing in its direction. It ridiculed the EKD as the NATO Church and began a campaign of relentless pressure for the church in the GDR to sever all ties.[34] How could the state cooperate in any way with a church whose clergy were blessing soldiers that pointed nuclear weapons in its direction? Meanwhile, despite its control of the media, education and relentless propaganda efforts, the GDR continued to hemorrhage citizens, as over 262,000 refugees left the country in 1957.[35]

32. Goeckel, *Lutheran Church*, 50. Moses, "Church Policy," 239.

33. Führer, *Und Wir Sind Dabei Gewesen*, 138.

34. Goeckel, *Lutheran Church*, 52. Moses, "Church Policy," 239.

35. Sollberg, *God and Caesar*, 261.

Act 4: Withdrawal from the Pan German EKD and the formation of the GDR Church Federation (Kirchenbund), 1958–1969: The Witness of Albrecht Schönherr

During this period the Cold War tension seemed to ratchet up to a further level of German anguish over nuclear brinkmanship. Moments of special alarm included the construction of the Berlin Wall (1961) and the Cuban missile crisis (1962). In response to the risk of internal disruptions, the GDR launched its notorious policy of *Abgrenzung* (separation), in which it tried to seal itself off from all Western contacts. However, the official policy of separation seemed only to increase people's desire to emigrate. By the time the government took the step of erecting a physical barrier against the West (the Berlin Wall) in August 1961, more than three and a half million Germans (one sixth of the population) had already left for the West.[36] *Abgrenzung* was particularly distressing for Christians in the GDR. No doubt many if not most agreed with Bishop Dibelius in preferring to live under a Western style democracy. Even those sympathetic to a more socialist form of government hardly wished to be separated from family and church connections in the other spheres of Germany.

This was also a period of dramatic political assassinations and large public protests. Perhaps the most shocking deaths were those of President Kennedy (1963) and in 1968 both his brother Robert Kennedy and Martin Luther King Jr. Not coincidentally, this was the time of escalation in the Vietnam War, which ignited student protest movements throughout Europe, including Berlin, Paris, and London. In 1968 the West German student leader of the Vietnam War protests, Rudi Dutschke, was nearly assassinated, and withdrew as a central political figure, eventually dying from his injuries in 1979.[37] In the years that followed, the Red Army Faction (earlier known as the Baader-Meinhof gang) became notorious for a string of kidnappings and assassinations of government and business figures. Also in 1968, the Democratic National Convention in Chicago was disrupted by riots on the streets between police and war protesters.

Though hardly center stage given the enormity of the events noted above, relentless pressure mounted on the church in the GDR to sever ties with the Protestant church in West Germany, the EKD. Eventually in 1969 a total withdrawal was formalized as the Protestants in the East formed their own Federation of Evangelical Churches in the GDR (*Bund der*

36. Pond, *Beyond the Wall*, 25.

37. Dutschke had close personal ties to Barth's friend, Helmut Gollwitzer, as well as Martin Niemöller, and was buried in the graveyard of St. Anne's church in Dahlem. Cf. Dutschke, *Wir Hatten Ein Barbarisches, Schönes Leben, Rudi Dutschke*, 429.

Evangelischen Kirchen or Kirchenbund). The question was: could the church in the GDR walk a narrow path between resistance and accommodation or would it inevitably come out clearly in resistance to the communist state?

In many respects the years from 1958 to 1969 were trench warfare between church and state. Though the search for a third way was never abandoned, it was not without its fierce critics. In his book *Authority* (*Obrigkeit*) published in 1959, Bishop Dibelius of Berlin argued that Paul's instructions for Christians to submit to the state (Romans 13) did not apply to the GDR because a totalitarian state is not ordained by God and so could not be seen as a legitimate order.[38] Dibelius concluded there was no possibility of the church's service to the state within such a social order. Not surprisingly, the GDR denounced Dibelius as a *persona non grata*. Once the wall was built, Dibelius was simply refused reentry to the GDR after traveling to the West on church business. The mirror opposite of Dibelius's strategy was a meeting on July 21, 1958, where Minister-President Otto Grotewohl met with a group of clergy to agree on a communiqué, demonstrating mutual respect.[39] At that meeting, the state promised to respect the Christians' observation of their civic duties according to their faith. Unlike Dibelius's fierce attacks on communism, here was instead a public document in which the church expressed readiness to respect the socialist path and the state expressed a response in kind.

It was during this period of tension that Barth published his influential "Letter to a Pastor in the GDR," where he encouraged the church in the GDR to be an example of a church that is *for* not *of* the people, to be the church in "God's beloved (deeply beloved!) East."[40] In his reply, Pastor Johannes Hamel, whose impactful student ministry had caused him constant harassment and even arrest, nevertheless held out a vision that the church should be neither an enemy, a capitalist fifth column within a Marxist society, a Marxist appendage, nor fellow travelers within. Rather it must learn how to declare good news *within* the Marxist world. Otherwise it would have no credibility.[41]

At this time Bonhoeffer's former Finkenwalde student Albrecht Schönherr began to assume increasing responsibility. When Dibelius was refused GDR reentry, he was initially succeeded as bishop by Kurt Scharf. But given that Scharf also was part of "the NATO Church" he too was soon refused reentry back to the GDR after a visit in the Western zone. With Scharf's

---

38. Goeckel, *Lutheran Church*, 62. One wonders how Dibelius regarded the Roman Empire at the time Paul wrote his epistle to the Romans?

39. Althausen, "Churches in the GDR," 6.

40. Barth and Hamel, *How to Serve God in a Marxist Land*, 64, 65.

41. Ibid., 110, 126. Cf. Sollberg, *God and Caesar*, 148, 168.

approval, Schönherr was elected interim moderator of the Eastern Synod in 1967. Eventually, he was officially elected as bishop responsible for the Eastern side in 1972.[42] As a member of the Weissensee Study group, Schönherr had already disassociated himself from the anti-communist strategy of Dibelius. Earlier, in 1964, the Weissensee group had issued a manifesto entitled *Seven Theological Theses on the Freedom of the Church to Serve*. The *Seven Theological Theses* was a response to a document from 1963, *Ten Articles about the Freedom and Service of the Church in the GDR*, which sought to firmly distance the church from any form of accommodation to the state, such as, for example, the Christian Democratic Union (CDU), a nominally independent political party that had tried (unsuccessfully) to mobilize Christian citizens to support socialism in the GDR.[43] Schönherr and the Weissensee pastors argued that God's love makes Christians free to cooperate in the social order and to take responsibility. "Christians and non-Christians work together at the task of creating internally a human and just order and a lasting peace in the relations among peoples and states."[44]

For Schönherr, Dibelius's politics of resistance was too embedded in Luther's two kingdoms doctrine, with its separation of the working of the world from the church in a rigid dichotomy of law versus gospel.[45] It was this kind of isolation between spheres which Barth had earlier identified as the reason why so many Lutherans happily accepted the Nazi state without asking many questions. In Dibelius's case, the stark contrast he offered between church and world reinforced a separation in which no constructive engagement with the state was possible. As Moses puts it, the strategy of Dibelius was to brand the state as illegitimate, even criminal, withdraw into a ghetto and wait for it to self-destruct.[46]

42. Oestreicher, obituary of Bishop Albrecht Schönherr (April 2, 2009).

43. In Switzerland, Barth's response to the *Ten Articles* was mixed. While he agreed with the call to refuse all "optimistic accommodations, coordinations and identifications of the church" and the world (63), he regretted its lack of theological substance. For example, he asked, why did the document speak of the Church's "freedom and service" as if these two items remained in an unresolved separation? Why not speak instead of "freedom *for* service," which would have sounded a clear and "joyous roar of the Lion of Judah"? (68). As we will see, that roar would only be sounded ten years later in a 1972 address to the synod by his former assistant, Heino Falcke. Cf. Barth, "Ten Articles on the Freedom and Service of the Church, Text and an Evaluation" in Barth, *Fragments Grave and Gay*, 63, 68.

44. Quoted in Goeckel, *Lutheran Church*, 63. From theses 5 and 7.

45. Althausen, "Churches in the GDR," 8.

46. Moses, "Church Policy," 240. Elsewhere Moses complains that the Weissensee Group unfortunately employed Bonhoeffer to absorb the church *into* the state, with Marxism accomplishing the purposes of the gospel. Cf. Moses, "Bonhoeffer's Reception," 286. Unfortunately Moses virtually reduces Schönherr's efforts to the acquiescence

Though he did not invent the phrase, Schönherr expressed an approach which came to be known as "the Church in socialism." At the height of the Cold War he rejected the anti-communist strategy that the church should subversively cooperate with the forces of capitalist freedom to eliminate socialism. Instead he pursued the hope that socialism could be reformed *according to the gospel.*[47] For all its controversy and its potential for misuse by those seeking to reduce the church to a bureau of state, Schönherr's approach had one real strength, viz. its clear rejection of a false identification of the gospel with anti-communism. This error had already been lamented in 1947 by the Council of Brethren at Darmstadt for blinding the church to its social responsibilities and for contributing to its seduction by Nazi anti-communism. But anyone sympathetic to Dibelius considered Schönherr guilty of false accommodation; acquiescing in the trampling of human rights and co-opted by the secret police (Stasi). However, to be fair, Schönherr never defended the behavior of the GDR toward the church. Rather he wanted the church to pursue an open relationship with the state rather than to work, whether openly or clandestinely, to undermine it by encouraging emigration or overthrow it for a capitalist alternative.[48] To borrow the language of others, Schonherr desired the church to stand up to the state with its back unbent (Barth) and to speak directly to the state, not indirectly through the filter of the media (Führer).

Schönherr himself best described the narrow path between accommodation and resistance which he sought for the church. His essay on the fortieth anniversary of Bonhoeffer's death credited his teacher as the primary influence in the effort to live as a pastor in a Marxist society.

> That I could respond to the past in this way is something I owe to Dietrich Bonhoeffer. . . . I regard it as one of my chief responsibilities to pass on to others what I learned from Dietrich Bonhoeffer. I am convinced that he can still be of help to many.[49]

Schönherr began his essay by describing his service in the Confessing Church, as having given the Nazis a "little bit of resistance." He tells how,

---

of a sycophant.

47. Goeckel, *Lutheran Church*, 74. The term had a mixed nuance of meanings. Others influential figures such as Bishop Rathke of Mecklenburg, described it with a distinctive nuance that included standing up against injustice. Also some like Falcke and Bishop Krusche of Saxony understood it in terms of social and political criticism by the church, but within the context of a general approval of socialism. Cf. Goeckel, *Lutheran Church*, 174.

48. Althausen, "Churches in the GDR," 9.

49. Schönherr, "Dietrich Bonhoeffer," 1090.

after being drafted into the Nazi war effort, he became a POW in Italy when Germany capitulated. But as the war ended, his conscience was far from clear. He found himself in deep agreement with the Stuttgart Confession of Guilt. He had become personally convinced that unless one honestly faced the past, and took responsibility for one's own role, one could not move into any future except one which repeated the past and succumbed to the same temptations, "perhaps with different names."[50]

For Schönherr, the aspect of Bonhoeffer's Christology that most impacted his conversations with the state, was the manner of his speaking not of Christ as an idealist philosopher who crafts a "harmonious world view" nor a Christ of the individualist "who guarantees strength for life, happiness and eternal salvation" but rather "the Biblical Christ who is faithful to the earth," who "brings salvation and healing from suffering and death, liberation from guilt and sin, liberation from the forces which are destroying the earth, among which war and injustice are the most terrible."[51]

The words, *Christ as faithful to the earth*, are worth further comment. Though Schönherr affirmed a belief in Christ as guarantor of an individual's salvation, his frame was far larger: Christ's passion included the entire created order. That is why, following Bonhoeffer, he refused to compartmentalize his faith as only of individual, private or religious significance. Schönherr movingly writes:

> Christ's manger stands on the earth, his cross is rammed into the earth, his grave is dug into the earth. Because God became human in Christ, there is only the one reality, which includes God, world and human persons. Bonhoeffer's thought was not like ours, divided among different realities: employment and family, economy and politics.[52]

It was Bonhoeffer then who inspired Schönherr to believe in a Christ who was neither under church protection nor church control. Quite the contrary, Christ was Lord of the church—but not just the church. He was

> the Lord of the earth—but not in triumphing power; rather as the crucified, the one who suffers by us and with us. Expressed another way: Christ is the person for others. And his divinity lies precisely in that, and not in the glory of total power.[53]

50. Ibid.
51. Ibid.
52. Ibid., 1091.
53. Ibid.

When this Christ leads the church and is the content of the church's message, the mission of the church will always undergo the same imprint. If Christ is the person for others, "then his people must form the church for others."[54] Moreover, a church *for* others includes the Church *with* others. For the church in the GDR, Schönherr urged the others should not be seen as inferiors but as partners. Yes, partners even with Marxists and secularists! How is this possible? Schönherr's answered: "When the center is clear, then the boundaries can be open. The church for others must participate in the human life of the community, not as a master, but as a servant."[55] At the church synod of 1970, Schönherr's influence was clear as it dared speak of cooperation with the Marxist, citing Darmstadt for naming the church's earlier failure to cooperate with the Marxists in opposing the Third Reich.[56]

Finally, Schönherr reflected on the title of Bonhoeffer's volume of letters from Tegel prison. In English the title is drably translated *Letters and Papers from Prison*. But in German the theme is precisely paradoxical: *Widerstand und Ergebung* (Resistance and Submission). The title expresses Bonhoeffer's personal struggle as a disciple in the Third Reich. No narrow path between these two words can be found by some abstract definition or prearranged plan. As Bonhoeffer wrote, for the Christian, *both* exist and *both* must be practiced. "Faith demands this elasticity of behavior."[57] This was the theme that now guided Schönherr's narrow path of witness to the gospel for the church within socialism. Earlier, for Dibelius and Scharf, the GDR's political pressure to separate from the West German Church (the EKD) was unacceptable. But Schönherr took a more pragmatic approach. Do our ecclesiastical structures help us accomplish our mission? Frankly, as a *missional* structure for the church in the GDR, he sensed the EKD had lost its usefulness. A painful separation was needed in order that the church might be free to carry out its ministry concretely in the socialist order of the GDR, and to do so not as an alien threat but instead as accompanying Christians along a difficult way in a socialist and atheist society.

Implicit in this approach, Schönherr committed himself to accompanying non-Christians as well, helping to preserve their rights and dignity in

54. Ibid.

55. Ibid.

56. Goeckel, *Lutheran Church*, 116. Looking back on Bonhoeffer's relevance for Christian witness in the GDR, Schönherr argued that Bonhoeffer was taken more seriously in the GDR than in the Federal Republic. Quoted in Huber, "Inspiration, Controversy, Legacy," in Green and Carter, *Interpreting Bonhoeffer*, 12.

57. Quoted from a letter of February 21, 1944, in Schönherr, "Dietrich Bonhoeffer," 1094.

concrete ways.[58] In the end, Schönherr argued that the success of his policy would be on the ground, not in theory. Would local Christians bear faithful witness? This would be the proof of the pudding. In an essay reflecting on the legacy of the Barmen Declaration for the GDR, Schönherr pointed to its second thesis, Christ's claim on our whole life, and interpreted his own political struggle in the GDR in its light. We see from these two essays how Schönherr linked his obligation to Bonhoeffer with Barth by saying that the church's political responsibility simply reflects the Lord's own path when he intervened on behalf of those on the margins of life and ministered to those who were weak, who had no lobby group to defend their rights.[59]

Act 5: GDR Ambivalence toward the New Church Federation (Kirchenbund), 1969–1971

With Cold War tensions ever growing, the year 1970 witnessed a fresh initiative by West Germany's newly elected chancellor, Willy Brandt, to change the climate. His policy of *Ostpolitik* led to signing the Warsaw Treaty whereby West Germany gave up any claim to lands ceded to Poland and Russia after the war. Such a relinquishment was a step Adenauer had always refused.[60] Despite such Western initiatives, however, the GDR government always responded to Schönherr's strategy with great ambivalence. While his openness toward the goals of a socialist society created a sense of mutual respect and the opportunity for dialogue, his criticisms, for example, of the Russian intervention in the Prague Spring, his ongoing ties with the West through ecumenical relations—set off alarm bells. In retrospect, it seems the government mostly sought ways to manipulate Schönherr's model to restrain dissent rather than engage in a genuine conversation about the social order.[61]

Writing in 2009, Führer likened the notion of "the church in socialism" to walking on a knife-edge between conformity and resistance, in which the church sought to define herself neither in opposition nor in the conformity desired by the government. Events, however, would turn the church increasingly toward resistance. As it happened, less than twelve years from SED chairman Erich Honecker's historic conversation with Schönherr, the GDR ceased to exist. But the church's conciliatory attitude to its former enemy/

---

58. Schönherr, "Legacy of the Church Struggle in Contemporary Germany," in Locke and Littell, *Remembrance and Recollection*, 104.

59. Ibid., 101.

60. Weizsäcker, *From Weimar to the Wall*, 176.

61. Goeckel, *Lutheran Church*, 113, 147.

partner did not end with the crumbling of the Berlin Wall. Though largely unknown, when Honecker was forced to abdicate as a result of the 1989 events, the only place of refuge he could find was neither a Dacha of his Soviet comrades nor a holiday home belonging to the communist party (SED), but with the family of a local evangelical pastor, Uwe Holmer, in the village of Lobetal.[62] Holmer offered Honecker and his wife a room in his home and for two months their families lived together until Honecker's cancer required further hospitalization. The message sent by Pastor Holmer's act of mercy had both personal and political implications for a people tempted to revenge. Holmer's hospitality was especially poignant given that none of his children had been allowed entrance to university studies due to their Christian faith.[63]

Act 6: Between Ambivalence and Limited Rapprochement, 1971–1972: Heino Falcke's Theology of Freedom

In 1972 Chancellor Willy Brandt's *Ostpolitik* strategy led him to sign the Basic Treaty with the GDR. It meant that West Germany now legally acknowledged the separate existence of the GDR.[64] As part of this agreement, travel and visitation restrictions for families were significantly eased, while at the same time both Germanys were admitted to the UN as independent nations. Sadly, GDR church and government relations continued to be severely strained. In particular, two main areas of conflict erupted: education and military training. When children of pastors and others refused participation in the secular youth confirmation, the government closed their opportunities for further education. This was accelerated in 1971 after Honecker replaced Walter Ulbricht as general secretary of the SED and launched a new emphasis on ideology.[65] The previous year, university students, in addition to fulfilling their previous military service, were required to serve an additional minimum of thirty days annual training.[66] This created fresh tension since after the Nazi era, the tradition of German militarism had come under deep suspicion from young Germans. Tightened restrictions on church events followed. Only meetings conducted by those in full-time

---

62. Pierard, "Religion and the East German Revolution," 506.

63. Führer, *Und Wir Sind Dabei Gewesen*, 142, 143. For further details about this unlikely sharing of life together, see Huber, *Meine DDR*, 277–80. Honecker's wife, Margot, had been the secretary for education in the GDR since 1955.

64. Weizsäcker, *From Weimar to the Wall*, 157, 177.

65. Goeckel, *Lutheran Church*, 182.

66. Ibid., 189.

church employment were permitted. Only rooms normally used by the
churches were permitted.[67] Valid events were specifically itemized: worship
services, communions, baptisms. The intention was clear: reduce church activity to rituals increasingly isolated from social life. Even the use of jazz in
worship was forbidden by the state out of concern that such modern music
would appeal to youth.[68] Not surprisingly, such measures took an increasing
toll on church participation. From 1965 to 1973 baptisms dropped nearly
in half; attendance at religious education and confirmation by one third.[69]

Nevertheless, during this grim time of increasing tension, the "clear
and joyous roar of the Lion of Judah" Barth had hoped for was sounded.
In 1972 Heino Falcke gave the keynote address to the synod meeting in
Dresden, entitled "Christ Liberates—therefore, the Church for Others." He
chose to focus on the most controversial value (or lack thereof) within the
socialist system—freedom. Because of it impact, it bears special attention.

Heino Falcke: Freedom within Socialism

First and foremost, for Falcke the church must not allow Christ's liberating
action to be isolated in a narrow religious sector. This was not possible in any
case since Christ had penetrated to the depths of all human life by his death
and resurrection. By entering into the utter depth of human suffering, Christ
had become the brother of all humanity in its poverty, marginalization and
especially with all victims of religious or social oppression.[70] But in dying and
rising, Christ had neither simply brought history to an end, nor had God's
kingdom openly arrived. Was the liberation announced by the gospel simply
something for the future? Falcke's answer: "The freedom of Christ still takes
the form of the cross, though through the power of a great hope." Through
this form Christ's freedom now intervenes and even redeems human movements for freedom, *including the one promised by the socialist movement.*

67. No doubt Führer was well aware of these rules during his years at Leipzig.

68. Goeckel, *Lutheran Church*, 191–95. In his autobiography, Saxony evangelist
Theo Lehmann describes his encounter with jazz music and the sense of freedom it
provoked among people whenever he used it in public worship in East German society.
As a society severely regulated by hierarchical regimentation, jazz shocked the listener
with its spontaneous structures. Lehmann recalls that when he first heard the Negro
spirituals which gave birth to jazz, "I feared my skull would split open." Using jazz as an
accompaniment to his evangelistic events attracted many young people, and sparked
real alarm in the SED. Lehmann, *Blues Music and Gospel Proclamation*, 61.

69. Goeckel, *Lutheran Church*, 236.

70. Falcke, "Christ Liberates," 167.

For Falcke, the key to Christ's liberating intervention was love. In the first place, we become free when we encounter a love that accepts us unconditionally. This is what liberates us from a prison of self-centeredness into a new confidence that we are no longer God's enemies, but adopted as the brothers and sisters of God's own Son.[71] In the wake of this intervention, freedom can no longer be simply construed in terms of independence or self-autonomy or based on a hunger for self-achievement driven by a need for acceptance by others. Indeed Christ liberates us from the fear of not being successful, of not being needed and hence abandoned. Falcke borrowed Niemöller's phrase, Christ has become our gracious neighbor who seeks us out for our own sake, and accepts us and supports us even in the solitariness of our death.[72]

> It is because Christ liberates us from the pressure to achieve that he makes possible new action, which no longer has to prove itself but can focus completely on the task in hand and on the neighbor. Because the root of this freedom is love, it includes the neighbor.[73]

Such a freedom enables us to take responsibility, rather than be oppressed by authoritarian powers or rather than being obsessed with obtaining security through transient things such as technology, weapons, and consumerism—all symptoms of fear-based ideologies. To discover the freedom of the children of God is to find release from such self-imposed immaturity.[74] And in this release, one discovers the capacity to be free *for the other* not for self-chosen ideologies. Again, how is this possible? It is possible because "we received freedom as love." It is love which releases in us "freedom for others and with others."[75] The strong awareness *of the other* with its deep sense of responsibility *for others* is a gift of freedom granted by the love of God.

From this basis in Christ's freedom, Falcke proceeded to address socialism directly. It need no longer be construed as freedom's enemy. Indeed, why shouldn't the church help to design a socialism in which the commitment is to be a self in community instead of a self in isolation?[76] Why must freedom be framed any longer in terms of separation from others, or independence of others? Because of the cross of Jesus, we may instead see freedom as a way of being available *for* others. In this way Falcke explored

71. Ibid., 168.
72. Ibid.
73. Ibid.
74. Ibid., 169.
75. Ibid., 170.
76. Ibid.

the possibility of a fundamental compatibility and even theological support for a socialist society. However, such a society would be profoundly different than the socialism of the SED in the GDR!

But not just socialism. The gospel way of freedom is a way of being for the entire global village, releasing us from whatever forms of bondage we are in. Here Falcke confronted the socialist state. He urged that the policy of separation or demarcation (*Abgrenzung*) which had become fundamental to the GDR for many years, be done away with. He reasoned that to seek "inner stability by sealing ourselves off from the outside world" blocked the way of being for others,[77] turning relative differences into forces which divided peoples, turning freedom into a "reward for conformity with group behavior."[78] The contrast with the way of Jesus could not be more radical. Jesus broke through borders. Jesus made himself available to those who were excluded. His love liberated from the pressure to seal ourselves off from others. His love frees us to view our neighbor differently, yes, even our enemies. This was the freedom that could be a new starting point whenever we think about taking sides in any and all disputes, domestic or political.

Further Questions for the Marxist

Falcke also addressed the Marxist claim that Christianity had made an ideology out of suffering when it should have protested and resisted oppression. Clearly, the church shared real common ground with Marxism in standing in solidarity with the oppressed. But Falcke asked, was it really the case that Marxism stood in solidarity with those who suffer—particularly those who suffered in a Marxist society? Was it not rather guilty of avoiding this side of reality? "Whoever needs to repress suffering in order to remain optimistic and relish his or her work is not free."[79] To be *for others* was to be in solidarity with *all* who suffer. Falcke reminded the synod that not long ago an entire nation had ignored the concentration camps in its midst during the persecution of the Jews. So now the church must not ignore or minimize those who suffer in today's society. That is why the church can and indeed must challenge "the paralyzing dogma" that things cannot be changed for the better. People were free only when they could hope. "Fear and striving for security become ingenious in the technology of war, in strategies of deterrence and in all forms of self-assertion. But God's promise releases the

77. Ibid., 171.
78. Ibid.
79. Ibid.

creativity of a love that becomes resourceful for others and for new forms of living together."[80]

Further Questions for the Church

After raising such critical questions to the Marxists, Falcke raised several urgent questions for the church. Why, he asked, did the church still appear to so many to be a closed society, not one for others? Why did she find it so difficult to practice the love which transcended boundaries? Why was the church so inhibited in speaking with Marxism and being a part of socialist society? Certainly being *for* others needn't mean being *like* others, but "why does our being different not express itself more clearly as being there for others in solidarity and love?"[81] Why shouldn't Christians as people in the minority toil as team players or must they only be team captains? Falcke showed no inclination to spare the church criticism, especially since the church always lived from the hope that she was ever summoned to change increasingly for the better. So let the church be free to serve; free to find a Word that doesn't oppose the world, but creatively explores life together. Let the church be free to learn from the social sciences as it sought to serve in complicated areas of modern life such as urbanization, or in developing countries affected by racism. "This is because the love that demonstrates solidarity *has* to raise these issues, and keeping oneself properly informed is part of the service of the Word."[82]

Concretely, what then should the church's responsible action in socialism look like? If it was only the proclamation of the Word, religion would be only a leisure-time activity. This would demote and marginalize the church instead of releasing it to be a liberating force within the social order. No, the Christian is free to hope that socialism can be re-visioned in the light of Christ's promise. Of course, it was well known that socialism began as a protest and a struggle against the misery of people who were oppressed and claimed it would abolish all oppression and bring a realm of freedom. "But the cross and resurrection of Christ make us critical of such exaggerated claims."[83] Christ's solidarity with those who suffer, his promise of freedom to the suffering—this also frees Christians to participate in socialism's protest against misery and share in the task of changing inhuman situations. So Christians are free to join in building up a socialist society when it cre-

80. Ibid., 172.
81. Ibid., 173.
82. Ibid., 175.
83. Ibid., 178.

ates more justice, and serve others within its structures. "In the promise of Christ, we will tirelessly remind our society of our committed hope for a socialism that can be changed for the better."[84] So let the Christian participate in building a better socialism in a spirit of "joyful service" (Barmen, article 2) rather than as heavy demand.[85] Concretely, the church can do this by becoming a voice for the weak and disadvantaged, whether for nearby neighbors who lacked the productivity potential or for neighbors far away in the so-called third world, where help might take the form of socialist models with a clear no to "neo-colonial dependency and exploitation."[86]

Summons to Socialism: Promote Freedom, Sponsor Sabbath

Falcke advised the socialist party that it would do well to become a sponsor of freedom as an aid to growth in self-responsibility instead of categorizing some as holding a wrong point of view and in need of reeducation and indoctrination. Within a communist system, the church must be free for open discussions with people of different opinions. This didn't mean the church should leave its own teachings behind, but rather that it is free to engage in conversations because it believes it can be led more deeply into the truth through such conversations. In this way the church could offer a space for critical debate, a place for free speech, an openness to radical questioning and a readiness to learn without fear. This would be a contribution of the utmost importance to creating a responsible partnership in society.[87]

Last but hardly least, Falcke asked, what should be the place of leisure in a society which championed the worker rather than the owner of capital? From the gospel we learn that only in the context of Sabbath is human work experienced not as the pressure to achieve but as a response to the gift of God's acceptance. Only the context of Sabbath sets our work free to be humane, not toxic through drivenness. Human toil only becomes more than a burden when it is accompanied by a day of rest, a day which teaches workers the meaning of celebration and festivity. Even on his way to the cross Jesus paused for a meal with his disciples in order to join with them in a foretaste of freedom. Each time the church celebrates the Lord's Supper, it remembers the freedom Christ distributes to the community, pausing to join him at his table where "even the inadequate disciples are accepted." Rising from this table, Christians join their suffering in solidarity with the oppressed, and

84. Ibid., 178.
85. Ibid., 179.
86. Ibid.
87. Ibid., 180.

join the Risen One in renewed action. This rhythm of work and rest grants disciples a true taste of freedom "in the very midst of history."[88]

Consequences

Moses rightly interprets Falcke's "freedom speech" as both a milestone and an act of defiance, a classic instance of the church practicing a "critical loyalty" to the State.[89] Falcke's address cast a vision of a freedom that moved society toward social responsibility as an expression of love: the freedom to love the other. And though it raised a radical challenge to socialism, it was not without challenge for the Western capitalist notion of freedom as the unencumbered pursuit of self-interest! It was also no small contrast to the SED's friend/foe thinking, which cut off people from one another instead of creating neighbors. At once Falcke described a freedom that was both compatible and even supportive of socialism and yet in tone more critical than simply a reassuring word spoken from "the church in socialism." He proposed a path between the "crippling alternatives" of opposition in principle to socialism and uncritical co-optation. He hoped that even in disappointment with the status quo, Christians might remain active and involved in society, working to improve socialism.[90]

How did the SED respond? In the immediate aftermath of his address, Falcke was refused permission to travel to international ecumenical events. Rather than receiving Falcke's *critical* solidarity as solidarity, it only heard criticism. It took special offense at the idea of improving socialism.[91] It sounded too much like Czechoslovakia's "socialism with a human face" which Soviet tanks had flattened four years before. The speech was not permitted publication in the GDR. It was not even permitted to be distributed with official synod papers. However, it circulated the old fashioned way, hand to hand in duplicated form.[92] Later Falcke's travel restrictions were

88. Ibid., 183.

89. Moses, *Reluctant Revolutionary*, 247. Moses suggests that Falcke is much more influenced by Bonhoeffer's *Ethics* than Barth's reflections on freedom. This contrasts sharply with Brown, who notes that Barth's theology of freedom was carefully worked out in the volumes of *Church Dogmatics* while Falcke served as Barth's assistant. Brown, "Introduction to Heino Falcke," 161. Moreover, Brown sees in Falcke a clear distancing from any notion in Bonhoeffer's prison writings that the church needed to adapt to a secular "world come of age." Rather "through Christ human beings are liberated to become *people* come of age, capable of freely assuming responsibility."

90. Goeckel, *Lutheran Church*, 175.

91. Ibid., 176.

92. Brown, "Introduction to Heino Falcke," 162.

rescinded and he became an ongoing participant in ecumenical conversations, in particular playing a crucial role in the World Council of Churches meetings in Vancouver, 1983.[93]

Act 7: Walking the Knife Edge between Submission and Resistance, 1973–1978[94]

Increasingly, local churches now grew subject to ideological pressure. The severity of this pressure led many to be critical of the Schönherr approach as too accepting of the status quo.[95] After all, Schönherr had said that the real test of "the church in socialism" would be local. And the local church became the place of relentless tension as the church sought to create a space in socialism for reconciliation, dialogue, participation and community. In the tension of the time, local churches sought to empower people to be human, to live out a model of nonviolence, while learning to speak to the state, as Barth would say, with a straight back. At times the sheer contrast of the church's approach with that of Marxism was painfully awkward, especially as in the East German state, Marxism seemed to require conformity and secrecy.[96] Tension only mounted as the brief descriptions which follow indicate.

The Helsinki Accords

In 1975, the GDR, along with the United States and the rest of Europe, signed the Helsinki Accords. Helsinki sought to lesson Cold War tensions by guaranteeing territorial boundaries, rejecting the use of threats of force, encouraging collaboration in technology and culture and guaranteeing respect for human rights. It contained a significant endorsement of freedom of conscience and freedom of religion. Schönherr noted that even though Honecker (and Ulbricht before him) perpetuated a great deal of injustice, he never undertook systematic genocide and never actively worked toward

---

93. Cf. Brown's introductory remarks to Falcke's essay, "Ecumenical Assembly," 184.

94. Goeckel suggests the title "Deepening Rapprochement," but given the movement of the nation toward confrontation on the streets, this description doesn't do justice to the conflictual nature of this period, including the increased local pressure on churches. The German title of Bonhoeffer's *Letters and Papers from Prison*, "Submission and Resistance," seems more fitting.

95. Goeckel, *Lutheran Church*, 238.

96. Steele, "At the Front Lines of the Revolution," in Johnston and Sampson, *Religion*, 140.

war.[97] On the other hand, the state insisted that basic social rights such as education and work were conditional upon meeting socialist obligations. The church rejected these conditions.[98] In reaction, the state increasingly saw the church's independent voice as a threat. It began to promote the traditional "two kingdoms" Lutheran approach to church and state. Thus, for example, Gerhard Bassarak, the professor of ecumenics at Humboldt University, argued that the state was responsible for welfare; the church for salvation.[99] This tidy division of labor was a clear retreat to the era of church prior to Barmen. Meanwhile, the state heightened its ideological campaign and discrimination against Christians in education.

The Death of Pastor Brüsewitz

On August 18, 1976, Pastor Oskar Brüsewitz went to the pedestrian zone in front of the Michaelskirche in the village of Zeitz with two handwritten notes on his backpack that said, "Radio message to all: the Church in the GDR accuses communism! Because of oppression in schools in children and young persons."[100] Then he doused himself with gasoline and lit the fire. He died four days later. Brüsewitz's self-immolation was a desperate protest against the repressive nature of the communist regime. Though the state promptly labeled him a psychopath, a vigorous, grief-stricken debate was provoked within in the church. It led the church to more resistance and less acceptance of state oppression.[101] In retrospect his action anticipated the future public demonstrations against the regime.

The Growth of Secular Dissent

The revocation of folk musician Wolf Biermann's citizenship following his concert in West Germany, the request by one hundred thousand for permission to emigrate under the new Helsinki guidelines, a dramatic youth riot at a Berlin rock concert, all in 1977, gave evidence of the state's growing fear of internal developments.

97. Schönherr, "Legacy of the Church Struggle in Contemporary Germany," in Locke and Littell, *Remembrance and Recollection*, 107.

98. Goeckel, *Lutheran Church*, 215.

99. Ibid., 221.

100. Quoted in Führer, *Und Wir Sind Dabei Gewesen*, 172.

101. Goeckel, *Lutheran Church*, 239–40, interprets Brüsewitz's suicide note as expressing frustration with the lack of support for local Christians by church leaders overly concerned with keeping on good terms with the state, a clear rebuke to Schönherr.

Meeting with Erich Honecker, March 6, 1978

All the above led to the arrangement of a formal meeting between Honecker and Schönherr. The church hoped that it could be seen in a new light by the state and in turn the state hoped it could be perceived differently as well. Honecker wanted from the church a positive declaration of solidarity. Concessions to the church included access to television, with quarterly broadcasting, as well as access to its members in prison.[102] Schönherr wrote, "We counted it a success when the GDR head of state Erich Honecker, acknowledged the work of the church in diaconic institutions and for reconciliation among nations. . . . But a famous meeting with Honecker in 1978 after a great effort meant permission to organize pastoral care in prisons and nursing homes."[103] Despite this success, an undertow of secularism and ideological pressure further depressed church attendance. Participation in confirmation declined 35 percent from 1965–1973, baptisms dropped 46 percent.[104] By 1974 church membership had dropped from 82 percent in 1946 to below 50 percent.[105]

Act 8: 1978–1989, The Freedom to Be a Church for Others

We have seen how the launching of the peace prayers in Leipzig came during a time of increasing tension between East and West. However, concurrent with this increasing tension, a different note was also sounding. Inspired by Chancellor Willy Brandt and his advisor Egon Bahr, a consensus had gradually (and not without fierce disagreement) emerged, known as *Ostpolitik*. To put it simply, it was the conviction that positive change and eventual reunion was more likely—not through confrontation and attempts to create instability in the GDR—but rather through small steps of reconciliation, including trade agreements, lessoning of travel restrictions, and financial aid.[106] Perhaps Germans were uniquely aware of the contradictions between living amid increased bellicosity between Russia and the United States on the one hand while their own politicians were seeking ways to increase cooperation and communication between the two Germanys on the other. Then unexpectedly into the mix came Mikhail Gorbachev, the new Soviet

---

102. Goeckel, *Lutheran Church*, 241.

103. Schönherr, "Legacy of the Church Struggle," in Locke and Littell, *Remembrance and Recollection*, 101, 103.

104. Goeckel, *Lutheran Church*, 236.

105. Burgess, *East German Church*, 45.

106. Weizsäcker, *From Weimar to the Wall*, 226.

president, with his policy of *Glasnost* (openness, transparency). Like Brandt and Bahr's *Ostpolitik* but with the greater leverage of a superpower, the Cold War logic of ever-growing tension and confrontation met a different approach, whose reforming possibilities could not be predicted. Would the launching of the peace prayers in Leipzig be drowned out by the increasingly bellicose Cold War rhetoric? Would they be caught up and amplified by these other, reconciling currents? Who could predict?

As our study of church and state relations began with the Leipzig *Nikolaikirche*, it is fitting to bring this study to an end by returning to Leipzig and to examine the nonviolent revolution as it happened. Leipzig became the unforeseen, unplanned center for how the church in local situations would gather and accompany various grassroots groups to create a partnership that rendered the imperial style of GDR socialism inoperable.

The final years leading to German reunification can and indeed should be considered from many angles. However, in describing the final decade of the GDR, my primary lenses will come from the dramatic insider's account of Christian Führer.

8

From the Sanctuary to the Street

In the past for the most part the Church for a long time had for its motto, "throne and altar" with power and violence joined and thus lost sight of Jesus. In reality, in the purpose of Jesus, altar and street belong together!

—CHRISTIAN FÜHRER[1]

In effect, the fate of the East German regime was decided on the Leipzig Ring on four successive Monday evenings between September 25 and October 16, then confirmed in Berlin between Saturday, November 4 and Thursday, November 9.

—CHARLES S. MAIER[2]

We had everything planned. We were ready for everything. Except for candles and prayers.

—HORST SINDERMANN[3]

CHRISTIAN FÜHRER ARRIVED AT Leipzig's *Nikolaikirche* in 1980 following twelve years of pastoral work in the village of Lastau. The son of a faithful

---

1. Führer, *Und Wir Sind Dabei Gewesen*, 263. "*Nicht Thron und Altar gehören zusammen, sondern Straße und Altar.*"

2. Maier, *Dissolution*, 139.

3. Reportedly spoken in retrospect by Horst Sindermann, president of the People's Chamber. Führer, *Und Wir Sind Dabei Gewesen*, 219.

Lutheran pastor, Führer's sense of call to pastoral ministry came early. Later, during his theology training in Leipzig, he wrote his master's thesis on Bonhoeffer's theology. By the time he had completed his ministerial training, Führer was convinced that to preach the gospel amid the increasingly bellicose rhetoric of the Cold War and escalating rearmament, one must find ways to bear witness to peace. Bonhoeffer had convinced him that words were not enough. "Pray and do righteous action."[4] However, in the late 1970s the state had introduced military training as a required subject as early as the ninth and tenth grades of school. This meant that the church in the GDR could not simply blame NATO for its aggression; its own government was invested in an increasingly militaristic approach to foreign relations, reaching all the way down to youth education. Many local churches in the GDR responded with a wide variety of grassroots projects on peacemaking.[5] Given this context, it was not surprising that in his first year at Leipzig, Führer introduced a day of repentance, which included "a peace minute." He also regularly addressed the theme of peacemaking with young people in his confirmation classes as an essential of Christian discipleship.[6]

The Launch of the Peace Prayers (Friedensgebet)

As I noted in the introduction of this study, a defining moment in Leipzig came with a notice sent to the youth in the community inviting them to an evening meeting at 10 p.m. on the theme of peace. Expecting but a handful, Führer was shocked when over a hundred youth walked into the church, most of whom were not Christians but were eager to discuss peace-making. Unabashed, Führer calmly led them right to the center of the church and after a few introductory remarks, laid a wooden cross on the floor and invited anyone who wished, Christian or non-Christian, to express or name a concern, light a candle and set it on the cross. Though Führer's first surprise was the large number of youth in attendance, it was not his biggest surprise of the evening. Instead of two or three extroverts speaking up, *everyone* shared. The youth held nothing back. Things that couldn't be voiced elsewhere in the GDR poured out—pressure at school, struggles with parents, the obligation to enter the National Guard, the war of words between the Soviets and the Americans, on and on it went. Gradually as one after another opened up and lit a candle, the stark wooden cross became a cross of shining light glowing in the darkness. It was as if the emerging brightness around the

4. Ibid., 102 ("Beten und Tun des Gerechten").
5. Goeckel, *Lutheran Church*, 256, 257.
6. Führer, *Und Wir Sind Dabei Gewesen*, 104.

cross released a sense of hope that slowly filled the room. The young people were exhilarated to share together a feeling of being heard, supported, in what became for each person there an unforgettable atmosphere of freedom and honesty. It only ended after several hours with a joyful singing Führer described as "God-roaring."[7]

Thus was sown in the *Nikolaikirche* the mustard seed of a revolution. The church began to open its doors to a variety of special interest groups who had little or no previous connection to it. Nor was the *Nikolaikirche* isolated in offering support and conversation to outside groups. Many GDR churches wrestled with their political responsibilities as part of bearing witness to the gospel. In these developments, Führer credits the youthful critics of the regime, especially their hunger to address themes which not only included peace, but also social justice, human rights, ecology and the integrity of creation, the very themes raised earlier by Heino Falcke,[8] and widely explored by the ecumenical church during those years. Throughout the GDR, churches explored such topics. By 1982 Führer decided to schedule a weekly meeting on Mondays at five o'clock p.m. to address and to offer prayers centered on such themes. He called the gatherings *Friedensgebet* (prayers for peace).[9] The topics of the Monday prayers ranged from personal issues and community concerns to special attention to global emergencies.

Meanwhile, during these years an acute anxiety developed in Germany regarding the ongoing Cold War. It was a time when in America, despite (or perhaps because of) being the richest country in the world with the strongest economy, there had grown a pervasive fear that somehow the Soviets were winning the arms race. The conventional wisdom, which had grown in the '60s and '70s that parity existed, was replaced with a sense of inferiority. A new round of escalation began when President Brezhnev stationed new intermediate range missiles, SS-20s, pointing toward Europe.[10] In December 1979 NATO reciprocated by installing intermediate nuclear missiles in West Germany. The same month the Soviet Union invaded Afghanistan. In response, the United States spent billions to arm and train insurgents in that country.[11] Back and forth it went. In 1980 and 1984 Ronald Reagan was elected twice on the foreign policy platform that nuclear superiority must

---

7. Führer, *Und Wir Sind Dabei Gewesen*, 114–15.

8. See ch. 7.

9. Führer, *Und Wir Sind Dabei Gewesen*, 117.

10. Weizsäcker, *From Weimar to the Wall*, 198.

11. Goeckel, *Lutheran Church*, 257. Chalmers Johnson has documented the delayed and unintended consequences of this investment. Cf. Johnson, *Blowback*, 10–13.

be restored.[12] Moreover, his Strategic Defense Initiative (a.k.a. Star Wars) seemed intended to restore the practicability of atomic warfare, beyond the stalemate of mutual deterrence.[13] By May 1984, East and West Germans faced the stark reality of escalating numbers of American and Soviet nuclear missiles facing each other all across the East and West German boundary zone. The ongoing nuclear build-up combined with President Reagan's dramatic rhetoric (the Soviet Union as the "Evil Empire") was hardly reassuring to Germans. It contributed significantly to an unprecedented anxiety. In response to the stress, a peace movement emerged on both sides of the border, including public protest marches.[14]

As the movement spread, the church did not keep to the sidelines. In 1982 *The Berlin Appeal* was circulated by Berlin Pastor Rainer Eppelmann and supported by longtime SED party member turned critic Robert Havemann. It called for the withdrawal of occupation troops from and neutralization of both Germanys. In its wake, Pastor Eppelmann was put in detention, although eventually the church was able to gain his release.[15] That same year the church synod, meeting in Halle, publically released a statement condemning the logic, spirit and practice of nuclear deterrence.[16]

Despite the protests, marches for peace and calls for disarmament on both sides of the border, missiles deployments only increased in alarming numbers in both East and West Germany. One consequence in the East was a wave of gloom, not only toward the possibility of change, but also toward any hope of positive initiatives coming from the Western democracies.[17] Pond describes it as a wave of self-pity and sense of abandonment that swept over Germany.[18] It seemed that Germany was stuck with a series of nuclear weapons on either side that could hit little but Germany. There were times in these years when the Monday prayers dwindled to fewer than ten people. But Führer and the church council determined to carry on regardless. "After all, Jesus said he would be present whenever two or three were gathered in his name. And even when we were down to six, we still had twice as many as the required number Jesus promised! So go ahead."[19] Modest numbers were not unusual until 1988.

---

12. Pond, *Beyond the Wall*, 45.
13. Von Weizsäcker, *From Weimar to the Wall*, 225.
14. Pond, *Beyond the Wall*, 35–42.
15. Goeckel, *Lutheran Church*, 263.
16. Ibid., 264.
17. Führer, *Und Wir Sind Dabei Gewesen*, 188.
18. Pond, *Beyond the Wall*, 52.
19. Ibid., 189.

This cultural mood of gloom during this increasingly chilling phase of the Cold War was the context in which the *Nikolaikirche* initiated a ministry of welcome to everyone, including many non-Christians, who wished to pray, preach or simply groan for peace. Führer's hope was to interrupt the gloom, send a clear signal of *no* to military solutions, and engage in the one public act still within the church's right—the freedom to pray for peace in church. In doing this, the church was adopting an independent line from the state, challenging the logic of armament escalation, whether from the GDR or from NATO. Many churches began to engage in a variety of creative responses to the militarism pervading the regime. As Führer noted, had Leipzig acted alone and uniquely, there never would have been a peaceful revolution.[20] Eventually Führer opened the church for daily prayer, not just Mondays. And people came. He made a signboard and attached it outside the entrance that read: "Nikolai church—open for all (*Nikolaikirche—ofen für alles*)."[21]

Swords to Ploughshares

The church's witness for peace in a time of massive military spending inspired the admiration and stirred the idealism of many young people. Largely due to the militarism that pervaded the generations both under the Nazis and earlier under the Kaiser, a strong aversion to the German trademark of a strong military had grown among the youth culture in Germany. Various mottos expressed the hopes for a future without the dominance of a militarist mindset hanging over the nation. One motto especially came to dominate the popular consciousness of the peace movement among young people: *Swords into Ploughshares*. Führer found it more than coincidental that a phrase from the Old Testament prophet Micah was now the most important logo of the growing peace movement. For him, its original context as prophecy was the secret behind its ongoing relevance.

> In the last days the mountain of the LORD's temple will be established as the highest of the mountains; it will be exalted above the hills, and peoples will stream to it. Many nations will come and say, "Come, let us go up to the mountain of the LORD, to the temple of the God of Jacob. He will teach us his ways, so that we may walk in his paths." The law will go out from Zion, the

20. Führer, *Und Wir Sind Dabei Gewesen*, 121. Cf. Swoboda, *Revolution of the Candles*, 40, 48, 65, where Swoboda independently describes a variety of events and pastors, including numerous Baptists, who departed from their traditional isolation from political events to take risks in Dresden and Halle as well as Berlin.

21. Führer, *Und Wir Sind Dabei Gewesen*, 118.

word of the LORD from Jerusalem. He will judge between many peoples and will settle disputes for strong nations far and wide. They will beat their swords into plowshares and their spears into pruning hooks. Nation will not take up sword against nation, nor will they train for war anymore. Everyone will sit under their own vine and under their own fig tree, and no one will make them afraid, for the LORD Almighty has spoken.[22]

The church staff at the *Nikolaikirche* mobilized its use by duplicating large numbers of clandestine felt patches, which students then sewed onto everything from schoolbags to jackets.

But something unexpected happened which ironically accelerated the movement. The government took great offense that a symbol was being popularized and distributed by the creativity and vision of a movement outside the official chain of command. They determined to come down hard, forbidding the symbol to be shown or worn in schools or any other public place. Orders went out for its removal from any public display. This reactionary decree became a source of escalating tension and frequently ridiculous police harassment whenever a young person chose to express even a small amount of nonconformity by wearing this sign. Führer himself was once stopped by police for having such a sticker on his briefcase. The police removed it and threatened him with arrest for "open disparagement of the state."[23]

Of course the whole situation was ironic. The GDR was officially supportive of military nonaggression and nonproliferation treaties. In fact, the

22. Micah 4:1–4.
23. Führer, *Und Wir Sind Dabei Gewesen*, 148.

source of the drawing on the patches was none other than the sculpture by the Russian artist Vuchettich, which the Soviet Union had given to the United Nations Headquarters in New York in 1959.

"Why go on about the Russians?" Führer chided the SED officials.[24] Adding to the absurdity, a picture of this symbol was included in a book given to every graduate of the state's youth confirmation program. Hence while the police tore off the patches from their jackets, they warmly bestowed a book, which included the same symbol in a state sponsored celebration ceremony.

24. Ibid., 146.

As it happened, the ongoing harassment only served to guarantee the symbol's incredible popularity with the youth. It also significantly bolstered the church's street credibility for its role in distribution, display and championing of its powerful symbolism.

The state's constant need for total control even over the peace movement was seen in other venues as well. One incident involved a march for peace in memory of the much-respected critic of the arms race, the assassinated Swedish prime minister Olof Palme. Führer described a cat-and-mouse game as the church youth maintained their own identity during the rally and march, instead of simply participating in an anti-NATO piece of propaganda.[25] Führer was convinced the furor over prohibiting independent symbols such as "Swords to Ploughshares" had the effect of embedding this emotionally charged biblical prophecy into the imagination of the entire population of the GDR, including the police. Like the peace prayers themselves, this evocative logo became another piece of the puzzle, which would eventually lead to something much greater than the sum of the parts.

Internal Struggles: Grassroots Groups, Emigration Seekers and Stasi Provocateurs

Every January, the GDR commemorated with a festival the martyred communists of a previous era, Rosa Luxemburg and Karl Liebknecht. But in 1988, a group of dissidents dared to reinterpret this event with their own banners. In particular they chose to reappropriate Luxemburg's famous lines, "Freedom is always and exclusively freedom for the one who thinks differently."[26] Mass arrests followed. The following week, the *Nikolaikirche* council prepared a weeklong prayer vigil on behalf of the arrested. The church council's consensus decision inspired the admiration of dissidents in the community and led directly to increased attendance at the Monday peace prayers. However, at the same time tensions were growing between the various dissenting groups. Among the many groups who had attached themselves to the church, the grassroots groups were the most deeply committed to changing socialism as a system of governance. They were the people in greatest sympathy with the call of Heino Falcke and others, to work for a better socialism. While the grassroots groups were much admired, the admiration tended to be at a distance, since their efforts earned them special attention from the secret state surveillance known as the Stasi.[27]

25. Ibid., 152–57.
26. Ibid., 158.
27. Ibid., 161.

Much larger was the group, which had given up on the GDR and simply wanted to leave as soon as possible. Both groups had attached to the church as a place of support but they did not coexist easily. During one *Friedens-gebet* a violent verbal exchange took place between these groups within the sanctuary, interrupting the prayers. The situation quickly deteriorated into a parliamentary debate rather than a prayer meeting. Convinced the Stasi provoked the conflict, Führer abruptly stood up and cancelled the service. This event occurred during a time the state was increasing pressure on the church to terminate the peace prayers on the grounds that they were misusing the church for political purposes. Meanwhile the mood of the country seemed to grow more hostile to the state, which only caused attendance at the peace prayers to dramatically increase. Führer had no doubt the Stasi were arranging provocative behaviors designed to create an atmosphere of irreparable conflict within the various groups. That Führer's suspicions were not unfounded is evidenced by a recent conservative estimate that 500,000 GDR citizens were paid agitators.[28] Provocations took many forms, including one service (not at the *Nikolaikirche*) in which the Lord's Prayer was mocked.[29] As the pastor, Führer took it upon himself to hold these divergent threads of the peace prayer tapestry together—and also to deal with the provocateurs. At the same time the state relentlessly increased the pressure at local and national levels to stop the peace prayers altogether.[30]

In many respects, people seeking to emigrate were the "least of these" in the GDR. They were considered traitors by the government and quitters by those committed to changing the country for the better. They were persecuted by their employers, demoted or even laid off. They had nowhere else to turn. Their one hope was to receive permission to leave the country—the very thing the wall was built to make impossible. For Führer, there was no doubt that a "church for others" could not abandon those at the bottom of status and worth in the country. Their inclusion was a witness to the reconciling gospel in a society organized around policies of strict boundaries (*Abgrenzung*) and ideological purity. But it was not easy to include them and grant them a voice in the prayers and planning, keep the grassroot groups on board, all while sifting through the Stasi provocateurs. The more the émigré seekers sensed church support, the more their attendance at the prayer services increased. The more attendance increased, the more desperate the state grew to halt the prayer services once and for all. The government considered them to be nothing more than a front for

---

28. Bytwerk, *Bending Spines*, 81.

29. Führer, *Und Wir Sind Dabei Gewesen*, 190, 194.

30. Ibid., 160, 163.

counterrevolutionary hostility to the state.[31] Meanwhile the émigré seekers' despair and depression made them quite vulnerable. In responding to their pastoral needs, Führer set up a special support group for all those waiting to emigrate. The church was their sole space of hope in a society in which they felt otherwise completely marginalized. Many times the honest prayers of sadness and lamentation they uttered stirred people deeply—that such things were daringly expressed both in community and before God.[32]

In addition to grassroots organizations and émigré seekers, Führer had one other group to contend with. This group in fact objected to the presence of both other groups. They were the circle of devout Christians, who began to grumble about the growing stream of non-Christians attending the Monday prayers. In pastoral conversations, Führer reminded them of Jesus' parable of the prodigal and the elder brother, and the Father's insistent welcome for both. One of the happier anecdotes Führer records is how this circle realized the shabbiness of its attitude and had a change of heart.[33]

Inevitably with the spike in Monday attendance the *Nikolaikirche* moved to the center of Stasi attention as a primary subversive lair of counterrevolution. When later, Führer accessed his own Stasi files, he not only read reports of how the Stasi deliberately sought to isolate him within the church and interfere with his leadership, he also discovered that twenty-eight Stasi agents were assigned to work on his case![34] He was labeled as someone unwilling to compromise.[35]

Throughout this entire time of growing conflict, there was one theme Führer never compromised but insisted on for any group which joined in the prayers as part of the church: nonviolence. He was certain that only by teaching and practicing quite faithfully this theme from the heart of the Sermon on the Mount, would any real transformation of the system be possible. For Führer, this nonviolence was centered on personal loyalty to Jesus himself.[36] This was the threshold for any real hope of change. Of course, this approach was not without its critics, but for Führer it was nonnegotiable because it came straight from Jesus and without it, the church would simply cease to be the church.

31. Ibid., 164.

32. Ibid., 168.

33. Ibid., 171.

34. From an interview with Führer reported in the film documentary *One Fine Day*, written and directed by Klaas Bense (2011).

35. Führer, *Und Wir Sind Dabei Gewesen*, 178–79.

36. Ibid., 182. Thus Bonhoeffer's instinct for the significance of Gandhi's strategy of nonviolence, as an adaptation of the Sermon on the Mount for the present day, was proved by Führer to be correct. Bonhoeffer, however, never found a way to implement it.

An Unexpected Ending

After years of weekly peace prayers, with the costly practice of welcoming and including diverse groups of non-Christians, and attending to the pastoral dilemmas thus aroused, the end came abruptly and unexpectedly. On May 7 a local election took place in which it was declared that 98 percent voted yes for the one-party list. This fraudulent result created a sensation because somehow independent observers had monitored the election and such results were clearly a farce. Nationwide protests (and arrests) quickly followed.[37]

Once again, the state responded by ratcheting up pressure on the peace prayers. But the numbers of participants only swelled. Along with each movement toward change and accompanying every fresh act of courage required, the participants were also accompanied by a single, constant emotion: fear. As Führer confessed, "Fear became my constant companion. Day and night. Always. I could only overcome it because always my faith was just a bit bigger than my fear."[38] Through it all, with support from his wife, Monika, the church council and a clear sense that his activity was for the "purposes of Jesus" he endured the continual provocations and threats.

Behind all the intimidation and warnings from the state was a fundamental allegation: the church was being misused for political purposes, indeed for the counterrevolutionary purpose of undermining the socialist order. How did Führer respond to this repeated accusation? Increasingly, he grew convinced that the church possessed a "limited political mandate." This had been the theme of a conference he attended as a synod representative in 1986.[39] From the perspective of our fifty-year study of the church in Germany, the origins of this awareness can be traced back to Barmen. Along the way we have also noted significant improvisations upon this theme, which included the solidarity in guilt declared at Stuttgart, Barth's advocacy of a third way between Cold War partisans, and the public opposition to German rearmament among many church leaders. To these we can add a crucial practice added by Führer: respect or submission to the state meant he would not hide anything about what he was seeking to accomplish. Nor would he try to embarrass the state in any way. That was why, when numbers began to swell in 1988, he declined all interviews with the Western press. When they grumbled, he replied, "What we have to say to the GDR we do not say by way of the Western press. We say it to their face."[40] The point was not to subvert and agitate indirectly,

---

37. Ibid., 184. See also Swoboda, *Revolution of the Candles*, 33.

38. Führer, *Und Wir Sind Dabei Gewesen*, 184–85. In his autobiography, Führer devotes a chapter to three different health crises he endured in his ministry (237ff.).

39. Ibid., 191.

40. Ibid., 193.

but to be always accessible and open to the authorities. If he believed criticism was required according to the church's political mandate, it was never for effect or to try to belittle the state. But as numbers grew, state provocations increased to the breaking point.

The combustible moment came when Pastor Friedrich Magirius, the superintendent of the Leipzig churches, and co-pastor with Führer of *Nikolaikirche*, decided to remove the local pastor Christoph Wonneberger from his role of coordinating the prayers, a responsibility Wonneberger had held since 1987. Wonneberger had granted some groups more program autonomy than Führer admits he himself was always comfortable with. Nevertheless, Magirius's intervention was highly contentious. At first, it placed a gloomy sense of disempowerment upon the various groups who now lost their highly valued sense of freedom under Wonneberger. While Führer anguished over their sense of hurt, he agreed with Magirius that the Monday prayers needed clearer structure to protect them from the intensifying state accusations which were now on the verge of shutting them down as counterrevolutionary politics hiding inside the church's protective space. Führer's response was to design a structure for the prayers and their planning, requesting compliance from the various grassroots groups. In order to address the heightened pressure and increased state provocation, the plan included a clear hierarchical structure under supervision by the church council.[41] Eventually, after a painful gap of several months, Führer was much relieved when full participation by all groups began afresh in March 1989. So it came to pass that only months before the turning point of October, the various grassroots groups and émigré seekers were again together under the roof of the church, joining in prayer and in the weekly reading of the Sermon on the Mount.

In Führer's mind, the crisis had been resolved through leaning once more on the theme of the church's political mandate as essential to its witness to the gospel, a mandate which had nothing to do with notions of freedom derived from any ideology. The structure and content of the peace prayers needed to clearly reflect the gospel, out of which the church was "open to all." But the church was never "open for everything" that might include strident speeches against the state or expressions of hopelessness or the advocacy of atheism. Führer had used the internal crisis as an opportunity to clarify the meaning of the *Friedensgebet* as prayers according to the gospel of Christ's reconciling death—the foundation of the peace prayers.[42]

41. Ibid., 195–98.
42. Ibid., 190, 196.

The Final GDR Birthday Party

Meanwhile, the GDR was preparing for an ostentatious fortieth birthday celebration on October 7, 1989. All the arrangements were accompanied with
a sense that the country must be kept under tight control. One sign of the
government's anxiety came in the form of a summons Führer received to the
civil court in August. There he was berated by the public prosecutor for being
"naïvely exploited by the Western security services and capitalist foreigners,
used to damage the society." In effect he was told, "You have been the rudder
of the peace prayers for a long time. Now we are asking you to bring this fuss
to an end."[43] As it happened, the Monday prayers were on summer break and
the plan was to resume the first Monday of September (Sept 4), which just
happened to be the first day of the annual Harvest Fair in Leipzig. The coincidental timing meant many Western journalists would (quite unusually) have
access to the entire city, a worrisome contingency of serious concern for the
city officials. Just days before the prayers, Führer and the church council were
strongly urged to wait a week until the fair was over. Since plans had already
been made, the council saw no reason to wait. With a remarkable display of
courage under pressure, the council refused to postpone.

On the evening the peace prayers recommenced, Magirius preached.
In attendance (thanks to the Harvest Fair) were various West German
television cameras. At one point a quick-witted student grabbed a sheet of
paper and stuck in front of the cameras the words: "For an open country
with free people." It only took ten or fifteen seconds before a troupe of Stasi
tore it down and threw the youth to the floor, all with the cameras running. After the service, over twelve hundred demonstrators gathered in the
church courtyard. It became the lead story in the evening news, viewed in
the West as well, giving extraordinary publicity throughout the country to
Leipzig and the *Nikolaikirche*.

The state's response to such unwanted publicity? The following Monday, September 11, the police aggressively arrested hundreds of those
seeking to walk in a demonstration following the prayer meeting. During
the entire next week there was a triple police chain around the church. To
those inside, Führer urged, "Don't let the non-violence be stuck here in the
church, take it out into the streets and squares. Don't jostle, don't push, so
nobody comes to harm. In no case, respond with violence, lest you become
exactly like those outside and leave the steps of Jesus."[44] As people left the
sanctuary that evening, they were brutally manhandled and arrested for

43. Ibid., 201.
44. Ibid., 204.

no cause. By arrangement, they shouted out their names to witnesses, who wrote them in the church windows for everyone to see. People put candles and flowers on the pavement in front of the windows, and walked past to light candles in solidarity and prayer for those arrested. Almost at once the windows became a kind of spontaneous place of pilgrimage for the city. The authorities telephoned Führer demanding he clear away the candles, flowers and lists of names. He tersely replied to the instructions: "Already more or less everything is prohibited us in this land. But sorrow and pain cannot still be forbidden. Clear these things away yourself."[45] The only response he heard was a click on the phone line. Watching the waves of brutal arrests moved Führer deeply. At the next prayer service, he wore his funeral suit as a sign of mourning. More brutal arrests and intimidation continued on the days from the 11th to the 18th and also on the 25th. Once again, those arrested had their names listed in the windows. Pilgrims kept returning to light candles and leave flowers. It created an atmosphere in the city that was impossible to describe.

At the September 25 prayer service, Pastor Wonneberger and a human rights group prepared a moving prayer service, in which Wonneberger uttered a sober warning should nonviolence be compromised in any way. "One thing is clear. The first injured policeman will lead inevitably to an escalation of violence that we at this point cannot even imagine."[46] Afterward some eight thousand people who had assembled in and around the church walked to the train station and sang, "We Shall Overcome."[47] It was too much for the government. On the 29th, Führer and Wonneberger were summoned to the public prosecutor. Accompanied by a church council representative, they received a final warning: "Unless you stop with these peace prayers, you will be arrested. We will tolerate no further provocation. You violate the law of the GDR. Your profession as pastors will give you no more protection."[48] The two pastors remained silent and departed. On October 2, the Leipzig prayers and demonstration swelled to over ten thousand and marched again along the city roads.[49]

Finally came Saturday, October 7, the fortieth anniversary celebration of the founding of the GDR. In Berlin, the celebrations included a one hundred thousand–strong torchlight parade reminiscent of old Nazi pageants, followed by a huge military display of tanks and missiles along Karl Marx

45. Ibid., 206.

46. Pfaff, *Extra-Voice Dynamics*, 103.

47. Führer, *Und Wir Sind Dabei Gewesen*, 207. Cf. Pond, *Beyond the Wall*, 93.

48. Führer, *Und Wir Sind Dabei Gewesen*, 207–8.

49. Pond, *Beyond the Wall*, 101.

Boulevard. Meanwhile more than five thousand peaceful demonstrators were severely beaten near the Gethsemane Church by three thousand security forces. Provocateurs instigated fights. The pattern was replicated all over the country.[50] That day in Leipzig, as people simply passed by the church, out of nowhere appeared the white helmets of the riot police. With tears of helplessness, Führer watched from the windows of his office as people were beaten and thrown into trucks. But he also noticed that people did not in any way hit back. He wondered if this pattern would happen in two days' time at the Monday prayers.[51]

As if there was not already enough to worry about, that day Führer read in the newspaper an article entitled, "Hostility to Government Tolerated No Longer." The article stated that all counterrevolutionary behavior must come to an end, if necessary with weapons in hand. The hardened sentiment of the article, penned by a military authority, surpassed his worst fear. That evening, the aggressive arrests continued without pause. Again and again, people were grabbed simply for walking past the church windows, dragged and hurled into trucks as over two hundred arrests were made.

The next morning was Sunday, October 6. After morning services, an unusually large number of medical doctors were present and requested a conversation with Führer. They reported many fractured collarbones from people in police custody. More disturbing, they reported that for the next day, Monday, blood reserves had been requested for possible gunshot wounds. This was a sign that the "Chinese solution" had been chosen by the authorities, to end the public acts of protest once and for all. "Chinese solution" was shorthand to describe the tragic events earlier that year on June 4 at Tiananmen Square in China, where hundreds and possibly thousands of people had been shot and killed.

Monday, October 9, 1989: "We were ready for everything, except for prayers and candles."

Despite the threats and warnings, Führer anticipated large numbers would risk attending the prayers on Monday. Thus he had arranged for the neighboring Thomas Church and the Reformed Church (whose service was being led by the Catholic Chaplain, Father Bernhard) to be open for a prayer service as well. All day long Führer's telephone rang without pause. Most calls came from worried people. "There will be shots tonight. You should cancel the prayers." Some were anonymous threats to burn down the church

---

50. Ibid., 107.

51. Führer, *Und Wir Sind Dabei Gewesen*, 209.

if they held another peace prayer. Führer arranged with the sexton that they would stay behind after the prayers that evening, keeping the doors open in case people needed to run back in.[52] More phone calls informed Führer that schools were closing early and workplaces had urged people to stay home that evening, as no one could guarantee anyone's safety. From a military source there was a message informing them that the SED leader, Erich Honecker, had given word-of-mouth instructions that Leipzig and the *Nikolaikirche* were to be stopped. The chief of security, Erich Mielke, had sent a telegram to leaders of all serving units, for offensive measures to be taken to prevent and resolve anticipated riots. The message was not subtle: after tonight, the alleged counterrevolution would be over. One piece of phoned information was especially helpful for Führer as he prepared: over a thousand SED party members had been deployed to go to the church at midday to participate in the prayers. "Arrive there early; that way there will be no room for others."[53]

When at 2 p.m. the sexton excitedly informed him the sanctuary was already nearly full, Führer was not surprised. Explaining to the sexton what had been reported over the phone, Führer went across to the church as the sexton shut off the galleries. In the friendly way of pastors, he greeted the Comrades (*die Genossen*), gave them a brief history of the church and its architecture. He reminded everyone the church was open for all, and then with humor, noted that since the prayers didn't start until 5 p.m. and since workers can only arrive by 4 p.m., he was going to close the galleries temporarily so a few Christians and workers could still fit! Many smiled against their will. "He understands. He knows who we are."[54] Signs were placed in the windows to inform people of the other nearby churches where prayers would also be held.

When the 5 p.m. start time arrived, the church was overflowing, but the service went smoothly. The hundreds of Comrades sat quite calmly in the nave. Though they had taken others' places, Führer was aware that they were exposed to the gospel that evening and its radical message. This was something he never took lightly whenever the Stasi were near; listening to the Sermon on the Mount could impact spies as well as students. Words like "love your enemy" rather than "down with the opponent" were not without effect in this charged atmosphere. Before the benediction, a statement was read out requesting everyone to act calmly with a promise to explore in dialogue together ways to improve the country. The same message was spoken

52. Ibid., 214.
53. Ibid., 215.
54. Ibid., 217.

at the other churches and also over the radio by the well-known director of the Leipzig orchestra, Kurt Masur.

Instead of Violence

As Bishop Hempel gave the benediction, he strongly urged everyone, including the many visiting Comrades, not to use violence, not to create provocation, not to respond to violence. As the doors opened and two thousand people went out of the church, Führer saw an unforgettable sight: outside ten thousand people had been waiting! All total in all the churches, more than seventy thousand people had come out to the prayers and the demonstrations. Given the threats and rumors sweeping the city, an astonishing number of people had turned out to risk their lives. Only gradually could the church empty as people squeezed into the surrounding crowds and made room for each other. Many carried candles. As Führer notes, when you carry a candle, you need both hands, one to keep it from blowing out. There is no hand available for a rock or a stick. The candle option is the nonviolent option.[55]

Of course, as always there was fear. It was as if on that evening in October the people of Leipzig went to the prayers and demonstration as to their funeral.[56] The evening was a war of nerves; at every corner of every street, the people were vulnerable to provocation by the Stasi, or an impulsive act by a zealous demonstrator to start something, and of course everywhere was the surrounding presence of multiple military units armed with live ammunition.[57] Each step was an act of courage. But there was also an emotion of hope as the train of people moved slowly though the inner city, from the church to the Opera House, around the ring road and on to the central train station. As they walked along together, the miracle happened all around them. "The Spirit of Jesus' non-violence gripped the masses with a peaceful power."[58] Demonstrators engaged the army, the troops, and all those in uniform in conversation. Around the Stasi headquarters, demonstrators laid a ring of candles around the entry steps. Others wore sashes that read, "No violence!" (*Keine Gewalt!*).[59]

That night East Germany was transformed by a peaceful revolution. Central Committee member Horst Sinderman was reported to have said in retrospect, "We had everything planned. We were ready for everything.

55. Ibid., 218.
56. Swoboda, *Revolution of the Candles*, 186.
57. Pond, *Beyond the Wall*, 114.
58. Führer, *Und Wir Sind Dabei Gewesen*, 218.
59. Ibid., 219.

Except for candles and prayers."[60] Even though Mielke had ordered the security to take offensive action to eliminate any *potential* for riot, the spirit of nonviolence had accompanied the people from the sanctuaries into the streets and proved itself there. "Outside was the proof!" as Führer had reminded people many times at the prayers. Meanwhile, crucial to the miracle that evening was a fundamental human ingredient: no one lost face. No one was humiliated. No group triumphed over another group. The nonviolence was a complex, collaborative web that joined together all the parties.

Leipzig's collective decision to reject violence is worth pondering. As Führer put it, here was a nation trained in the ways of violence over many decades, a people who had launched two world wars, who had perpetrated unspeakable violence against Jesus' own race. And in the midst of such a history, a peaceful revolution was birthed on German soil.[61] The next day, a Comrade who had stationed herself in the church phoned Führer to thank him. Her preconceived opinion about the church as a tool of the capitalists had shifted. She now grasped that the party had lied to her and had used her. This discovery now meant she must take a new look at other areas of life, including within her family. For Führer, this was evidence of God's humor, that he brought committed atheist-communists to the church in their hundreds so they could experience the peace prayers for themselves. It was not a strategy Führer would have ever arranged.[62]

Late in the evening, Führer and Magirius sat together and listened to the reports as they came in one after another of how not one event of violence had occurred—not at any corner, not at any street, not at any part of the entire evening's march. They also learned that from the tower of the Reformed Church, cameramen had secretly filmed the entire demonstration. It was smuggled out to West German media the next evening. The news broke out everywhere and thus without consultation or strategy, the peace prayers and peaceful demonstration in Leipzig was reported throughout Europe. Over the next weeks the demonstrations that followed lifted the GDR system off its hinges. In those days as Führer sought to grasp the proportion of what was occurring, he remembered an advent sermon Bonhoeffer had preached about Mary's *Magnificat*: "He has put down the proud, taken them from their thrones and lifted up the lowly." Here, said Bonhoeffer, is not the tender, gentle, dreamy Mary we see in pictures, but the most passionate, wildest, most revolutionary song that was ever sung.[63] He also

---

60. Ibid.

61. Ibid., 220.

62. Ibid.

63. Quoted by Führer, *Und Wir Sind Dabei Gewesen*, 223. For Bonhoeffer's complete

kept pondering the Apostle Paul's words, that in the weak, the power of God was made mighty (2 Cor 12:9). These ancient words now burned with actuality. On October 9, the city of Leipzig demonstrated that all chain reactions are not negative. After that night, there was to be no more violence. On the following Mondays, demonstrations would climb to over 200,000 people marching peacefully around the central ring road.

Events now unfolded rapidly as success followed success. On October 18, Honecker was forced by the SED Central Committee to resign, replaced by Egon Krenz.[64] On November 4 the largest mass demonstration in German history took place as half a million people assembled at Berlin's Alexanderplatz to condemn the regime. Then came the unexpected and dramatic moment of November 9, when through a series of bureaucratic blunders, the Berlin Wall itself was opened. People were permitted to come and go without permission and paperwork.[65] But the demon of fear didn't depart overnight from the people and system that was the GDR. Over the next days there were widespread rumors that reactionary forces among the secret police and the military might organize a political coup and a civil war would surely break out. Through it all, the church continued to be a strong, calming presence to ensure that demonstrations everywhere remained peaceful.[66] Just as importantly, the church played a crucial role in facilitating a peaceful transition to democracy following the collapse of the SED government. The credibility of church leaders meant that they were entrusted with a major role in the transition government from November 1989 until the first and final free election in the GDR of March 18, 1990. Even the local staffing and arrangement for the March election were largely due to the volunteer work of the churches.[67] In the end, the party urging rapid reunification won the majority, the Christian Democratic Union (CDU). On October 3, 1990, the union was official and the GDR was history.

Church and State: Concluding Thoughts on the Church's Political Mandate

German reunification had never been Führer's goal. In fact, he wished reunion had gone at a much more deliberate pace, for then perhaps the entire

---

sermon, see "Sermon on Luke 1:46–55, December 17, 1933," in Bonhoeffer, *London*, 342.

64. For many of the following details, see Pierard, "Church and the Revolution," 49.

65. Führer, *Und Wir Sind Dabei Gewesen*, 245. Pond, *Beyond the Wall*, 131.

66. Burgess, *East German Church*, 93.

67. Goeckel, "Evangelical-Lutheran Church," 3.

nation would have properly weighed the unique contribution the East had given to the new Germany, namely, a lived journey of nonviolence that changed a corrupt system. The failure to fully weigh the significance of this achievement was in his view, a "fatal mistake."[68]

If Führer had a "political" goal, it was simply a belief in the church's "limited political mandate": the church was there to "insert itself for people in difficulty."[69] In the GDR this seemed to include much of the population, who found themselves constantly coerced by an oppressive system. But as we have noted, in the People's State, the most reviled persons, "the least of these," were those seeking to emigrate. They were especially vulnerable and in need of help from "a church for others." At great cost, Führer had invested himself to ensure that the church would not abandon them. That the church actually became such a place—a church for émigré seekers, regime critics, SED members, Stasi, soldiers, Christians and non-Christians—that was the real miracle of those days. "The Church united them all under the outstretched arms of the crucified and risen Jesus Christ."[70] All those who experienced this enacted parable of the church's political responsibility would not see the church ever again in quite the same way.

68. Führer, *Und Wir Sind Dabei Gewesen*, 249–50.

69. Ibid., 224.

70. Ibid., 225.

Epilogue
Unlearned Lessons, Hopeful Anticipations

Even amongst men who would hardly claim to be numbered with original thinkers, the policy of referring back to the primary Christian truths may precipitate new things and prove to be a starting-point of historical change.

—HERBERT BUTTERFIELD[1]

The fact is that none of us predicted that unification of the two states would come about in the way that it did. . . . With their non-violent acts, the revolutionaries of 1989 have given all Germans a new consciousness of freedom. This has not wiped out the past. But it has added a decisive chapter to our history.

—RICHARD VON WEIZSÄCKER,
PRESIDENT OF THE FEDERAL REPUBLIC OF GERMANY,
1984–1994[2]

When the great hope is present,
small hopes must always arise for the immediate future.

—KARL BARTH[3]

---

1. Butterfield, *Christianity, Diplomacy and War*, 3.
2. Weizsäcker, "Facing the Past," 75–76.
3. Barth, *CD*, IV/1, 121 (rev. ed.), quoted in Hunsinger, *Karl Barth*, 223.

WE HAVE EXPLORED THE neglected theological and historical backstory to the church's role in giving birth to Germany's peaceful reunification. In retrospect, are there lessons still waiting to be learned a quarter century later?

Almost immediately, two lessons were quickly grasped. John De Gruchy, the South African theologian, had been for many years actively involved in the movement against apartheid. As he watched the breaking news on television he recalls, "I knew that meant the beginning of the end of apartheid."[4] With the center of communism collapsing, it would be impossible for the South African government to justify itself any longer as the bastion against communist expansion in Africa.

Second, its impact was seen in Moscow in the street resistance that followed the attempt to overthrow President Gorbachev. Numbers similar to the Leipzig march of October 9 accompanied Boris Yeltsin as he climbed upon a tank outside the House of Parliament and withstood a military putsch by Soviet hard-liners. Astonishingly, only two lives were lost as the government that ruled since Lenin was swept from power. Two years previously, these Russian citizens had witnessed the collapse of the GDR. "Leipzig's demonstrators had shown that when the small minority of those with civil courage reaches a certain mass and intersects with demoralization in the power hierarchy—change is possible."[5]

Long-term lessons from Germany's story are more contested, however. A common error of historical logic is to see events like the nonviolent reunification of Germany as in retrospect inevitable. But anyone who lived through these times remembers well enough that the world watched in astonishment that such a peaceful yet transformative event was taking place. No one anticipated these changes, let alone predicted them. Moreover, the central role of the church largely went unnoticed. In the United States, the official separation of church and state tends to shroud the role of the church in public life and inflate the achievements of secular agencies and ideals. That the media missed this story was less the result of a conspiracy of wealthy media moguls than the consequence of secular plausibility structures that informally censor our news. But the results show the limits of interpreting history through the lens of a narrow secularism. The fact is that without the church there would have been no actual community seeking to live out of Jesus' mission that God's will be done on earth as in heaven. There would have been no higher claim upon dissenters to refrain from revenge; no solution to Germany's totalitarian dilemma beyond another round of violence.

4. Quoted from a speech De Gruchy made in Leipzig several years later, in Brown, "Berlin Wall."

5. Pond, *Beyond the Wall*, 237.

There would have been only a dysfunctional, corrupt ideological regime with its tentacles of control brutally silencing pockets of angry resistance.

There is probably a more primary reason for the relative silence about the church's role. Given the vast investment in military operations during the Cold War, it must have been very difficult to grasp that the breakthrough to freedom occurred through peaceful means rather than the ways in which a long series of administrations in Washington devoutly invested the nation's treasure. As a result, the courage of a statistically small number of pastors, Christian believers and seekers of justice to change a corrupt governmental system has yet to be fully comprehended. One purpose of this study has been to present this story from the perspective of that numerically small but spiritually powerful assembly who were at the center of these unexpected events.

Forgiveness and Foreign Policy

Perhaps the primary Christian truth that enabled Germany to experience redemptive possibilities was that the church's witness helped birth forgiveness within public life. Immediately after World War II Barth had insisted that a paramount responsibility of the Allies was to pursue justice *with* mercy. Without mercy, the future would be just another spiral of victor's justice, more commonly known as revenge. Forgiveness was the implicit message behind the Marshall Plan's decision to reinvest instead of permanently punish a defeated enemy.

By contrast, the eponymous plan of President Roosevelt's secretary of the treasury, Henry Morganthau Jr., claimed the true lesson of World War I was the Versailles Treaty's insufficient punishment of Germany (see ch. 5). However by the summer of 1947, newly appointed Secretary of State Marshall, was convinced of a different lesson, not one pointing to the need for collective punishment and permanent degradation of a fallen nation but the need for collective reinvestment in both friends and adversaries in order to rebuild Europe. What might have happened to Germany and its neighbors had the Morganthau Plan become permanent policy makes for grim speculation. How a defeated state in the heart of Europe might have bled into and destabilized its neighbors has resonances with the current malaise in Iraq. On a smaller scale, the dismal consequences of the policies of collective punishment, economic degradation and military occupation have been on display for decades in Israel's policy toward Palestine.

Of course a committed secularist may without contradiction prefer to diminish the role of the church in the GDR to that of a benign landlord providing rent-free facilities for dissenting groups. But from the perspective of the pastors and the church struggle we have studied over a fifty-year span of time, a secular frame lacks sufficient explanatory power. What we have seen is that, in the face of unprecedented military expenditures on both sides, the Cold War in Germany was resolved through the nonviolent presence and pressure of those, who, inspired by Bonhoeffer's vision of a church for others, partnered with an unlikely and awkward variety of grassroot groups, and together rendered the communist government inoperable. Even though the combined budgets of all the churches and all the grassroots movements barely registered as a figure on a spreadsheet, in the end their modest numbers were decisive in a way that turned Stalin's old jibe at the pope ("How many divisions does the pope have?") on its head. Most commentators in the West have yet to give proper credit to the ordinary citizens of the GDR who, without a NATO-style Western military intervention or a fifth-column style secret operation, ended a dictatorship without firing a shot or breaking a window. Indeed, the failure to grasp the meaning of this accomplishment may be the primary reason why American foreign policy has attenuated into an endless series of military interventions and defense budget expansions. As the saying goes, when the only tool in your toolbox is a hammer, every problem looks like a nail.

Retrospective on the Cold War

The contribution of the church suggests a reassessment of the Cold War itself is overdue. Unfortunately the West's response to German reunification and the collapse of the Soviet Union, has mostly been self-congratulation. The political scientist Francis Fukuyama famously proclaimed that civilization had reached the "end of history" as liberal democracies and free market capitalism had shown themselves to be the final form of human government.[6] Such triumphalist assessments soon translated into support for President George W. Bush's preemptive invasion of Iraq to mop up the victory of democracy and free markets, and steer history's triumphant dynamics into the heart of the Middle East. However, the now decade-long dysfunctional state of affairs in Iraq and the spread of anarchy in neighboring Syria and Libya suggests that history has more turns and twists than the architects and apologists of the Iraq war imagined. However, Butterfield's proposal offers an alternative to Cold War partisanship: when the church creatively implements "primary Christian truths," history can still become the theater of redemptive possibilities.

6. Fukuyama, *End of History*.

Hidden Costs of the Cold War

Earlier, I suggested the Cold War was a proxy war for a conflict that runs through every human heart, every business owner, every government employee, whether a custodian or a president. In moments of grave conflict, the methods and motives of the "winners" may contain sufficient errors that victory becomes pyrrhic, sowing tares that, unchecked, spoil the harvest. In this light, President Eisenhower's 1961 farewell address merits fresh reading. Eisenhower chose a moment of American military and economic dominance to depart from office with a warning.

> Until the latest of our world conflicts, the United States had no armaments industry. American makers of plowshares could, with time and as required, make swords as well. But now we can no longer risk emergency improvisation of national defense; we have been compelled to create a permanent armaments industry of vast proportions. Added to this, three and a half million men and women are directly engaged in the defense establishment. We annually spend on military security more than the net income of all United States corporations. This conjunction of an immense military establishment and a large arms industry is new in the American experience. The total influence—economic, political, even spiritual—is felt in every city, every Statehouse, every office of the Federal government. We recognize the imperative need for this development. Yet we must not fail to comprehend its grave implications. . . . In the councils of government, we must guard against the acquisition of unwarranted influence, whether sought or unsought, by the military-industrial complex. The potential for the disastrous rise of misplaced power exists and will persist. We must never let the weight of this combination endanger our liberties or democratic processes. We should take nothing for granted.[7]

Clearly something about the way America was waging the Cold War had unsettled the man whose 1953 "cross of iron" speech had set a high standard for postwar realism about the tragic consequences of defining national security in simplistic terms of military build-up.[8] In retrospect,

---

7. Eisenhower, "Farewell Address," January 17, 1961.

8. "Every gun that is made, every warship launched, every rocket fired signifies, in the final sense, a theft from those who hunger and are not fed, those who are cold and are not clothed. This world in arms is not spending money alone. It is spending the sweat of its laborers, the genius of its scientists, the hopes of its children. The cost of one modern heavy bomber is this: a modern brick school in more than 30 cities. It is two electric power plants, each serving a town of 60,000 population. It is two fine, fully equipped hospitals.

the outer danger of communism mirrored an inner threat that America might become a society in which a militarized foreign policy aligned to an ever-expanding national security network would become its defining feature. Though the specific communist threat seceded, history has colluded in providing a new global enemy suitable for playing the role of evil adversary in what has become a permanent drama for American foreign policy.

Beyond the repetition of engaging with a (new) evil empire, there is also a concrete connection linking yesterday's Cold War to today's war for the Middle East. At the time of this writing, the insurgent forces America fights in Afghanistan use weapons supplied by the United States during the 1980s when President Reagan sent billions of dollars in military aid to the Pakistan mujahidin to defeat the Soviet Union.[9] Moreover, throughout the 1970s and 1980s, America's Middle East policy mirrored its Cold War strategy of heavy investment in military solutions. Repeatedly it preferred to support the religious right in the local Middle East societies over the secular left who shared any sympathy with the Soviets. As left-wing groups were marginalized or imprisoned by United States–supported military governments, oil money from the conservative Saudi regime busily spread the Wahabi version of Islam. The close link between these missions and what is known today as Isil or Isis is not a secret.[10] Thus in interwoven ways, today's Middle East wars are the fruit of a policy which has yet to learn the lessons of the Cold War's ending, at least, those lessons taught by the trail of pastors we have studied.

We are left then with a more complicated scenario than the popular version of a virtuous West as the victor in the Cold War. In this context, we should recall the nuclear-laden anxiety of "mutually assured destruction" in which the Leipzig events transpired. In retrospect, the relentless Cold War exhortations for "self-defense, the stronger the better" were not benign policies. The same toxins which affect our personal lives when we have an argument with a friend or colleague can, if unchecked, pressure nations into aggressive overreactions infected with pride. If one is not careful, mutual exaggerations and inflated rhetoric can demolish a once-valued relationship. By reacting self-righteously to a conflict, we face the danger that by endlessly escalating our defenses we become the mirror image of the enemy

---

It is some 50 miles of concrete highway. We pay for a single fighter with a half million bushels of wheat. We pay for a single destroyer with new homes that could have housed more than 8,000 people. This, I repeat, is the best way of life to be found on the road the world has been taking. This is not a way of life at all, in any true sense. Under the cloud of threatening war, it is humanity hanging from a cross of iron." Eisenhower, "Cross of Iron," April 16, 1953.

9. Goodman, *National Insecurity*, 385–86.

10. Cf. Bacevitch, *Limits of Power*, 46. Also cf. Lalami, "To Defeat Isis."

we so zealously resist. In the Christian tradition, the seriousness of this predicament has been central in its ethical teaching. It is why Jesus insisted we first take the log out of our own eye before we remove the speck from our enemy's. It is why enemy forgiveness lies at the heart of Christ's message and mission to the world, epitomized by the cross.

A Theodicy of Church-State Relations

To mention the cross in the context of a retrospective on the Cold War is also to remove the Cold War from the presumption of its central role as the prelude to the "end of history." A Christian telling of history would transfer the Cold War from such a pedestal and see it rather as a proxy war for the conflict between good and evil that runs through each person and through every government in every passing era. As Barth would remind us, the turning point in history was not the dawn of the Enlightenment, nor the victory of the Allies over Germany, nor the triumph of American democracy and capitalism over totalitarian communism, but rather the triumph of Jesus over his enemies on the cross.

Had we asked a theologian of the early church to set the scene for this central event; we might ask how dangerous was the world at that moment and how malevolent was the situation into which Jesus entered? The church's reply was revolutionary within its ancient setting. "How bad are things? God has been crucified. That's how bad." The passing of time should not remove the scandal implicit in the origins of the gospel. Alone among the major religions Christianity "has as its central event the suffering and degradation of its god."[11]

Unfortunately familiarity with the crucifixion narrative can keep us from noticing the revolutionary social consequences of its depiction of God. The claim of Christianity is that the entire project of creation was at such risk that the Author intervened personally, yet did so, not by raw power but in the vulnerability of love, as befitting God's true nature. The crucifixion of Jesus is what happened in our world when humanity was confronted with the head-on intervention of truth, goodness and beauty into our desperate situation. This is why of all people, Christians should be the least sentimental about the consequences of even modest efforts to make an impact for good in such a world. Even in small ways (and they are usually embarrassingly small), when Christ-followers risk imitating Jesus' way of life, the costs are cruciform. Yet for believers, death is not the final destination; only a penultimate station on the road to freedom (Bonhoeffer). It is for this very

11. Gascoigne, *Christianity*, 7.

reason that the cross cannot be avoided if we are to escape a superficial interpretation of history. Just as Christians should not be surprised that humanity's existential warfare between good and evil continually erupts into external wars (of which the Cold War was not the first and won't be the last), we can still be hopeful that redemptive possibilities will continue to confront us—though not without cost.

Of course Christians are not alone in addressing the crisis of what happens when genuine goodness encounters a fallen world. Plato has already taught us that true goodness puts our world on trial. Should true goodness visit our world, how would it fare? From his story about Socrates and Athens, the answer is clear: goodness was murdered. Similarities with the story of Jesus are not by chance; they are there, according to C. S. Lewis, because goodness is what it is, and because the fallen world is what it is.[12]

Here is where Christian theodicy casts a probing light on the Cold War. Writing in 1953, the British historian Herbert Butterfield declared the greatest menace to the world of his day was the conflict "between giant organized systems of self-righteousness—each system only too delighted to find that the other is wicked—each only too glad that their sins give it the pretext for still deeper hatred and animosity."[13] Whether ancient or modern, wars of righteousness are especially prone to justify hatred, torture and the refusal to compromise. These are the same qualities that constitute the deadliest features of today's war for the greater Middle East. In wars of righteousness, each side considers the other an evil empire. Blind to the log of evil in their own system, adversaries see with precision the corrupting splinter in the system of the rival. The result? We live in the illusion we are laden with virtue and our opponents are mostly if not utterly evil. Into this cycle of mutual hatred the church's unwelcome witness is to risk the difficult act of loving the enemy, the sole practice that interrupts the spiral of revenge and the spirit of self-righteousness. If Barth was correct, and the primary way the church serves the state lies in modeling its own life according to the coming kingdom, then the church's post-World War II role in creating peace through reconciliation, instead of peace through vengeance and punishment, was a life-giving legacy offered to both sides.[14] The Stuttgart Declaration embodied this lesson. It was the church's initiative at Stuttgart which opened a space for the Allies to invest in the Marshall Plan rather than the Morganthau.

12. Lewis, *Reflections on the Psalms*, 88.

13. Butterfield, *Christianity, Diplomacy and War*, 43, 26.

14. Barth, "Christian Community and Civil Community," in *Community, State and Church*, 186.

In this light we must lament the self-inflicted toxins disseminated by the Cold War's use of exaggerated fears and the dehumanization of its opponents. This approach reached its zenith in the anti-philosophy known as anti-communism. However, President von Weizsäcker's caution that Germans tended to forget or minimize the crimes of the Nazi past contains an implicit warning for those in the West whose agenda is driven by a self-righteousness that refuses to temper justice with mercy. "Anyone who closes his eyes to the past is blind to the present. Whoever refuses to remember this historical inhumanity is prone to new risks of infection."[15]

Alternatives to Self-Righteousness

Is it possible that a successful politician at the center of a great political struggle can awaken to the danger of self-righteousness, of how prone we are to project our own evil onto the enemy? Can there come a moment in the history of a great clash, where an awareness dawns that the war against the other is to a significant degree an interior crisis projected outward? Arguably Gorbachev was such a politician, one who did not simply double down on attacking the traditional capitalist enemy but instead asked awkward questions about Soviet society. We should not be surprised that such a leader found his fiercest resistance at home. To the extent Gorbachev approximated a Socratic presence within the Soviet system, the challenges he raised provoked an attempted coup by hardliners, leading to his loss of power, not only for himself but later for the very system whose self-scrutiny he represented and which was rejected.[16]

Suppose we apply the same logic to the other great superpower of the era, the United States? Suppose a Cold War politician began to sense that the ideology of anti-communism was doing more damage to Western society than communism itself could ever do? What if someone at the center of the military-industrial-congressional system at the height of the Cold War underwent a change of heart? Such a person might approximate a Socratic presence within that system.

This is the supposal recently raised by the Catholic theologian James Douglass, under the influence of his late friend, the Trappist monk and

15. Weizsäcker, lecture of May 8, 1985, "Forty Years After the War," 20, in the appendix to *From Weimar to the Wall*, 381–96.

16. In a recent interview, Gorbachev has been forthright about his decision to avoid a civil war: "A split in society and a struggle in a country like ours, overflowing with weapons, including nuclear ones, could have left so many people dead and caused such destruction. I could not let that happen just to cling on to power. Stepping down was my victory." Gorbachev, "Man Who Lost an Empire," December 13, 2016.

author Thomas Merton. Writing shortly after John F. Kennedy's election, Merton confided to a friend that he was not very impressed with the new president's character: a "*Time* and *Life Magazine* sort of fellow, a cold warrior type." But Merton prophesied, were Kennedy to become a good man or make a turn toward depth, self-forgetfulness and compassion, he would be marked for assassination.[17] The evidence that Kennedy had a change of heart can be observed in his behind-the-scenes negotiations with Krushchev, his June commencement speech at American University and his plans to withdraw from Vietnam following his reelection.[18] Any further examination of Douglass's provocative book goes beyond the scope of this study. However, what is neither controversial nor speculative is the context of Kennedy's violent removal from office: the Cold War.

Indeed, it is a grim fact of Cold War history that the list of countries impacted by violent regime change is disturbingly lengthy. Investigative journalists have gradually uncovered the extent to which anti-communism became the rationale for American security agencies to engage in covert operations, including assassinations, against a series of governments, including democratically elected ones. A conservative list includes Iran (1948, 1953), Cuba (1961), Iraq (1963), Brazil (1964), Ghana (1966), Argentina (1966, 1976), Peru (1968, 1975), Bolivia (1971), Chile (1973), Uruguay (1973), and Ecuador (1976).[19] In addition, we should remember that during this period, South Africa was ruled by the fiercely anti-communist National Party, which in its efforts to defend itself from communism received its strongest backing from the United States right through to the Reagan presidency—despite the fact that it racially disenfranchised 90 percent of its population. All this reveals both the pervasiveness and the intensity of Western (and American-led) anti-communist activism. Barth was not guilty of hyperbole when he said a cloud of fear hung over the West. Allied to self-righteousness and hatred of communism, it fueled a series of aggressive engagements which included assassinations, coups d'état, and the violent suppression of dissent. For this inventory of behaviors American public institutions have yet to take responsibility. Such a list and our corporate shrug of the shoulders about accountability painfully remind us that the line between good and evil runs through every human society, not simply between East and West. One result

17. Quoted from Merton's letter to W. H. Ferry, in Douglass, *JFK*, 11.

18. Kennedy's remarkable behind-the-scenes exchanges with Kruschev have been described by Norman Cousins, who served as a courier. Cf. Cousins, *Improbable Triumvirate*. Kennedy's intention to withdraw from Vietnam has been documented both by his secretary of defense, Robert McNamera, and also by his friend and speech-writer, Theodore Sorenson. Cf. McNamera's *In Retrospect* and Sorensen's *Kennedy*.

19. Chung et al., *Liberating Lutheran Theology*, 21.

of our ongoing avoidance of responsibility is that public confidence in the integrity of our political leaders and institutions has suffered severe self-inflicted damage. A democracy in which the basic systems of governance engage in large-scale deceit, including covert operations against other elected governments, in critical ways ceases to function as a government of the people, but only of certain powerful and somewhat hidden elites. The list of nations impacted by such behaviors, including possibly our own, suggests that America's decision to interpret itself as the military and moral victors of the Cold War, has been at a cost to democratic institutions and a humane society much greater than the public consensus has yet to acknowledge. In retrospect, the West is still waiting for the kind of leadership which the Stuttgart Declaration, the bold sermons of Niemöller and the witness of Barth, Bonhoeffer and their students prophetically offered Germany. Instead, our repeated military initiatives are unwelcome evidence that we are immersed in a fresh surge of national self-righteousness. Of course our exertions are encircled by the rhetoric of spreading (or defending) freedom, democracy, justice and peace. But despite the progressive rhetoric, the large profits involved combined with the military methods are evidence of a nation infected with imperial ambitions.[20]

A New Cold War?

Recently, with the events surrounding the Ukraine, fears have grown that American/Russian relations have crossed the threshold into a new Cold War. In his old age, Mikhail Gorbachev has issued a series of warnings that unless these two nations recover the will and the courage to work, plan and negotiate with mutual respect, it is quite possible there could be a tragic return to the old fears and mistrust that formerly characterized relations.[21] Russian scholar Stephen Cohen is more pessimistic than Gorbachev. For Cohen, the proof that the Cold War ended was the fact that Russia granted Germany permission to reunite and join NATO. However, despite Western promises, a series of NATO expansions under Presidents Clinton, Bush and Obama have created a fundamental loss of trust in America's non-aggressive intentions. Amid NATO's expansions, a further sign of the erosion of trust came with President George W. Bush's decision to unilaterally withdraw from the 1972 Anti-Ballistic Missile Treaty, an agreement upon which Russia had based its security since the days of Brezhnev and Nixon. In 2008 a proxy war between Russia

---

20. Wright, *God in Public*, 5, 60.

21. Gorbachev, "I Am Truly and Deeply Concerned" (interview), January 2015.

and the United States occurred in Georgia.[22] Today's Ukrainian conflict offers further evidence that a new Cold War is upon us. That twenty-five years after the end of communism, after President Reagan's declaration in January 1989, "The Cold War is over," we seem caught up in a new Cold War reveals the vulnerability at the heart of all international political achievements, especially when the personal egotism of political leaders is inflamed by a national egotism tutored by a media that promote a national self-righteousness instead of empathy and mutual respect.

Unlearned Lessons for the Church?

Are there unlearned lessons for the church in America as well as the state? The more we come to terms with our mistaken zealotry during the Cold War, the more we will begin to oppose a simplistic advocacy for what has become a perpetual war for American hegemony in the Middle East. What if various church councils and leaders offered public acknowledgments, that is, confessions, about our Cold War past which echo the candor of the Stuttgart Declaration? In doing so, the church would be bearing witness that it serves One Master only, not a two-headed church-and-state divinity. An encouraging foreshadowing of this worth remembering is the "change of heart" interview given by evangelist Billy Graham in 1979. In the wake of many conversations with Christian leaders around the world, Graham spoke out candidly about rejecting the necessity of the nuclear arms race. Even further, he acknowledged his own Cold War mistake:

> There have been times in the past when I have, I suppose, con-
> fused the kingdom of God with the American way of life. . . .
> But the kingdom of God is not the same as America, and our
> nation is subject to the judgment of God just as much as any
> other nation.[23]

Graham's change of heart is a harbinger that the church in American might still helpfully confess that with our endorsement much evil was performed in fighting the Cold War; that our chosen weapons were so mingled with hate and fear they cast a long shadow of self-righteousness over our conflicts up to the present, including the embarrassing revelations of American violations of the Geneva Convention against torture in Iraq.

22. Cf. Cohen, *Soviet Fates and Lost Alternatives*, 170.

23. Quoted in "Change of Heart," 2. Cf. also Gibbs and Duffy, *Preacher and the Presidents*, 259. Gibbs and Duffy detail the alarm in the Reagan White House when in 1982 Graham chose to attend a Peace Conference organized by the Russian Orthodox Church in Moscow.

Notwithstanding personal confessions like Graham's, the church in the West has never called out the ways our governments and elected officials exaggerated threats, incited fears, and spoke lies in order to manipulate public support for Cold War policies. Perhaps at this late date the opportunity no longer exists for the church to acknowledge colluding with such tactics in the name of preserving Western society. But perhaps it is not too late for the church to reframe the ending of the Cold War—not as a victory for democracy and capitalism, but as an open invitation to repentantly take responsibility for the bilateral abuses of power and incitements to fear and hate which diminished mutual respect and the willingness to honestly negotiate differences with our adversaries. Without such public confession by the church, the current Washington establishment may remain deaf to the lessons of Leipzig.

Unlearned Lessons for a Reunited Germany?

As for Germany itself, with his typical candor Führer identified two lamentable consequences of German reunification. In his first visit to West Berlin after the wall came down, he encountered a form of materialism that was clearly far more seductive than the atheistic version formerly available in the Eastern zone. As the West's consumer-style materialism poured into the East, people became pathologically dependent on the newly erected twin secular temples: the banks and the department stores. As a firsthand observer, Führer saw how people in the West commonly used their freedom: they became debtors to their banks and credit cards.[24]

The other distortion Führer observed was the maldistribution of wealth. How ironic, he noted, that when the banks suffered devastating losses in 2008, billion-dollar packages rescued them through collective support from investors and taxpayers. But when there were profits the sharing was suspended. Führer's warning to Western capitalism is that its current predatory form is failing to provide a future legacy any better than Nazism or Soviet-style socialism.[25] The West's idolatry of the free market means that today the church limps between two opinions; serving the gospel on Sunday and the gods of the market for the rest of the week. This has compromised the church's witness, exchanging its prophetic role for that of bank chaplain. Will the church remind those who idealize free market economics that no system has sainthood, that it too must be humanized for the purposes of Jesus? Who outside the church will dare to stand up to this challenge and in-

24. Führer, *Und Wir Sind Dabei Gewesen*, 247.
25. Ibid., 253.

tervene? "You are the salt," said Jesus. "You, who else?"[26] A similar message came a year prior to the 2008 crash from Heino Falcke, when he warned that the church was more vulnerable to seduction by the "friendly embrace" of capitalism than it had ever been by socialism. "It was then a question of making socialism more human, now it's a question of making capitalism more human." But Falcke cautioned that such a transformation was "not possible within the neo-liberal principles that are in force today."[27] In the few years since Führer's autobiography was published, the polarization of wealth distribution has only increased. However, Führer lived long enough to read the 2013 apostolic exhortation *Evangelii Gaudium* of Pope Francis, in which the pope added his weighty pastoral office and communication gifts to address the same issue.

> How can it be that it is not a news item when an elderly home-less person dies of exposure, but it is news when the stock mar-ket loses two points? . . . In this context some people continue to defend trickle-down theories which assume that economic growth, encouraged by a free market, will inevitably succeed in bringing about greater justice and inclusiveness in the world. This opinion, which has never been confirmed by the facts, ex-presses a crude and naive trust in the goodness of those wielding economic power and in the sacralized workings of the prevailing economic system. Meanwhile, the excluded are still waiting.[28]

A Church for Others—Hopeful Anticipations

The observant reader has noticed that this study does not end on a note of triumph. Nevertheless, amid the complexities and unresolved tensions, there is much in this story that gives pause to cynics and encouragement to believers. For in the story of the church in Germany and its confrontations with totalitarian governments, we are witnesses to an immense and unex-pected achievement. For a brief moment Bonhoeffer's vision of a "church for others" became a reality. When Christian Führer opened himself to Jesus' spirit of forgiveness he was able meet Stasi and the Comrades in a spirit of mercy not vengeance. The willingness to forgive the adversary was ev-erywhere implicit in the turn toward nonviolence rather than the spiral of violence on the streets of Leipzig. Had the people been tutored to insist on

26. Ibid. (my translation).

27. Falcke, "German Protestant Warns Churches."

28. Pope Francis, *Evangelii Gaudium*, ch. 2, paragraphs 53, 54.

paybacks, the reactivity of the soldiers and police could have easily led to carnage on a grotesque scale. Miraculously, in a nation addicted to violence, a peaceful revolution was waged and won.

However, Führer later queried: in the church's rush to unify with the church in the West, had it ever really opened itself to Bonhoeffer's insight?[29] In pondering this space somewhere between an astonishing fulfillment and a missed opportunity, it is worth recalling Führer's personal response to the Stasi, particularly to the hundreds who strategically filled up the *Nikolai-kirche* on the afternoon of October 9. Theologically speaking, to be indwelt by the spirit of Jesus, confounds the natural distinction between one's adversaries and one's friends. In a limited but truth-bearing way, it reflects the forgiveness of the cross by which God turned enemies into friends. Whenever the church lives out of this reconciling event, it creates a sense of wonder, almost bewilderment, especially when it includes the enemy—the other in his and her most distressing guise.

The theme of reconciliation with the enemy has continued to be an acute issue given the extent to which the church in the GDR had been a complicit society of informers and Stasi agents. It bore a certain analogy to the German Christian subversion of the church during the Nazi period. The church in the Eastern sector suffered real embarrassment and a loss of moral authority when the Stasi files were opened and the spy lists included the names of pastors and bishops for everyone to see.[30] But if we remember the "solidarity of guilt" confessed at Stuttgart, we will not be overly distressed. Nevertheless the church should never minimize its complicity, for to do so would be akin to the avoidance of responsibility decried by Niemöller. As we have noted (ch. 5), Niemöller's challenge to take personal responsibility helped to embolden the better angels of the later student movement in West Germany to actively participate in democracy, to be willing to go, as student leader Rudi Dutschki put it, on a long, reforming march into institutions in contrast to many of the older generation who were content simply to repress past complicity, which only led to a loss of confidence in tarnished Western institutions.[31]

A final statistic exposes how vulnerable was the church's political witness before the state. According to Steven Pfaff, the number of local pastors in Leipzig who provided any shelter or assistance to political groups of any kind was about 10 percent—the same percentage as those who served as informants for the Stasi.[32] In other words, pastors like Christian Führer, as

29. Führer, *Und Wir Sind Dabei Gewesen*, 264.

30. Conway examines the details of this sad legacy in "Coming to Terms," 383.

31. Burgess, *East German Church*, 118.

32. Pfaff, *Exit-Voice Dynamics*, 87.

with Bonhoffer, Niemöller and Barth before him, were never numerically ascendant. Yet in the years leading to 1989, they were enough to make the difference.

Statistics also reveal that reunification did not bring about any visible church revival in Germany, not even a bump in church affiliation. In fact, the member rolls declined. Legally speaking, the church was given new privileges, including a raise in clergy salaries to match Western German levels as the new revenue stream of the West German church tax became the law of the land.[33] However, when the church updated its rolls, many departed in order to avoid paying the tax. No more than 10 to 20 percent of the population remain formally affiliated. In the West meanwhile, numbers stayed similar despite higher rates of affiliation.[34] Thus the new legal and financial privileges did not lead to any obvious missional advances. Most of the fresh revenue went into expensive and long overdue church building repairs or the upgrading of clergy salaries. The latter benefit in particular came with a double edge, as it served not only to alienate the clergy from their economically disadvantaged parishoners, but led to shrinking the number of clergy in many areas, since they now commanded West German levels of salary which declining roll numbers could not afford! When Superintendent Magirius retired in 1994, he was not replaced even though Führer's workload had increased significantly due to the success of the Peaceful Revolution. The stress which resulted led to a period where he was incapacitated for weeks.[35]

Thus after all the numbers are duly scrutinized and interpreted, Führer would no doubt reminds us that the lower numbers of the current day tell as much about the reality of Christian faith in Germany today as the higher numbers did during the throne and altar glory years of the Kaiser. The fact remains that despite the modest numbers, despite forty years of wilderness in the GDR, a little flock of church emerged with the kind of freedom grounded in the narrative surrounding Jesus. It was a freedom based on service, not attenuated into acquisitive impulses or *quid pro quo* reckonings. The fact remains that in cities and villages all over the GDR, a critical mass of churches experienced a freedom *for* others. There were enough pastors and people like Führer and *Nikolaikirche* to take the risk of embracing the vision that Bonhoeffer first described during his prewar pastorate in

33. Ziegler, *Doing Theology*, 192.
34. Burgess, *East German Church*, 134.
35. Führer, *Und Wir Sind Dabei Gewesen*, 214–42.

London, a way of preaching the gospel that made the Sermon on the Mount central not peripheral.[36]

Thus two realities remain in collision. On the one hand, a return to "the primary truths of Christianity" (Butterfield) enabled the remarkable historical achievement of 1989, adding a new chapter to Germany's story. On the other, there has been no "happily ever after" triumph for the church, neither in the former Eastern sector nor the Western. Should this mingled story of redemption and dissonance surprise or discourage us? One recurring note of this study has been the typically modest numbers of those small groups and pastors who bore witness to the church's mission. Despite the odds, their words and deeds in a broken but beloved nation helped to bend the arc of history toward the kingdom of God. Despite many and at times morbid failings, the church in Germany became, in Lesslie Newbigin's fine phrase, a sign, an instrument and a foretaste of the kingdom of God,[37] and did so in a most unlikely situation. Whenever this happens, in situations local or international, the church performs its unique service to the state, not with its back bent in subservience (Barth), nor when it tries to be conspiratorial, but when it is open for all (Führer), when it holds governments and economic structures accountable to be servants of the people, not their masters. Whenever the church risks enacting parables of final victory, it will by grace share in the overcoming of present evil with good. It will never do so just for the sake of the church alone, but also for the sake of others. This remains how the church enacts its confession and performs its God-given political mandate in each new contemporary moment.

Let us end this study of church and state relations in Germany where it began—by returning to the witness of Christian Führer, who died on June 30, 2014, a year after the passing of his beloved wife, Monika, only months before the twenty-fifth anniversary of the events which shook the GDR free from its totalitarian foundation. In a 2013 interview with the local newspaper, Führer was asked to respond to the critics who were freshly accusing him of being a social romantic and an incurable optimist. "I heard the same thing in the days before Oct. 9, 1989," he said. "At that time they said, 'You

36. Letter to Reinhold Niebuhr, in Bonhoeffer, *London*, 183. This of course became a prominent feature of Bonhoeffer's experiment in seminary training at Finkenwalde and frames the argument of his book *Discipleship*. See ch. 1 of this present study.

37. Newbigin, "Does Society Still Need the Parish Church?," in *Word in Season*, 48–65.

don't really think that your candles and prayers can change something?' But history saw things differently."[38]

38. Quoted in Eddy, "Christian Führer" (obituary), *New York Times*, July 1, 2014.

Appendix I

Theological Declaration of Barmen, May 1934[1]

An Appeal to the Evangelical Congregations and Christians in Germany

THE CONFESSIONAL SYNOD OF the German Evangelical Church met in Barmen, May 29–31 1934. Here representatives from all the German confessional churches met with one accord in a confession of the one Lord of the one, holy, apostolic church. In fidelity to their confession of faith, members of Lutheran, Reformed, and United churches sought a common message for the need and temptation of the church in our day. With gratitude to God they are convinced that they have been given a common word to utter. It was not their intention to found a new church or to form a union. For nothing was farther from their minds than the abolition of the confessional status of our churches. Their intention was, rather, to withstand in faith and unanimity the destruction of the confession of faith, and thus of the Evangelical Church in Germany. In opposition to attempts to establish the unity of the German Evangelical Church by means of false doctrine, by the use of force and by insincere practices, the Confessional Synod insists that the unity of the Evangelical Churches in Germany can come only from the Word of God in faith through the Holy Spirit. Thus alone is the church renewed. Therefore the Confessional Synod calls upon the congregations to range themselves behind it in prayer, and steadfastly to gather around those pastors and teachers who are loyal to the confessions.

1. http://www.presbyterian.org.nz/about/statements-of-faith/the-barmen -declaration-1934.

Be not deceived by loose talk, as if we meant to oppose the unity of the German nation! Do not listen to the seducers who pervert our intentions, as if we wanted to break up the unity of the German Evangelical Church or to forsake the confessions of the Fathers! Try the spirits whether they are of God! Prove also the words of the Confessional Synod of the German Evangelical Church to see whether they agree with holy scripture and with the confessions of the Fathers. If you find that we are speaking contrary to scripture, then do not listen to us! But if you find that we are taking our stand upon scripture, then let no fear or temptation keep you from treading with us the path of faith and obedience to the Word of God, in order that God's people be of one mind upon earth and that we in faith experience what he himself has said: "I will never leave you, nor forsake you." Therefore, "Fear not, little flock, for it is your Father's good pleasure to give you the kingdom."

THEOLOGICAL DECLARATION CONCERNING THE PRESENT SITUATION OF THE GERMAN EVANGELICAL CHURCH

According to the opening words of its constitution of July 11 1933, the German Evangelical Church is a federation of confessional churches that grew out of the Reformation and that enjoy equal rights. The theological basis for the unification of these churches is laid down in Article 1 and Article 2 (1) of the constitution of the German Evangelical Church that was recognized by the Reich government on July 14 1933:

Article 1. The inviolable foundation of the German Evangelical Church is the gospel of Jesus Christ as it is attested for us in holy scripture and brought to light again in the confessions of the Reformation. The full powers that the church needs for its mission are hereby determined and limited.

Article 2 (1). The German Evangelical Church is divided into member churches (Landeskirchen).

We, the representatives of Lutheran, Reformed, and United churches, of free synods, church assemblies, and parish organizations united in the Confessional Synod of the German Evangelical Church, declare that we stand together on the ground of the German Evangelical Church as a federation of German confessional churches. We are bound together by the confession of the one Lord of the one, holy, catholic, and apostolic church. We publicly declare before all evangelical churches in Germany that what they hold in common in this confession is grievously imperiled, and with it the unity of the German Evangelical Church. It is threatened by the teaching methods and actions of the ruling church party of the "German Christians" and of the church administration carried on by them. These have become more and more apparent during the first year of the existence of the German Evangelical Church. This threat consists in the fact that the theological basis on which the German Evangelical Church is united has been continually and systematically thwarted and rendered ineffective by alien principles, on the part of the leaders and spokesmen of the "German Christians" as well as on the part of the church administration. When these principles are held to be valid, then, according to all the confessions in force among us, the church ceases to be the church and the German Evangelical Church, as a federation of confessional churches, becomes intrinsically impossible. As members of Lutheran, Reformed, and United churches we may and must speak with one voice in this matter today. Precisely because we want to be and to remain faithful to our various confessions, we may not keep silent, since we believe that we have been given a common message to utter in a time of common need and temptation. We commend to God what this may mean for the interrelations of the confessional churches. In view of the errors of the "German Christians" of the present Reich church government which are devastating the church and also therefore breaking up the unity of the German Evangelical Church, we confess the following evangelical truths:

1. "I am the way, and the truth, and the life; no one comes to the Father, but by me." (Jn 14.6) "Truly, truly, I say to you, he who does not enter the sheepfold by the door, but climbs in by another way, that man is a thief and a robber . . . I am the door; if anyone enters by me, he will be saved." (Jn 10.1, 9)

Jesus Christ, as he is attested for us in holy scripture, is the one Word of God which we have to hear and which we have to trust and obey in life and in death.

We reject the false doctrine, as though the church could and would have to acknowledge as a source of its proclamation, apart from and besides this one Word of God, still other events and powers, figures and truths, as God's revelation.

2. "Christ Jesus, whom God has made our wisdom, our righteousness and sanctification and redemption." (1 Cor 1.30)

As Jesus Christ is God's assurance of the forgiveness of all our sins, so, in the same way and with the same seriousness he is also God's mighty claim upon our whole life. Through him befalls us a joyful deliverance from the godless fetters of this world for a free, grateful service to his creatures.

We reject the false doctrine, as though there were areas of our life in which we would not belong to Jesus Christ, but to other lords-areas in which we would not need justification and sanctification through him.

3. "Rather, speaking the truth in love, we are to grow up in every way into him who is the head, into Christ, from whom the whole body [is] joined and knit together" (Eph 4.15, 16).

The Christian church is the congregation of the brethren in which Jesus Christ acts presently as the Lord in word and sacrament through the Holy Spirit. As the church of pardoned sinners, it has to testify in the midst of a sinful world, with its faith as with its obedience, with its message as with its order, that it is solely his property, and that it lives and wants to live solely from his comfort and from his direction in the expectation of his appearance.

We reject the false doctrine, as though the church were permitted to abandon the form of its message and order to its own pleasure or to changes in prevailing ideological and political convictions.

4. "You know that the rulers of the gentiles lord it over them, and their great men exercise authority over them. It shall not be so among you; but whoever would be great among you must be your servant." (Mt 20.25, 26)

The various offices in the church do not establish a dominion of some over the others; on the contrary, they are for the exercise of the ministry entrusted to and enjoined upon the whole congregation.

We reject the false doctrine, as though the church, apart from this ministry, could and were permitted to give itself, or allow to be given to it, special leaders vested with ruling powers.

5. "Fear God. Honour the emperor." (1 Pet 2.17)

Scripture tells us that, in the as yet unredeemed world in which the church also exists, the state has by divine appointment the task of providing for justice and peace. [It fulfils this task] by means of the threat and exercise of force, according to the measure of human judgment and human ability. The church acknowledges the benefit of this divine appointment in gratitude and reverence before him. It calls to mind the kingdom of God, God's commandment and righteousness, and thereby the responsibility both of rulers and of the ruled. It trusts and obeys the power of the Word by which God upholds all things.

We reject the false doctrine, as though the state, over and beyond its special commission, should and could become the single and totalitarian order of human life, thus fulfilling the church's vocation as well.

We reject the false doctrine, as though the church, over and beyond its special commission, should and could appropriate the characteristics, the tasks, and the dignity of the state, thus itself becoming an organ of the state.

6. "Lo, I am with you always, to the close of the age." (Mt 28.20) "The word of God is not fettered." (2 Tim 2.9)

The church's commission, upon which its freedom is founded, consists in delivering the message of the free grace of God to all people in Christ's stead, and therefore in the ministry of his own Word and work through sermon and sacrament.

We reject the false doctrine, as though the church in human arrogance could place the word and work of the Lord in the service of any arbitrarily chosen desires, purposes, and plans.

The Confessional Synod of the German Evangelical Church declares that it sees in the acknowledgement of these truths and in the rejection of these errors the indispensable theological basis of the German Evangelical Church as a federation of confessional churches. It invites all who are able to accept its declaration to be mindful of these theological principles in their decisions in church politics. It entreats all whom it concerns to return to the unity of faith, love, and hope.

Appendix II

The Stuttgart Declaration
Declaration of the Council of the Evangelical Church in Germany October 19, 1945

THIS TEXT OF THE Evangelische Kirche in Deutschland is frequently referred to as the Stuttgart Declaration of Guilt

The Council of the Evangelical [Protestant] Church in Germany welcomes representatives of the World Council of Churches to its meeting on October 18–19, 1945, in Stuttgart.

We are all the more thankful for this visit, as we know ourselves to be with our people in a great community of suffering, but also in a great solidarity of guilt. With great anguish we state: through us has endless suffering been brought to many peoples and countries. What we have often borne witness to before our congregations, we now declare in the name of the whole Church. We have for many years struggled in the name of Jesus Christ against the spirit which found its terrible expression in the National Socialist regime of tyranny, but we accuse ourselves for not witnessing more courageously, for not praying more faithfully, for not believing more joyously, and for not loving more ardently.

Now a new beginning can be made in our churches. Grounded on the Holy Scriptures, directed with all earnestness toward the only Lord of the Church, they are now proceeding to cleanse themselves from influences alien to the faith and to set themselves in order. Our hope is in the God of grace and mercy that he will use our churches as his instruments and will give them authority to proclaim his word and in obedience to his will to work creatively among ourselves and among our people.

That in this new beginning we may become wholeheartedly united with the other churches of the ecumenical fellowship fills us with deep joy.

We hope in God that through the common service of the churches the spirit of violence and revenge which again today is tending to become powerful may be brought under control in the whole world, and that the spirit of peace and love may gain the mastery, wherein alone tortured humanity can find healing.

So in an hour in which the whole world needs a new beginning we pray: "Veni Creator Spiritus."

Bishop Wurm

Bishop Meiser

Superintendent Hahn

Bishop Dibelius

Professor Smend

Pastor Asmussen

Pastor Niemöller

Landesoberkirchenrat Lilje

Superintendent Held

Pastor Niesel

Dr. Heinemann

Representatives of the Allied Churches led by W. A. Visser't Hooft (Netherlands) included:

George Bell, Bishop of Chichester, England

Gordon Rupp, England

Samuel Cavert, USA

S. C. Michelfelder, USA

Pierre Maury, France

Hendrik Kraemer, Netherlands

Alphonse Koechlin, Switzerland

Stewart Herman, former pastor of the American Church in Berlin[1]

---

1. http://www.ccjr.us/dialogika-resources/documents-and-statements/protestant -churches/eur/752-ecg1945.

Acknowledgments

Two PAPERS WERE READ at conferences which later became the introduction and chapter 6: "Lessons from Leipzig, 1989: Prayer and Peacemaking," American Academy of Religion, Newberg, Oregon, May 2, 2008; and "The German Church and the Cold War: The Search for a Third Way," Conference on Faith and History biennial conference, Newberg, Oregon, October 9, 2010.

A revised portion of chapter 5 was published as "The Stuttgart Declaration of 1945: A Case Study of Guilt, Forgiveness and Foreign Policy," in *Trinity and Transformation: J. B. Torrance's Vision of Worship, Mission and Society*, edited by Todd Speidell (Eugene, OR: Wipf and Stock, 2016), 157–74.

An abridged version of the introduction was published as "Reflections on Pastor Christian Führer of the Nikolai Church in Leipzig," News and Notes, *Contemporary Church History Quarterly* 20 (2014), http://contemporarychurchhistory.org/2014/09/reflection-on-pastor-christian-fuhrer -of-the-nikolai-church-in-leipzig.

Apart from the support of many groups and persons this book would not have seen the light of day. First of all, I am grateful to George Fox University for the privilege of leading five church history study trips to Europe with my wife, Sue. GFU also granted me a sabbatical in 2008 in which I was able to initiate the research for this book.

Out of this opportunity flowed the gift of fellowship and generosity from a whole number of laity, pastors and educators. In particular, I gratefully acknowledge the following:

Dr. Marcus and Doris Müller, whose warm hospitality introduced us to contemporary Christian witness in Germany, first at the Waldensian Retreat Center in Torre Pellice, Italy, and later at the YMCA in Munich, Germany, and at Chrischona, in Basel, Switzerland.

Pastor Tim Buechsel, for his heartfelt translation of our meeting with Christian Führer and for ongoing conversations.

Alke and Georg Goosmann, for generous welcomes to the St. Anne's Church in Dahlem and the Niemöller manse.

Knüt Hämmerling and Burckhard Scheffler at the Bonhoeffer House in Berlin, whose competence and friendliness have blessed many pilgrims.

The Taize prayer group that meets at the Segenskirche in Prenzlauer Berg, especially:

Dorothea Frärks, for her kindness, hospitality and friendship.

Stephanie Sippel, who sacrificed time with her young family to offer kindness, hospitality and invaluable service in arranging a memorable program for our students.

As for the writing of the book, I must record my gratitude to those who read portions of the text and whose suggestions and corrections have been invaluable. They are living reminders to me of the communion of saints who are eager to serve one another.

Dr. John S. Conway	Walter Fields
Dr. Mark Brocker	John Hodges
Dr. Stephen Brown	Dr. Javier Garcia
Dr. Gary Burge	Dr. Marilee Newell.
Dr. Andrew Chandler	

I must also mention with gratitude those whose encouraging and instructive conversations along the way supported my research and writing:

Dr. Paul Anderson	Dr. Ulrich Lincoln
Dr. Jeremy Begbie	Dr. Bob Mayo
Father Seraphim Bell	Dr. Richard Pierard
Dr. Irv Brendlinger	Brother John of Taize.
Dr. John de Gruchy	

I am grateful for the students of George Fox University who traveled with me to Germany, and who put up with the many inconveniences of international travel and a directionally impaired tour leader with nearly endless good spirits. It has been a privilege to have joined you in a modern pilgrimage to the living sources of faith in Europe.

My final two thanks are for those without whom this book could not have been written. First, I cannot imagine having ventured forth on the study tours in Europe over many years without the presence and practical skills of my beloved wife, Sue.

Finally, I am indebted to the faithful witness of Pastor Christian Führer and his wife, Monika, whose hospitality to our student group (and so many others) at the *Nikolaikirche* awakened me to ask fresh questions about church and state relations in Germany hidden behind the miracle of 1989.

Bibliography

Althausen, Johannes. "The Churches in the GDR between Accommodation and Resistance." *Occasional Papers on Religion in Eastern Europe* 13 (1993) 1–20.

Arendt, Hannah. *Eichmann in Jerusalem: A Report on the Banality of Evil.* London: Penguin, 1992.

Bacevitch, Andrew J. *The Limits of Power.* New York: Metropolitan, 2008.

Bacque, James. *Crimes and Mercies: The Fate of German Civilians under Allied Occupation, 1944–1950.* Vancouver: Talonbooks, 2010.

The Barmen Declaration. 1934. http://www.presbyterian.org.nz/about/statements-of-faith/the-barmen-declaration-1934.

Barnett, Victoria J. "Barmen, the Ecumenical Movement, and the Jews: The Missing Thesis." *Ecumenical Review* 61 (2009) 17–23.

———. *For the Soul of the People: Protestant Protest against Hitler.* New York: Oxford University Press, 1992.

Barth, Karl. *Against the Stream: Shorter Post-War Writings, 1946–1952.* London: SCM, 1954.

———. *The Church and the Political Problem of Our Day.* London: Hodder and Stoughton, 1939.

———. *Church Dogmatics.* Vol. III, *Doctrine of Creation.* Pt. 2. Edinburgh: T. & T. Clark, 1960.

———. *Church Dogmatics.* Vol. IV, *Doctrine of Reconciliation.* Pt. 1. Edinburgh: T. & T. Clark, 1960.

———. *Community, State and Church.* Introduction by Will Herberg. Gloucester, MA: Smith, 1968.

———. *Fragments Grave and Gay.* London: Fontana, 1976.

———. *The German Church Conflict.* Richmond: John Knox, 1965.

———. *Karl Barth Letters, 1961–1968.* Grand Rapids: Eerdmans, 1981.

———. *The Knowledge of God and the Service of God according to the Teaching of the Reformation.* London: Hodder and Stoughton, 1938.

———. *A Letter to Great Britain from Switzerland.* London: Sheldon, 1941.

———. *The Only Way: How Can the Germans Be Cured?* New York: Philosophical Library, 1947.

―――. *Protestant Theology in the Nineteenth Century: Its Background and History.* London: SCM Press, 1972.

―――. *Revolutionary Theology in the Making: Barth-Thurneysen Correspondence, 1914–1925.* John Knox, 1964.

―――. *Theological Existence Today! A Plea for Theological Freedom.* London: Hodder and Stoughton, 1933.

―――. *Theology and Church: Shorter Writings, 1920–1928.* New York: Harper & Row, 1962.

―――. *The Theology of Schleiermacher: Lectures at Göttingen, Winter Semester of 1923/24.* Edinburgh: T. & T. Clark, 1982.

Barth, Karl, and Johannes Hamel. *How to Serve God in a Marxist Land.* New York: Association, 1959.

Beller, Hava Kohav, director. *The Burning Wall: Dissent and Opposition Behind the Berlin Wall.* Documentary film. 2002.

Bense, Klaas, writer, director. *One Fine Day.* Documentary film. 2011.

Bentley, James. *Martin Niemöller, 1892–1984.* New York: Macmillan, 1984.

Bergen, Doris L. *Twisted Cross: The German Christian Movement in the Third Reich.* Chapel Hill: University of North Carolina Press, 1996.

Beschloss, Michael. *The Conquerors: Roosevelt, Truman and the Destruction of Hitler's Germany, 1941–1945.* New York: Simon and Schuster, 2002.

Bethge, Eberhard. *Dietrich Bonhoeffer.* London: Collins, 1985.

Bettis, Joseph. "Barmen: What We Have Learned and What We Have Yet to Learn." In *The Church Confronts the Nazis: Barmen Then and Now,* edited by Hubert G. Locke, 145–84. Toronto Studies in Theology 16. Lewiston, NY: Mellen, 1984.

Bonhoeffer, Dietrich. *Berlin, 1932–1933.* Dietrich Bonhoeffer Works 12. Minneapolis: Fortress, 2009.

―――. *Discipleship.* Dietrich Bonhoeffer Works 4. Minneapolis: Fortress, 2001.

―――. *Ethics.* Dietrich Bonhoeffer Works 6. Minneapolis: Fortress, 2005.

―――. *Letters and Papers from Prison.* Dietrich Bonhoeffer Works 8. Minneapolis: Fortress, 2010.

―――. *London, 1933–1935.* Dietrich Bonhoeffer Works 13. Minneapolis: Fortress, 2009.

―――. *Sanctorum Communio.* Dietrich Bonhoeffer Works 1. Minneapolis: Fortress, 1998.

Brandt, Willy. *My Life in Politics.* New York: Viking, 1992.

Brown, Stephen. "Introduction to Heino Falcke." *Ecumenical Review* 56 (2004) 160–65.

―――. "The Berlin Wall Fell in Many Places." World Council of Churches website, Nov 5, 2009. http://www.oikoumene.org/en/press-centre/news/the-berlin-wall-fell-in -many-places.

Brueggemann, Walter. *Finally Comes the Poet—Daring Speech for Proclamation.* Minneapolis: Augsburg Fortress, 1989.

Burgess, John P. *The East German Church and the End of Communism.* New York: Oxford University Press, 1997.

Busch, Eberhard. *The Barmen Theses Then and Now.* Grand Rapids: Eerdmans, 2010.

―――. *Karl Barth: His Life from Letters and Autobiographical Texts.* SCM, London, 1976.

―――. *Karl Barth and the Pietists: The Young Karl Barth's Critique of Pietism and Its Response.* Downers Grove: InterVarsity, 2004.

Butterfield, Herbert. *Christianity, Diplomacy and War*. London: Epworth, 1953.

Bytwerk, Randall L. *Bending Spines: The Propagandas of Nazi Germany and the German Democratic Republic*. East Lansing: Michigan State University Press, 2004.

Calvin, John. *Institutes of the Christian Religion* 3.4.3. Philadelphia: Westminster, 1960.

Chadwick, Owen. *The Christian Church in the Cold War*. London: Penguin, 1992.

Chandler, Andrew. *George Bell, Bishop of Chichester*. Grand Rapids: Eerdmans, 2016.

———, ed. *The Moral Imperative: New Essays on the Ethics of Resistance in National Socialist Germany 1933–1945*. Boulder, CO: Westview, 1998.

Chang, Ha-Joon, *Bad Samaritans*. New York: Bloomsbury, 2008.

———, ed. *Rethinking Development Economics*. London: Anthem, 2003.

Chapman, Audrey R., and Bernard Spong, eds. *Religion and Reconciliation in South Africa: Voices of Religious Leaders*. Philadelphia: Templeton-Foundation, 2003.

Christmann, Brunhild, ed. *Germany: Seeking a Relevant Witness beyond Contrast and Assimilation*. Gospel and Culture Pamphlet 13. Geneva: WCC Publications, 1996.

Chung, Paul S., et al. *Liberating Lutheran Theology: Freedom for Justice and Solidarity with Others in a Global Context*. Minneapolis: Fortress, 2011.

Cobham, J. O. "The Significance of the Barmen Declaration for the Oecumenical Church." In *The Significance of the Barmen Declaration for the Oecumenical Church*. London: SPCK, 1943.

Cochrane, Arthur. *The Church's Confession under Hitler*. Pittsburgh: Pickwick, 1976.

Cohen, Stephen F. *Soviet Fates and Lost Alternatives*. New York: Columbia, 2011.

Conway, John S. "Coming to Terms with the Past: Interpreting the German Church Struggles 1933–1990." *German History* 16 (1998) 378–96.

———. "The German Church Struggle: Its Making and Meaning." In *The Church Confronts the Nazis, Barmen then and Now*, edited by Hubert G. Locke, 93–143. Toronto Studies in Theology 16. Lewiston, NY: Mellen, 1984.

———. "How Shall the Nations Repent?" *Journal of Ecclesiastical History* 38 (1987) 596–622.

———. "Kirche im Sozialismus: East German Protestantism's Political and Theological Witness, 1945–1990." *Religion in Eastern Europe* 13 (1997) 1–21.

———. *The Nazi Persecution of the Churches, 1933–45*. New York: Basic, 1968.

———. Personal correspondence with the author, July 18, 2014.

———. "The Political Theology of Martin Niemöller. *German Studies Review* 9 (1986) 521–46.

Cousins, Norman. *The Improbable Triumvirate: John F. Kennedy, Pope John, Nikita Krushchev*. New York: Norton, 1972.

———. *The Pathology of Power*. New York: Norton, 1987.

De Gruchy, John W., ed. *Bonhoeffer for a New Day*. Grand Rapids: Eerdmans, 1997.

———. *The Church Struggle in South Africa*. With Steve De Gruchy. Minneapolis: Fortress, 2005.

Dibelius, Otto. *In the Service of the Lord*. London: Faber, 1965.

Douglass, James W. *JFK and the Unspeakable*. New York: Orbis, 2008.

Dutschke, Gretchen. *Wir Hatten Ein Barbarisches, Schönes Leben, Rudi Dutschke*. Koln: Kiepenheuer & Witsch. 2010.

Eddy, Melissa. "Christian Führer, East German Whose Prayers Inspired Protests, Dies at 71." Obituary. *New York Times*, July 1, 2014.

Eisenhower, Dwight D. "The Cross of Iron." Address to the American Society of Newspaper Editors, April 16, 1953. Originally titled "The Chance for Peace." http://www.informationclearinghouse.info/article9743.htm.

———. "Farewell Address, January 17, 1961." Final TV Talk 1/17/61 (1). Box 38, Speech Series, Papers of Dwight D. Eisenhower as President, 1953–61. Eisenhower Library; National Archives and Records Administration.

Ericksen, Robert P. *Theologians under Hitler: Gerhard Kittel, Paul Althaus and Emanuel Hirsch*. New Haven: Yale University Press, 1985.

Evans, Richard J. *The Third Reich in Power*. New York: Penguin, 2005.

———. *The Third Reich at War*. New York: Penguin, 2009.

Falcke, Heino. "Christ Liberates—Therefore, the Church for Others (1972)." *Ecumenical Review* 56 (2004) 166–83.

———. "The Ecumenical Assembly for Justice, Peace and the Integrity of Creation." *Ecumenical Review* 56 (2004) 184–91.

———. "German Protestant Warns Churches against Being Kidded by Capitalism." *Ecumenical News International*, July 4, 2007. http://www.ekklesia.co.uk/node/5418.

Francis, Pope. *Evangelii Gaudium*. www.vatican.va.

Führer, Christian. "The Events in Fall 1989." http://www.nikolaikirche-leipzig.de.

———. Extended Interview. PBS, Religion & Ethics NewsWeekly. November 6, 2009. http://www.pbs.org/wnet/religionandethics/2009/11/06/november-6-2009-the-rev-christian-fuhrer-extended-interview/4843/.

———. *Protestant Lutheran Church of St. Nikolai in Leipzig: A Spiritual Church Guide*. Regensburg: Verlag Schnell & Steiner GMBH, 2006.

———. *Und Wir Sind Dabei Gewesen, Die Revolution, die aus der Kirche kam*. Berlin: Ulstein, 2008.

Fukuyama, Francis. *The End of History and the Last Man*. New York: Free Press, 1992.

Gascoigne, Bamber. *Christianity: A History*. New York: Carroll and Graf, 2003.

Gibbs, Nancy, and Michael Duffy. *The Preacher and the Presidents: Billy Graham in the White House*. New York: Center Street, 2007.

Goeckel, Robert F. "The Evangelical-Lutheran Church and the East German Revolution." *Occasional Papers on Religion in Eastern Europe* 10 (1990). http://digitalcommons.georgefox.edu/cgi/viewcontent.cgi?article=1585&context=ree.

———. *The Lutheran Church and the East German State: Political Conflict and Change under Ulbricht and Honecker*. Ithaca: Cornell University Press, 1990.

Goodman, Melvin A. *National Insecurity: The Cost of American Militarism*. San Francisco: City Light, 2013.

Gorbachev, Mikhail. "I Am Truly and Deeply Concerned." Interview with Matthias Schepp and Britta Sandberg. *Der Spiegel*, January 16, 2015. http://www.spiegel.de/international/world/gorbachev-warns-of-decline-in-russian-western-ties-over-ukraine-a-1012992.html.

———. "Mikhail Gorbachev: The Man Who Lost an Empire." BBC.com, December 13, 2016. http://www.bbc.com/news/world-europe-38289333.

Graham, Billy. "A Change of Heart." *Sojourners*, August 12, 1979. https://sojo.net/sites/default/files/images/A-Change-of-Heart.pdf.

Green, Clifford J., and Guy C. Carter, eds. *Interpreting Bonhoeffer: Historical Perspectives, Emerging Issues*. Minneapolis: Fortress, 2013.

Hart, Trevor A., ed. *The Dictionary of Historical Theology*. Grand Rapids: Eerdmans, 2000.

Herman, Stewart W. *The Rebirth of the German Church*. New York: Harper, 1946.

Hesekiel, George. *Bismarck: His Authentic Biography*. New York: Fords, Howard and Hulbert, 1877.

Hirschman, Charles, et al. "Vietnamese Casualties during the American War: A New Estimate." *Population and Development Review* 21 (1995) 783–812.

Hockenos, Matthew D. *A Church Divided: German Protestants Confront the Nazi Past*. Indianapolis: Indiana University Press, 2004.

———. "Martin Niemöller in America, 1946–1947: 'A Hero with Limitations.'" *ACCH Quarterly* 18 (2012). https://contemporarychurchhistory.org/2012/06/conference-paper-martin-niemoeller-in-america.

———. "On the Confessing Church's June 1936 Memorandum to Hitler." *Contemporary Church History Quarterly* 22 (2016). https://contemporarychurchhistory.org/2016/06/on-the-confessing-churchs-june-1936-memorandum-to-hitler.

Hoover, Arlie. *God, Germany and Britain in the Great War: A Study in Clerical Nationalism*. New York: Praeger, 1989.

Huber, Florien. *Meine DDR: Leben im anderen Deutschland*. Berlin: Rowohlt, 2008.

Hunsinger, George, ed. *Karl Barth and Radical Politics*. Philadelphia: Westminster, 1976.

Ising, Dieter. *Johann Christoph Blumhardt, Life and Work: A New Biography*. Eugene, OR: Cascade, 2009.

Jasper, Ronald C. D. *George Bell, Bishop of Chichester*. London: Oxford University Press, 1967.

Jehle, Frank. *Ever Against the Stream: The Politics of Karl Barth, 1906–1968*. Grand Rapids: 2002.

Jenkins, Philip. *The Great and Holy War: How World War I Became a Religious Crusade*. New York: HarperOne, 2014.

Johnson, Chalmers. *Blowback: The Costs and Consequences of American Empire*. New York: Holt, 2000.

Johnston, Douglas, and Cynthia Sampson, eds. *Religion: The Missing Dimension of Statecraft*. New York: Oxford University Press, 1994.

Jones, Tim. "Six Key Points about Greece's Debt." Jubilee Debt Campaign website, January 26, 2015. http://jubileedebt.org.uk/reports-briefings/briefing/six-key-points-greek-debt-weeks-election.

Jüngel, Eberhard. *Christ, Justice and Peace: Toward a Theology of the State*. Edinburgh: T. & T. Clark, 1992.

Keynes, J. M. *Economic Consequences of the Peace*. New York: Skyhorse, 2007.

Lalami, Leila. "To Defeat Isis We Must Call both Western and Muslim Leaders to Account." *Nation*, November 15, 2015. http://www.thenation.com/article/we-cannot-defeat-isis-without-defeating-the-wahhabi-theology-that-birthed-it/.

Lang, R. Clarence. "Imposed German Guilt: The Stuttgart Declaration of 1945." *Journal of Historical Review* 8 (1988) 55–78. First presented at the 8th IHR conference, Irvine, CA, October 1987. http://www.ihr.org/jhr/v08/v08p-55_Lang.html.

Lazarus, Stephen. "Pulling the Curtain Down: An Introduction to the Role of the East German Protestant Church in the Peaceful Revolution of 1989." *Many to Many*, issue 3, February 1993. http://thebigpicture.homestead.com/files/m2m3p29.htm.

Lehmann, Theo. *Blues Music and Gospel Proclamation: The Extraordinary Life of a Courageous East German Pastor.* Eugene, OR: Wipf and Stock, 2008.

Lewis, C. S. *Reflections on the Psalms.* London: Collins, 1969.

Lewy, Guenther. *The Catholic Church and Nazi Germany.* New York: McGraw-Hill, 1965.

Littell, Franklin H. "From Barmen (1934) to Stuttgart (1945): The Path of the Confessing Church in Germany." *Journal of Church and State* 3 (1961) 41–52.

Locke, Hubert G., and Marcia Sachs Littell, eds. *Remembrance and Recollection: Essays on the Centennial Year of Martin Niemöller and Reinhold Niebuhr and the Fiftieth Year of the Wannsee Conference.* Studies in the Shoah 12. Maryland: University Press of America, 1996.

Ludden, Jennifer, host. "Southern Baptists Apologize for Slavery Stance." *Faith Matters,* NPR radio, August 28, 2009. http://www.npr.org/templates/story/story.php?storyId=112329862.

Luther, Martin. "The Disputation Concerning Justification, 1536." In *Career of the Reformer IV,* edited by Lewis W. Spitz, 145–96. Luther's Works 34. Philadelphia: Fortress, 1967.

———. "The Freedom of a Christian." In *Three Treatises,* translated by W. A. Lambert, revised by Harold J. Grimm, 261–316. Philadelphia: Fortress, 1973.

Maier, Charles S. *Dissolution: The Crisis of Communism and the End of East Germany.* Princeton: Princeton University Press, 1997.

Marcuse, Harold. Niemöller Quotation Page. http://www.history.ucsb.edu/faculty/marcuse/niem.htm#news.

Marsh, Charles. *Wayward Christian Soldiers: Freeing the Gospel from Political Captivity.* New York: Oxford University Press, 2007.

Maschmann, Melita. *Account Rendered: A Dossier on My Former Self.* London: Abelard-Schuman, 1964.

McNamera, Robert S. *In Retrospect: The Tragedy and Lessons of Vietnam.* New York: Random House, 1995.

Merton, Thomas. *Peace in a Post-Christian Era.* Maryknoll: Orbis, 2006.

Mitscherlich, Alexander, and Margarete Mitscherlich. *The Inability to Mourn.* New York: Grove, 1975.

Morganthau, Henry, Jr. *Germany Is Our Problem.* New York: Harper, 1945.

Moses, John A. "Bonhoeffer's Reception in East Germany." In *Bonhoeffer for a New Day,* edited by John W. De Gruchy, 278–97. Eerdmans, 1997.

———. "The Church Policy of the SED Regime in East Germany, 1949–89: The Fateful Dilemma." *Journal of Religious History* 20 (1996) 228–45.

———. *The Reluctant Revolutionary: Dietrich Bonhoeffer's Collision with Prusso-German History.* New York: Berghahn, 2009.

Newbigin, Lesslie. "Does Society Still Need the Parish Church?" In *A Word in Season,* 48–65. Grand Rapids: Eerdmans, 1994.

———. *The Gospel in a Pluralist Society.* Grand Rapids: Eerdmans, 1989.

Niebuhr, Reinhold. *Essays in Applied Christianity.* Edited by D. B. Robertson. New York: Meridian, 1960.

———. "To America and Back." In *I Knew Dietrich Bonhoeffer: Reminiscences by His Friends,* edited by Wolf-Dieter Zimmermann and Ronald Gregor Smith, 165. New York: Harper and Row, 1966.

Niemöller, Martin. *Exile in the Fatherland: Martin Niemöller's Letters from Moabit Prison*. Edited by Herbert G. Locke. Grand Rapids: Eerdmans, 1986.

———. *Of Guilt and Hope*. New York: Philosophical Library, 1947.

———. "The Need and the Task of the Church in Germany." In *Best Sermons, 1947–48 Edition*, edited by G. P. Butler, 206–14. New York: Harper, 1948.

Niesel, Wilhelm. *The Gospel and the Churches: A Comparison of Catholicism, Orthodoxy and Protestantism*. Philadelphia: Westminster, 1963. http://www.archive.org/stream/gospelandthechur012840mbp/gospelandthechur012840mbp_djvu.txt.

Oestreicher, Paul. Introduction to *The Demands of Freedom*, by Helmut Gollwitzer. New York: Harper and Row, 1965.

———. Obituary of Bishop Albrecht Schönherr. *Guardian*, Thursday, April 2, 2009.

Parry, K. L., ed. *Congregational Praise*. London: Congregational Union of England and Wales, 1951.

Pfaff, Stephen. *Extra-Voice Dynamics and the Collapse of East Germany*. Durham: Duke University Press, 2006.

Pierard, Richard V. "The Church and the Revolution in East Germany." *Covenant Quarterly* 1 (1990) 43–52.

———. "Religion and the East German Revolution." *Journal of Church and State* 32 (1990) 501–9.

Piketty, Thomas. Interview with *Die Zeit*. Translated from the original German by Gavin Schalliol and published by the *Wire* in arrangement with *Die Zeit*. https://thewire.in/5851/thomas-piketty-germany-has-never-repaid-its-debts-it-has-no-right-to-lecture-greece/.

Pond, Elizabeth. *Beyond the Wall: Germany's Road to Unification*. Washington, DC: Brookings Institute, 1993.

Press, Eyal. *Beautiful Souls*. New York: Farrar, Straus and Giroux, 2012.

Rieger, Julius. *The Silent Church*. London: SCM, 1944.

Rumscheidt, H. Martin. Excerpt from "Europe Between Wars." *International Bonhoeffer Society Newsletter*, no. 97, fall 2009.

Schmidt, Dietmar. *Pastor Niemöller*. New York: Doubleday, 1959.

Scholder, Klaus. *The Churches and the Third Reich*. Vol. 1, *1918–1934*. London: SCM, 1986.

———. *The Churches and the Third Reich*. Vol. 2, *The Year of Disillusionment: 1934, Barmen and Rome*. London: SCM, 1988.

———. *A Requiem for Hitler*. London: SCM, 1989.

Schönherr, Albrecht. "Dietrich Bonhoeffer: The Message of a Life." *Christian Century*, November 27, 1985.

Shriver, Donald W., Jr. *Honest Patriots: Loving a Country Enough to Remember Its Misdeeds*. New York: Oxford University Press, 2005.

Sheldrake, Philip. *Pietism*. Atlanta: Westminster John Knox, 2005.

Sollberg, Richard. *God and Caesar in East Germany*. New York: Macmillan, 1961.

Sorensen, Theodore. *Kennedy*. New York: HarperCollins, 1965.

Spotts, Frederic. *The Churches and Politics in Germany*. Middletown, CT: Wesleyan, 1973.

Stassen, Glen H. *Just Peacemaking: Transforming Initiatives for Justice and Peace*. Louisville: Westminster John Knox, 1992.

St. Anne's Church in Berlin-Dahlem, Germany. Church Brochure. April 2009.

Swoboda, Jorg. *The Revolution of the Candles*. Macon, GA: Mercer University Press, 1996.

Tertullian. "On Repentance." In *Ante-Nicene Fathers*, vol. 3. Peabody: Hendrikson, 1994.

Thielicke, Helmut. *Notes from a Wayfarer*. New York: Paragon, 1995.

———. "Religion in Germany." *Annals of the American Academy of Political and Social Science* 260 (1948) 144–54.

Thomas, Nick. *Protest Movements in 1960s West Germany: A Social History of Dissent and Democracy*. New York: Berg, 2003.

Tolkien, J. R. R. *The Letters of J. R. R. Tolkien*. London: Allen and Unwin, 1981.

Torrance, J. B. "Covenant and Contract: A Study of the Theological Background of Worship in Seventeenth-Century Scotland." *Scottish Journal of Theology* 23 (1970) 51–76.

———. *Worship, Community and the Triune God of Grace*. Grand Rapids: InterVarsity, 1996.

Torrance, T. F. *Karl Barth: An Introduction to His Early Theology, 1910–1931*. Edinburgh: T. & T. Clark, 2000.

Varoufakis, Yanis. *And the Weak Suffer What They Must? Europe, Austerity and the Threat to Global Stability*. London: Bodley Head, 2016.

Visser't Hooft, W. A. *Memoirs*. Philadelphia: Westminster, 1973.

Weizsäcker, Richard von. "Facing the Past: An Essential Part of German Unification." In *Speeches for Our Time*, 1–12. German Issues 10. Washington, DC: American Institute for Contemporary German Studies, 1992.

———. *From Weimar to the Wall: My Life in German Politics*. New York: Broadway, 1999.

Weymar, Paul. *Konrad Adenauer*. London: Andre Deutsch, 1957.

Wright, Tom. *God in Public: How the Bible Speaks Truth to Power Today*. London: SPCK, 2016.

Yates, Timothy. "David Bosch: South African Context, Universal Missiology— Ecclesiology in the Emerging Missionary Paradigm." *International Bulletin of Missionary Research* 33 (2009) 72–78.

Ziegler, Philip. *Doing Theology When God Is Forgotten: The Theological Achievement of Wolf Krötke*. New York: Lang, 2007.

Züngel, Friedrich. *Pastor Johann Christoph Blumhardt: An Account of His Life*. Eugene, OR: Cascade, 2010.